TIM-BUNKER PAPERS

THE

TIM BUNKER PAPERS,

OR

YANKEE FARMING.

BY

TIMOTHY BUNKER, ESQ.,

OF HOOKERTOWN, CONN.

WITH ILLUSTRATIONS BY HOPPIN.

NEW YORK:

ORANGE JUDD AND COMPANY,

245 BROADWAY.

LOVEJOY, SON & CO.,
ELECTROTYPERS AND STEREOTYPERS,
15 Vandewater St., New York.

PREFACE.

These papers, begun in the interest of improved husbandry, without much method, and without any anticipation of their subsequent popularity, have been continued through twelve volumes of the *American Agriculturist*, in deference to the wishes of the senior editor and his numerous readers, rather than to the judgment of the writer. For the same reason they are gathered in the more convenient form of this little volume, in the hope that they may be still further useful. They are a humble attempt to represent the average wisdom of the Connecticut farmer, and the steady progress which this class is making in rural improvement and in the comforts and moralities of social life. The incidents herein recorded are fictitious in form rather than in fact, for they are the results of personal experience and observation, and are meant to represent the true drift of farm life in the land of Steady Habits. The teachings are believed to be in harmony with the best authorities in Agriculture and Horticulture, and with the earnest desire that they may cheer the workers upon the farm everywhere, and incite them to the best methods of husbandry and the noblest aims in living, they are submitted to the public.

TABLE OF CONTENTS.

THE TIM BUNKER PAPERS.

No. 1.—A STROKE OF ECONOMY.

The farm is a good school of economy in many repects. The age of homespun is yet fresh in the memory of many of the living, and its close calculations are yet visible on many a homestead. Time was less valuable in that age than in this, and money far less valuable now than then. But multitudes have not yet waked up to the fact, and often spend several dollars' worth of time to purchase what is not worth fifty cents at the market price. When every proprietor's time is worth two dollars a day in the legitimate business of planning and directing the labor on his own farm, he is in poor business, doing work which another will do for him at one-quarter of the price.

We have already begun to divide the labor of the farm, and have reaped very great advantage from it, and this division can be carried to a still greater extent with profit. The horse and the cultivator do a great deal of work once done by the hoe and human hands. No wise man will use the latter when he can avail himself of the former. The mowing machine is doing the work of a dozen men every fine hay day of July. How long will shrewd calculators break their backs over the old-fashioned scythe? Is it not about time to upset the old stumps, and put powder into the rocks that have been plowed, harrowed, hoed, and mowed around, for six generations? They have had their day, like other dogs, and should now be bidden to "get out." Labor is no longer the only or the cheapest equivalent for the farmer's wants. The question ought to be asked, how can this or that want of the farmer be met in the cheapest way? If a man wants information in regard to husbandry, he can get the best thoughts of our best cultivators at a much cheaper rate in the columns of our agricultural journals, than by visiting his neighbors to ask questions and make observations.

But Tim Bunker never thought of that. He has not much opinion of "that 'ere book farming." But Tim observes, and is quick at calculating an idea that he sees growing right out of the sod. "Them is the sort of ideas for practical farmers." He does not take the papers, but Deacon Smith, across the way, does, and offers to lend them, but Tim is so wall-eyed on the papers that he never accepts the offer. But he sees the Deacon's strawberries, and wonders if they would not grow in his soil. He plants, and succeeds. The Deacon sells in the next market town at twenty-five cents a quart—quite as much as he used to get for a bushel of apples. Tim thinks his strawberries look as good as the Deacon's, and he goes to market and brings home the cash. "In fact," soliloquises Mr. Bunker, "this business pays, and if folks will buy the strawberries at that price, I may as well raise them." The strawberry patch was realized last year, and a handsome sum of money with it. One of the coldest days last week Tim drove up to our door, after a long ride, which must have been tedious even with the excitement of fine sleighing and the music of the bells. Now, thought we, Bunker has certainly come to invest a dollar in book-farming. Not a bit of it. He had heard of our Lawton blackberries through the Deacon, and had come down to take a winter view of the brambles and to find out where they could be purchased. We were, of course, glad to see

Mr. Bunker, and gave him a dissertation on this fruit, relating our experience and mode of culture, and giving him the necessary directions for procuring the plants. Had he taken the *American Agriculturist*, he would have found in it much more information than we had time to give him, and in the last number no less than four parties advertising the plants for sale. Mr. Bunker's account stands thus with himself:

TIMOTHY BUNKER, *Dr.*

To time and use of horse - - . - -	$2.00
By information in February *Agriculturist*, *Cr.*	10
Balance - - - - -	$1.90

This is what we call a bold stroke of economy. Yet this account, foolish as it looks, is a good illustration of what is going on in many of the farming districts. Intelligent men will give two dollars to save ten cents in paper and type. We think they will do better to take the papers, and buy their information at wholesale price. Our time, however, was not lost with Mr. Bunker; for this article came of his visit, and we trust it will touch some of our readers in the right spot.—ED.

No. 2.—ORNAMENTAL TREES.

Tim Bunker says he would give one hundred dollars in clean cash if he had the Deacon's big elm tree in front of his house. It is a noble elm, planted a hundred years ago by the Deacon's grandfather, also a Deacon in the same church, when the sanctuary, with its square pews, high galleries, and sounding-board, was the type of all ornament tolerated in things sacred or secular. But the first Deacon loved shade and meditation, if he failed to appreciate the beautiful in trees, and so planted this elm and the row of maples that adorn the street leading from his house to the meeting-house. The elm now is a very majestic object, and probably no one passes under the shadow of its wide-spreading branches, and looks up into its leafy arches in summer, without admiring it and blessing the memory of its planter. The offer of so conservative a man as Mr. Bunker, is a good indication of its value. Even he would shell out the cash if he could rear such a noble creation in a day, in front of his dwelling.

A good many of his neighbors would give half as much for such an elm, but for some strange reason neither Mr. Bunker nor his neighbors plant ornamental trees, though they are plenty enough in the forests, and the nurseries have them in great variety for a mere trifle. It does not occur to them that time will make of the humblest sapling as lordly a tree and as graceful in its proportions as the big elm.

They have only to plant it in good soil, and guard it against injury, and nature will do the rest without compensation. Every year will add to its gracefulness, and to the value of the homestead which it adorns. The time has come when farmers should think more of planting ornamental trees as a matter of economy. They can be planted at the roadside with little disadvantage to the adjacent land. If maples are planted, they will, in a few years, be yielding sugar. If elms, they will soon turn a barren and uninteresting road into a graceful, shaded avenue, in the summer. It should be a part of the settled policy of every farmer to adorn all the roads leading through his farm in this manner. If he continues in possession, these trees will be objects of interest to make his home attractive as long as he lives. If he removes, his place will be more salable to any reasonable purchaser. We are sorry to make this latter supposition, but the truth is that a large majority of all the farmers in the East do not feel settled for life. They purpose, if they can ever sell their farms to good advantage, to look up a new home; and this feeling of unrest is the bane of all permanent improvement and ornament on the farm. We heartily wish our farming population, at least the middle-aged portion of them, could feel settled. They would then plant orchards and ornamental trees, and make their homes attractive. Let the good work be commenced this month.

No. 3.—TIMOTHY BUNKER, Esq.

This gentleman of the old school, whose name has repeatedly appeared in our pages, has elicited so much interest, that we give a brief sketch of his career, to satisfy the public curiosity. He now holds the office of Justice of the Peace, though he was so late in arriving at this honor, that everybody calls him Tim Bunker, just as they used to. He himself blushes at the title, and perhaps feels insulted if any of his old neighbors call him anything else. It is said, however, that his wife, in speaking of the husband of her youth to third persons, does sometimes give him the honors, but she is very careful never to call him Esq. Bunker in his presence.

He was born and bred in Connecticut, and is a product of her soil and institutions so unique, that it were impossible for Tim Bunker to have grown up anywhere else. He would have been quite another man. He lives in Hookertown, in the first ecclesiastical society, and all his ancestors for five generations back have been members of the church of the standing order in that ancient commonwealth. He is not himself a member of the church, but his orthodoxy is as vigorous and sturdy as the most devout member of the Puritan church where he worships. He reveres the institutions of religion, and is as punctual at the meeting-house on the Sabbath, as the preacher or the sexton. His model man is Deacon Smith, though he follows him afar off, both in horticulture and in religion. He is as zealous as the Deacon in the defence of the speculative doctrines of the church, and is quite as correct in his moral deportment. By all but his intimate friends, he is supposed to be a member, so correct is he in his opinions and practices. His personal appearance is somewhat striking. He is just about medium size, square built and stout, and though past fifty, can keep up with the smartest of his hands in the field at any kind of work. He has an open, manly face, expressive of benevolence, and his look does not belie his character. He is known far and near as an excellent neighbor, always ready to help at a bad job, to change work, to lend his horse or oxen, even when it is not quite convenient for himself. In dress he is always behind the times. The Sunday hat has been his for five years, and neither rim nor crown has changed with the changing fashions. His dress is of the same age, and the only trouble pertaining to dress that agitates him, is the apprehension that his habiliments will sometimes wear out in spite of his scrupulous care. A change of suit always goes hard with him, and it requires the most adroit management of his good wife to get him safely out of the old into the new. He has been in a condition which she calls "not fit to be seen" for a full year, before she can effect a change of Sunday suit.

In politics Tim Bunker was a whig until the last Presidential election, since which time parties have become so much split up, that for once he has found himself entirely at a loss. For his part he cannot see why folks want to keep changing about so, every few years. If the world ever gets finished and adjusted to a given position, he will be a supremely happy man.

He has always lived upon the ancestral farm, and by a life of industry has succeeded in buying out the other heirs, and now owns in fee simple all the paternal acres. He is a good sample of the old style farmer, shy of books and papers that treat of husbandry, and a frequent quoter of that old proverb "old birds are not to be caught with chaff." Tim, however, was once caught, if not with chaff, at least with something very like it.

Some five and twenty years ago, there was a Rohan potato fever that infected all Hookertown. Many of his neighbors who read the papers experimented with the article, and among the rest his model man Deacon Smith went into the speculation. Tim Bunker believed in practical farming, and as these potatoes were manifestly a reality, he bought of the Deacon a bushel of Rohans for ten dollars. This was pretty warm in the mouth, but as some sold for fifteen the same season, he was satisfied with his bargain. It was the last year of the speculation, and the fall crop was dull in the market, at a dollar a bushel. Tim Bunker rubbed his eyes with both his fore-fingers, when harvest came, and declared that he would never touch another new thing. But he has repented of that now, and adopted quite a number of new things that have been tested in the Deacon's garden. He is always certain to make the Deacon pay for his own experiments, and only adopts the new fruit or vegetable when he is certain it will pay. He has lately got wind of the Dioscorea Batatas. His neighbor lent him the nursery pamphlet in which the wonderful productiveness of that astonishing tuber was duly set forth. Tim digested its contents, and when he returned the pamphlet, very dryly inquired:

"Deacon, does not this make you think of the Rohan?" He will not purchase this year.

Conservative as he is, there is manifest progress with Mr. Bunker, and a real improvement is sure to find its way, in due time, to his farm. The debt and credit account of his adventure in pursuit of the blackberry plants as he read it in the Deacon's *Agriculturist*, struck Tim full in the face. He has not stopped thinking of it yet, and we hope to record his name, before a great while, upon our list of subscribers.

P. S.—The seed has borne fruit. We received the following letter this morning:

HOOKERTOWN, CONN., April 15, 1856.

DEAR SIR:—Inclosed please find $1 for the *Agriculturist* for one year. TIMOTHY BUNKER.

O. JUDD, Esq., New York City.

No. 4.—TIM BUNKER'S VIEW OF THE BIRD LAW.

Jeremiah Sparrowgrass left Hookertown for the commercial metropolis at the tender age of sixteen, thinking that his salvation would be effected and his fortune made forever, if he could find a situation as clerk in a dry good store. He found in the city the object of his lofty ambition, and, after a little roughing it, was duly installed as errand boy and professor of small jobs in a respectable establishment on Broadway. At the age of twenty-one Jeremiah is a clerk with a salary in the establishment where he commenced his mercantile life; a youth of promise in the esteem of his friends, and not slow in his own estimation. In May he took it into his head to visit his country cousins at Hookertown, and to regale himself a little with country sports.

Nothing seemed better adapted to his tastes than gunning, and he accordingly brought up from the city a fowling piece, that he might carry out his deadly intent. He had seen certain brave, chivalrous youths returning from the Jerseys, dressed with hunting cap and coat, and ornamented with powder flask, shot-bag and game pouch, the very pictures of genteel recreation. So the first morning after he had surprised Hookertown with his advent, he girded on his shooting toggery and military weaponry, determined to make the birds of his native parish smell gunpowder, and bite the dust. He had some obscure recollections that there was a prejudice against birds among the farmers on account of their pulling up corn, and thought he would be performing a very good deed, as well as exhibiting his own prowess, by destroying them. His whole memory of country life had become exceedingly impaired by his city residence, and he delighted to show his ignorance by asking questions upon topics that he was thoroughly instructed in when a boy of ten on the farm.

Passing Deacon Smith's orchard, Jeremiah Sparrowgrass, merchant of the city of New York, spied a robin redbreast, singing away right merrily with his bill in the air, as if his whole soul was exhaling in the melody. Beneath, in a fork of the tree, was his mate, with a nest full of birdlings, and surely a happier family group was not to be found anywhere in the country. Bang went the gun of Jeremiah Sparrowgrass, and that morning song was ended. It was owing entirely to the inexperience of the sportsman that a husband and lover was not also ended, and a whole brood bereaved of their natural protector. The report of the gun brought out Deacon Smith before the heroic Mr. Sparrowgrass had time to reload his piece and make a demonstration on the mother, who was fluttering and crying in a state of great apprehension in the tree tops. Jerry knew the Deacon as well as any boy knows his senior in a country church that he has always attended, but this morning affected ignorance, both of the Deacon and his robins.

"My dear sir, will you have the kindness to inform me what species of bird this is? I am making a collection of the feathered tribe for my *herbarium*, and should like to add this specimen to my list."

"This bird," replied the Deacon, "is known as the Condor of the Andes, the same kind that sometimes carries off calves."

Jeremiah Sparrowgrass, merchant of New York City, did not stop to finish loading his gun, but sloped in the most expeditious manner.

He crossed the road and struck into the cow pasture of Tim Bunker, thinking less, probably, of his *herbarium* and scientific attainments, than before he shot at the robin. Here he found birds more plenty than he had known them in his boyhood. A statute of Connecticut, enacted a few years since, which prohibits shooting certain varieties of birds on another's land, under a heavy penalty, proves a very efficient protection, and the birds have multiplied wherever the citizens have enforced it. Timothy Bunker, Esq., being a Justice of the Peace, and arriving at the honor somewhat late in life, had zealously enforced the law in his neighborhood, not only to maintain the dignity of the law, but to protect his own fields against the depredations of insects. Though a very conservative man, he could see the benefits of the law, and promptly warned off all intruders from his wood and swamp pastures, where the birds loved to congregate.

Jeremiah Sparrowgrass was first saluted by a bobolink from the stake of a rail fence:

"Link, link-ee, wink, wink-ee, sweetch, sweetch-ee-ee, wee, wee-ee-ee-ee." His fire brought down poor Bob

A NEW YORK SPORTSMAN IN HOOKERTOWN. Page 16.

O'Lincoln, a wounded, dying bird, and waked up Tim Bunker, who happened to be in the adjoining field planting corn. The genteel merchant, in pursuit of country pleasures, was just bagging his game when Esq. Bunker came up. Sparrowgrass had only got as far as "My dear sir, will you have the kindness," in his stereotyped speech of enquiry, when he was interrupted.

"Why, Jerry, is this you, out here in Hookertown agin, killing our birds. You ought to be ashamed of yourself, shooting a poor skunk blackbird. What harm has he ever done you? His song is a little crooked, I allow, but cold lead is not the stuff to straighten it with. It is the same song the Almighty gin him to sing, and he has as good a right to sing it as you have to measure tape. It is a most inhuman thing to kill birds when they are laying their eggs and hatching their young. Besides, Jerry, we've got a law agin it, and all good citizens ought to obey it. The birds are the best friends the farmers have, and we have learned better than to kill the crows, as we used to when they pulled the corn. Now, Jerry, put up your shooting iron and go straight home to widow Sparrowgrass's, and if you shoot another bird in these parts I'll have you fined before night."

Mr. Jeremiah Sparrowgrass withdrew immediately, being particularly disgusted that an old farmer should call a Broadway merchant "Jerry," and very much out of humor with the Connecticut bird law.

The statute, however, is likely to stand for some years to come.—Ed.

No. 5.—GUANO IN THE HILL AND NO PAPER.

We recently met a man, driving fast, with a very long face. He was in pursuit of the editor, and reining up his steed, he opened his complaint.

"I heerd tell great stories about the dewings of that foreign manure in your paper. Deacon Smith tried it and I seed the account of it in Tim Bunker's papers. So I sent down to York this spring and got a half ton of guano and put it on to my corn. I was detarmined to give it a fair trial, and slap'd a hull handful into every hill. I planted it more than three weeks ago, and it aint up yet; and I am plaguy 'fraid that aint the worst of it. Now I want to know what is the matter and what I shall dew."

"My dear sir, I see you do not take the papers, but only borrow Tim Bunker's paper occasionally, and do not half read that."

"True as gospel, Mr. Editor, but how did you know that?"

"Know it! Why your story convicts you of not taking the papers. You cannot find in the country an agricultural paper so poorly edited that it would not tell you better than to put guano into the hill, especially a whole handful. That is enough to rot a whole handful of corn."

"Dew tell!!"

"Your corn will never see the light, neighbor, and you must plant it over again."

"You don't say so!"

"You should have sowed your guano broadcast, and plowed it in immediately; then it would have been diffused equally in the soil, and would have given you a good crop."

"I never thought of that."

"You ought to have taken the papers. In this operation you see you have lost five days' work, worth, at least, five dollars, and it is now so late that your corn will not be nearly as good as it would have been planted earlier. You will lose at least five dollars on every acre of corn you plant, for want of this information about the proper method of using guano. Five dollars in loss of labor and fifteen in loss of time make twenty dollars, which would furnish you with at least a dozen of the best agricultural journals in the country, and pay the postage on them."

"I should not wonder if that was so."

We left our unfortunate friend, scratching his head, now radiant with a new idea. What the result will be, of course, we cannot tell. But we expect better things in the future. Hundreds of cases like this are to be found all over the country. Men hear of guano, and take it for granted it is of no consequence how they use it; they put it in by the handful and plant the seed directly upon it. Farmers should read and think more. It is very expensive to cultivate the soil without knowledge. Take the papers.—Ed.

No. 6.—TIM BUNKER ON MOSS BUNKERS.

Hookertown has been thrown into quite a ferment lately, by the arrival of numerous loads of fish from the shore for the purpose of manure. The muck heaps are in a ferment with the fish, and the people with the talk about them. As in all new enterprizes, there is a great difference of opinion, and almost every man is as decided in his views as if he had used moss bunkers from his boyhood. Some declare that the fish cannot be used without making an odor, more distinguished than all the spice groves of the tropics, and that the man ought to be prosecuted who will put moss bunkers in any field within a mile of the road. Others think the fish are good for nothing after they are put upon the land. There is nothing like the good old stuff right out of the barn-yard. But the majority are bound to try the article, as they agreed last winter to take, some fifty thousand, some sixty, and some a hundred thousand. They live too far from the shore to apply them fresh to the growing crops, and they are almost without exception putting them into heaps and covering them with peat and muck. As this latter article is abundant, they use five or six cords of it to one of the fish. Tim Bunker very early consulted Deacon Smith and the back numbers of the *Agriculturist*, and after thinking the whole matter over a few days, he came to the conclusion that he would go in for fifty thousand of the fish and run the risk of it. The very first load of the article he brought through the street he was hailed by Mr. Jotham Sparrowgrass, the uncle of Jeremiah of bird-killing memory. Jotham was wise in the ways of his fathers and knew all about the fish, for he had lived over on Long Island when he was a boy.

"Well, Squire Bunker, I suppose you think you are going to do a nice thing with them 'ere fish, but let me tell you, you don't know everything if you do take the papers. Fish pizens land. I've seen it tried time and again, and I never knew it to fail."

"How do you know that, Jotham?"

"Why, you see, sir, that paper is filling your head full of foolish notions. When I was a boy, my father and all his neighbors used to use fish; John Woodhull, Tom Tuttle, Ben Miller, and a lot more. They got mighty great crops for a few years, and then the land got to be so poor that fish didn't produce no more effect upon it than so much sand. They came to the conclusion fish pizened the sile, and I never have thought much of fish since."

"Well, Jotham, can you tell me if they used anything else besides fish for manure?"

"No, they didn't. You see fish was so plenty in Peconic Bay, all along the shores of Southold, that they thought it was of no use to cart dirt into their yards."

"Well, that was the trouble with them, Jotham, and the reason that the land run to sorrel and moss. Deacon Smith has studied into this matter a little more than I have, and the Deacon says that if we only use muck with fish, or if we turn in green crops occasionally, the land will grow better all the while, and produce great crops. He says the fish stimulate the soil to produce great crops of corn, oats, hay, etc., and immense quantities of carbonaceous matter are carried off, and the soil is soon exhausted, unless we put back the carbon in some way."

"I don't believe a word about your carbonates, Tim Bunker, and the other stuff you and the Deacon get out of the papers. I tell you fish will pizen the land, and Hookertown will be a desert in less than five years if you keep carting these stinking fish into town."

"But if fish spoil the land, Uncle Jotham, why do they keep using them on the Island? One town over there raised twenty thousand bushels of wheat and corn last year, rye and oats in great quantities, and it was just where they used fish in greatest abundance."

"I don't believe a word on't. That wheat crŏp, you see, was growed on paper. You can't raise wheat in this part of the country. The sile is too old."

"Well, Uncle Jotham, I see you are dead set agin the fish, but I have made up my mind to buy them, and I think I shall show you they won't spoil the land."

Timothy Bunker, Esq., touched up his span and ended the conference; while Uncle Jotham struck his cane upon the ground with great emphasis and tugged off, muttering as he went: "Who would have thought it! Tim Bunker using bony fish! It's no use; they pizen the sile."—Ed.

NO. 7.—TIM BUNKER ON SUBSOILING.

It has been stirring times in Hookertown recently, on account of the advent of the subsoil plow. Deacon Smith had one last spring, and if Barnum's elephant had come along with it, the team would not have made half the talk the plow made. Elephants they had all seen or heard of at the menagerie as a kind of monster never designed to run in opposition to horses or any other farm team. But a subsoil plow was "a new fangled consarn that the Deacon was gwine to poke into the yaller dirt to astonish the natives." It was entirely contrary to all well-established notions in this venerable community, and was looked upon as an intruder.

The Deacon's barn-yard was a scene for a painter when the neighbors dropped in to examine the new tool. Tim Bunker was there of course, and Jotham Sparrowgrass, Seth Twiggs, the smoker, John Tinker, and Tom Jones.

Esquire Bunker's views were not very definite as to the construction of the plow, and he wanted to know:

"Why, Deacon, where is the mold-board?"

"I should not wonder if it screwed on," responded Mr. Twiggs, half inquiringly.

"Now, what do you call that ere article?" asked Tom Jones.

"It is a mighty lean looking consarn, ain't it?" says John Tinker.

"And I guess the crops it will make will be leaner," chimed in Jotham Sparrowgrass. "You see, Deacon, I know all about these subsoilers. They tried an experiment when I was a boy, over on the Island. You know Ben Miller got a notion in his head that the fish manure all leached down into the sile, and that was the reason why we did not get any better crops after we had used

A SUBSOIL PLOW INSPECTED. · Page 22.

them a few years. So he took his old plain lot, and plowed two furrows in a place, and turned up the biggest sight of yaller dirt you ever laid eyes on. It looked for all the world like so many acres of Scotch snuff. The result was that he planted corn there, and did not get ten bushels to the acre. The land was spilt, and it is of no use to talk to me about stirring the subsile."

Argument of course was out of the question, and the Deacon showed his good sense by leaving the plow to speak for itself. He subsoiled a field properly, and planted with corn. He also induced Tim Bunker to try it on a patch of his garden where he was purposing to plant carrots and melons.

The month of July brought a drouth in Hookertown. Uncle Jotham's garden felt it severely, and he had plenty of neighbors to sympathize with him in his lamentations over withered vegetables.

Tim Bunker called him into his garden one day as he was passing.

"See here, I want you to look at my carrots, and see how green they are where I used the Deacon's subsoil plow. They are growing now as fast as if they had a plenty of rain, and over there is a piece in John Tinker's garden that looks as if the lightning had struck it. He put on a good deal more manure than I did, and you see the difference."

"Who would have thought it!" exclaimed Uncle Jotham. "I guess you have put on water."

"Have you seen the Deacon's garden? It is all as green as a leek, and nobody would think there had been no rain for three weeks. You see there is no getting round the facts, and I have made up my mind to try a subsoil plow this fall. It must be a great thing to guard crops against drouth, and I shall try on the piece of land that I sow with rye."

Jotham Sparrowgrass was much less voluble than usual during the call, and went home soliloquizing, "Wonder if Tim Bunker did water them carrots!"—Ed.

NO. 8.—TIM BUNKER GOING TO THE FAIR.

"Dew tell, Squire Bunker, if you're gwine to exhibit at the County Fair this Fall," said Seth Twiggs, as he lighted his third pipe, and took his hat. "I never was tu one of them Fairs in my life, but I have heern tell of the big squashes and cabbage, and I thought you would be after sending up some of your garden sass, it is so mighty nice." Seth had kept an eye on the subsoil plow after he found it had no mold-board, and occasionally looked into the Deacon's garden, as well as into Squire Bunker's.

"Shouldn't wonder if I did," replied Tim Bunker. "You see, I went up last year for the first time, not thinking it was worth while to take up anything to show. But I found when I got there that Hookertown was making as good a show as any other town in the county, and there were some things there that took premiums that I could have beaten, even before my garden had the subsoil plow in it. Wife planted a squash at the edge of the carrot bed, and the vine has a half dozen whoppers on it. The big one there will weigh a hundred and fifty pounds, and she declares 'that squash must be seen.' Then John has a bed of onions, some of them measuring six inches across; and some California potatoes weighing two pounds apiece. Our Sally is tip-top on bread-making, and says she is bound to take a premium, for the ministers are to be the judges, and will give a righteous award. The bees have

TAKING IN SQUASHES. Page 25.

done well this year, and whiter honey never was seen than we have in our boxes. The carrots of the subsoiled land of course must go up. I measured one the other day twenty and one-half inches long, and I think I can find a bushel of the same length and size. Yes, Sir, Mr. Twiggs, we shall all go up to the Fair to-morrow morning."—Ed.

NO. 9.—TIM BUNKER IN TALL CLOVER.

THE FAIR, AND HOW HE TOOK THE PRIZES.

"Taking in your squashes then, this morning, Esq. Bunker," said Seth Twiggs, as he looked over the garden fence, and saw Tim very busy. The smoke curled up from his pipe, and both hands were thrust into his waistcoat pockets, as he stood with his weight poised upon one leg, and both ears opened.

"Oh, it is you, is it, Seth," said Tim, as he deposited the last squash in the basket. Did you hear how I came off at the fair yesterday?"

"Not exactly. I kind o' thought it wouldn't be strange if them carrots of you'rn got a premium."

"Carrots, man! why I made a clean sweep, and got a premium on everything I carried. Had the grandest time I and my family ever experienced. You ought to have been there, Mr. Twiggs, to see Hookertown in its glory. First, you see, our town train was made up of seventy-one yoke of oxen, besides Jim Latham's steer train of five yoke, which the Committee said would not count. This was bigger than anything upon the ground, and took a prize. Then Deacon Smith's fat pair of cattle, that weighed five thousand pounds upon the hoof, could not be beat. He also had some South Down wethers that weighed near two hundred apiece, and were said to be the finest fat sheep ever exhibited in the State.

"But I was going to tell you how our folks came out. You see Mrs. Bunker's big squash, that grew there in the carrot bed, beat everything in the vegetable line for size. There was a fellow up from Shadtown, on the river, that tho't he was some punkins. But, la suz, Seth, his squash could not hold a candle to ours, by sixty weight. He said he manured with fish, and calculated he should make a clear sweep on the vegetables, squashes in particular. The fellow got a premium on potatoes, which seemed to comfort him some."

"Whurra for our side!" exclaimed Seth, swinging his beaver.

"But I hain't done with the women yet. You see our Sally made up a batch of bread out of the new wheat that I raised on Stone Hill. It was ground over to the city, so that the whole stuff was Connecticut manufacture, from top to bottom,—wheat, flour, yeast, and the girl that made it. And who'd 'a thought, Seth, that same loaf of bread took the premium."

"Didn't the gal blush when it was read off?" inquired Seth.

"I shouldn't wonder if she did; but whether it was about the bread, or one of the ministers that was on the Committee, I couldn't say. They do say that the young man they have just settled in Shadtown, is mighty fond of exchanging with our man, and that Sally's singing is very much to his mind. But that had nothing to do with the premium, for it never got round that the bread was made of Connecticut flour, until after the premiums were read off. Then, you see, I let the cat out of the bag, and told them that No. 5 was made out of our home-made flour by our Sally.

"John's onions, too, came out just as they were labeled,

No. 1, and the boy has got the money for them in his pocket. His Bremen geese were the largest exhibited, and the white Dorkings could not be beat. You know our Suffolk pigs; I had them all washed up the day before the fair, and they were clean enough to go into the pork barrel all alive. They were the best lot exhibited.

"There was a good deal of competition on the vegetables. One man brought a hundred varieties, and another ninety-one. My carrots were hard run, and the Committee declared that they were a good deal bothered to know how to decide, and I guess they were so. But you see my star was in the heavens that day, and my carrots took the prize. That is what I call doing pretty well. But it isn't a circumstance to what I shall do next year. I'm bound to lay myself out at the next fair."

NO. 10.—TIM BUNKER ON HORSE-RACING.

Our cut illustrating an "Orthodox Agricultural Exhibition in 1856," appears to have touched the right cord. We are glad to learn that it has met with such favor among our orthodox subscribers in Hookertown and vicinity. We give Mr. Bunker's letter entire.

HOOKERTOWN, Nov. 12, 1856.

To the Editor of the American Agriculturist.

I am not much used to writing letters of any kind, much less letters for the papers. But I see you are reporting considerable many of my sayings in your paper, and I thought if you were bent upon having my notions circulated, you might as well have them direct from the fountain head, as to have them come in a round-about way. I just want to say that there is nothing come out lately that has struck the fancy of the Hookertown people like that cut of the horse-race, in the last paper. At first I did not know but you was coming out in favor of these fast colts and "whurra boys" at our fairs, and I begun to think that I should have to drop the paper, if that was the case. You see, horse-racing is an institution agin which Connecticut people are dead set upon principle, and it is no kind of use to attempt to revive that old engine of the enemy in this enlightened age, even under the cover of an agricultural fair.

We have got a great notion of the County and State Societies, and of the Fairs that come off every fall. They please our vanity somewhat, and are doing a heap of good, in waking folks up to a better kind of farming. All sorts of folks come to them, and the better part of the community especially. It seems as if we had got one thing that we could all be agreed on. There is a considerable split on religion, and politics always stirs up a deal of bad feeling, especially such an exciting election as this we have just had. Now it seems to me that these fairs are just what we want to draw all kinds of people together, and to keep up good neighborhood. But just as soon as you bring in horse-racing, and make that a part of the fair, you see, a multitude of people wont stand it no how. It does seem as if the devil was always around when folks are trying to start a good enterprise, getting up something to knock it all over. You see, we have put down circuses, theatricals, etc., time and agin, and we don't believe in horse-racing as a moral institution, fix it up any way you will. Deacon Smith, you see, is a rural improver, goes in for good horses, fine cattle, and all that sort of thing. He went down to Boston to attend the horse show, supposing they were going to have a civil kind of time. Guess how mortified he was, when he got into the show and found jockeys, gamblers, and betting men around him, thick as flies in

Hookertown in fish time. You see the Deacon will not be caught in such a scrape agin.

Now I don't suppose there is any objection to having a track upon the fair grounds, and to driving horses around on a pretty good jog, but I can't see how it is going to make us breed any better horses to have a regular racing match, and to have all the gamblers and fancy men in the country drawn together to see the sport. It strikes me that gamblers would be made much faster than good horses by such brutal exhibitions.

Just to show you how the thing works, I will tell you about my John. You see the boy has been at work hard all summer, and I thought I would let him go down to Boston with the Deacon, to see the fine horses. When the boy came home, I found he had been making a bet on Ethan Allen, and was cracking about the horse as raging as an old gamester. You see the boy was young, and his father was not with him. It won't be safe for a man to take his family to the fairs, if they are going to be turned into race-courses. Good people will be dead set agin them, and the first thing we shall know, all the pulpits in Connecticut will be blowing away at the fairs for horse-racing and gambling. Now, you see, I don't belong to the meeting myself, and am not so good as I ought to be, but I can see the bearing of horse-racing on the morals of the community. When a man's boy gets to betting at a fair, you see, it brings the matter straight home, and there is no blinding a man's eyes to the facts in the case. If the ministers come out agin this kind of agricultural exhibitions, they will have the right on their side and will be certain to carry the day. It is no kind of use to approve a thing that is not right. So you see I was mighty glad to see that picture in your paper showing up the folly of horse-racing at the fairs. Mrs. Bunker put on her spectacles, and looked at it, and wanted to know of John if that looked anything like the Boston show. John rather blushed, and said "the thing was natural as life." I have had a dozen people in to borrow the paper, and Seth Twiggs, Bill Bottom, and Jake Frink, want to take it. I inclose three dollars—Send them "A Bakers Dozen."

Yours Agin Horse-Racing,

TIMOTHY BUNKER Esq.

NO. 11.—TIM BUNKER AT THE FARMERS' CLUB.

HIS VIEW ON CHINA POTATO AND MIXED PAPERS.

Hookertown has at length a Farmers' Club. It was organized just after Thanksgiving, and may be regarded as one of the permanent institutions of that happy people. The farmers in the land of steady habits are proverbially cautious, and not carried about by every "wind of doctrine," whether in husbandry or in religion. But when a thing is done, it is generally well done, and will last until there is good reason for doing it away. The thing had been talked of by Deacon Smith and the minister, Rev. Jacob Spooner, for at least a year beforehand. They both agreed it would be a good thing in every point of view, if the people could only be brought to attend it. But there were so few agricultural papers taken in the place, that they doubted whether there was interest enough felt in the matter to sustain weekly meetings. So they let the matter rest until a Club should seem to be called for by public sentiment.

Rev. Jacob Spooner, the able and efficient pastor of Hookertown, is somewhat past his prime, though one might easily take him for a man ten years younger than he is. For forty years he has held his office, and molded public sentiment upon all secular topics, as well as upon religion. He is a good sample of a Puritan pastor of the present generation. He is regarded as timid by many of his juniors in the ministry, and altogether too cautious in the positions he takes in regard to the novelties of the day. But this reserve is the result of experience and age. He has seen the breakers, and knows more of the perils of a minister's life than his younger brethren. He is undoubtedly conservative, but not from any lack of moral courage. He has sometimes gone before public opinion in his parish, and knows something of the difficulties of bringing over a community to new opinions and customs. He always means to move in the right direction himself, and in his later years has thought it best, on the whole, to work in private for any new measure on which he had set his heart, before he committed himself to it in public. His shadow fills the place pretty well, and he is sometimes a little afraid of it, but nobody ever knew him to hold back from a thing that was really good and praiseworthy. When public sentiment is prepared by his "in-door work," as he calls it, the measure is pushed with a good deal of vigor.

A Farmers' Club in Hookertown was a fixed fact in this man's mind a year ago, and the delay was only a wise way of making haste slowly. He wanted to say the right thing to Timothy Bunker, Esq., and his wife Sally, in his pastoral visits, and speak of the Club as a thing likely to turn up another season, if the farmers would take hold of it. He also had a few words to say to Seth Twiggs, John Tinker, and Tom Jones, and their neighbors, which would prove as good seed in good soil for his purposes.

These private talks of the minister, together with the fairs and the agricultural papers, had stirred up a good deal of interest in the community, so that everybody was prepared to see the notice stuck up on the sign post in Hookertown, in front of the meeting-house, that the farmers and cultivators would hold a Club meeting at the school-house, on the first Tuesday evening in December. The subject announced for discussion was the "Dioscorea Batatas, or Chinese Potato."

The appointed evening came, and the school-house, when the orthodox hour of early candle-light appeared, revealed some five and twenty of the farmers, mechanics, and professional men of the town.

Deacon Smith was appointed Chairman, and as the proceedings were not designed for the public, it was concluded to forego the usual ceremony of appointing a clerk. The Chairman laid the subject for discussion before the meeting, and called upon gentlemen for their views of the distinguished stranger.

He said the topic had excited considerable interest among cultivators, and a good deal had been said about it in the papers. A nurseryman of distinction had claimed for it remarkable virtues, and had threatened to drive out all known esculents with it from the country. Great pains had been taken to disseminate the tubers, and he had learned that some of the tin boxes were imported into Hookertown last spring. He had understood that gentleman would be present this evening, who would relate his experience. The meeting was open for remarks.

Judge Bronson said he supposed the allusion to the tin boxes probably meant him, and he had to confess that he parted company with an "X" last April for one of those articles. The contents, he said, were sand, and a dozen black looking articles, a little bigger than pepper-corns, that looked about as likely to sprout as so many crumbs of Indian bread. He said his faith leaned hard upon a pamphlet containing a beautiful illustration of the tuber and a glowing description of its virtues and productiveness. He thought it was worth trying, and had tried it quite as thoroughly as any case he had ever tried in Court, and by ordinary rules of evidence, he was constrained to pronounce the claims put forth a great humbug, whatever might be said of the tuber itself.

Rev. Mr. Slocum, of Shadtown, next addressed the meeting. This gentleman's exchanges with the Hookertown minister have been more frequent of late, and as he always stops at Esquire Bunker's, it is mistrusted that something beside the Farmers' Club made him stay over to attend this meeting. Perhaps Sally Bunker knows about that; your Reporter does not. He said that he had received one of the pamphlets which Judge Bronson had mentioned, and from what he could learn at the ministers' meetings, the work was pretty extensively distributed among the clergy last winter. Whether the operators in tubers thought that an unusual share of the green ones was to be found among the clergy, he could not say. Probably that view of their character had something to do with the liberal share of pamphlets bestowed upon them. He was happy to state, however, that very few of his brethren had been caught in the trap, and those who had fooled away their ten dollars were best able to bear it. Gentlemen who had tried the new yam in his parish were disappointed with its performance, and thought it a swindle.

This brought up old Jotham Sparrowgrass, the distinguished uncle of Jeremiah, the Broadway clerk, who made such a figure shooting robins and bobolinks last summer, in Tim Bunker's cow pasture, as the readers of the *Agriculturist* will remember. Jotham had grown envious of Esquire Bunker's recent improvements and notoriety, and also of his neighbors, and though he was always running out against book-farming and new-fangled notions, he determined that for once he would steal a march upon them, and astonish the natives with potatoes a yard long. As soon as he saw the notices of the Dioscorea in certain leading political papers, he determined upon a venture, and ordered a dozen through his nephew, Jeremiah Sparrowgrass—him of New York City.

"Swindle!" echoed Uncle Jotham, as he rose and struck his cane upon the floor, "there has not been such a piece of rascality afloat since the Multicaulus fever. I got caught *then* with a Chinaman, and vowed I never would have anything more to do with book-farming. But those stories in my New York paper looked so mighty plausible, that I was taken in agin. You see, if they had been in an agricultural paper, I wouldn't 've read 'em. But coming in a political paper, I thought they were all right. But I have now come to the conclusion that there is a mighty difference between potatoes and politics. A man sound in politics may be a blind guide in vegetables. Why, them things cost me nearly a dollar apiece, they did not half come up, and what did come up might as well have staid down, they were such thin, stringy, consarns. Potatoes a yard long, and a rod of ground supporting a family!! Why, at the rate mine yielded, it would take an acre of 'em to support a pig, and if the one our folks cooked was a fair sample, the pigs might have 'em in welcome."

Tim Bunker, Esq., here got the floor, and, with a side glance at Jotham, said: "It would be well if cultivators who were going into new things would take a reliable agricultural paper, published by men who understand the business, and have access to the best sources of information in regard to the novelties that come out. He was not caught in this humbug, thanks to the *American Agriculturist*, which gave timely warning to all its readers last winter. The fact is, there is too much of a disposition to mix up things in the papers. I think a political paper better stick to politics and news, and a religious paper stick to religion and missions, and when we have a farmers' paper, let the editor stick to his text, and not hash up potatoes with love stories. I don't mean to reflect upon any rural paper in particular. For my part, I want a simple diet in my paper as well as upon my table. Then I know pretty much what I have got before me, and it is all plain sailing.

But you see this China potato first got a going in a political paper, and folks swallowed it whole as if it was all according to Gunter. But you see, the fellow that wrote about it was a cute chap, cyphering up a good speculation for himself, instead of calculating for the good of the public. The fellow promised too much by half. If he had only said he had got a good thing, and wanted folks to try it, it would have looked more reasonable. But when he came to talk about its feeding all China, and that it was soon going to feed all America, it was going a leetle too far. The funniest part of the whole story was, that he expected ministers were such greenhorns as to believe the whole of it, just as if the doctrine of total depravity had never been heard of in Connecticut. I doubt whether he goes to meeting much. The only safe way for us to avoid humbugs is to take a good agricultural paper, and keep up with the times."

Meeting adjourned.

NO. 12.—TIM BUNKER ON AN OLD SAW.

Mr. Editor:—You need not think that any of my neighbors have grown envious of my getting the premiums, and rode me out on a rail, or on one of the above articles, tooth side up. And you needn't suppose I am going to write about a *saw*, though it's a very convenient tool about a farmer's workshop. But you see there is a saying, "Penny wise, pound foolish," that is always a see-sawing up and down in some folks' mouths, that they call an old saw, as they do all such like proverbs. I expect they call 'em so, because of the teetering process which such sayings are always undergoing. There is a deal of pith in 'em, as a rule, though they are made to apologize for pretty much all sorts of shortcomings. I am now going to bring out this old proverb, "Penny wise, and pound foolish," and putting it at one end of the plank, I mean to give some of the Hookertown people an airing on the other.

I wish some of our folks up here could look at themselves and their farming in a looking-glass, and just see what sort of work they are making. You see, every man thinks every man penny wise but himself. The looking-glass would often bring 'em right.

Uncle Jotham Sparrowgrass I s'pose never spent the value of fifty cents in his life for seeds of any kind before he went in for that China potato last year. He could not see, for the life of him, but what one kind of seed was about as good as another. The onion seed, and carrot and parsnip seed, that Mrs. Sparrowgrass always saved and stored away in an old basket in the pantry, always came up and bore something, though the onions might have been mistaken for leeks, they were so little, and the other roots were hardly big enough to make a spile for the cider barrel. Everything else in his garden was just so. The parsnips, cabbage, and beets, were all crossed, and *run out* as they call it, and there was hardly a decent vegetable in his garden for want of good seed. He could not afford to buy it when he had it in the house—used to talk about hurting his wife's feelings if he should not use the seed she had saved. That would have been less of a joke, you see, if he had always been careful of her feelings on other occasions. Well, you see, when he read those advertisements in that yellow-covered literature last spring, he altered his mind some about potato seed, and thought he would put in for a dozen at ten dollars. He was going to be a pound wise man, and show his neighbors some potatoes that were potatoes. Didn't he catch it, though! The Sparrowgrass family have hardly had potatoes on the table since. It is said they set bad on Uncle Jotham's stomach.

Now you see I tried this planting of seeds gathered from the odds and ends of the garden, for rising of forty years, and I think it is a penny wise business—my onions used to be scullions, my cabbages did not head well, and the tap-roots would often run to seed the first year. Last spring, you see, when I went down to the city to sell my beef cattle, I went to a first-rate agricultural store, and spent about *ten dollars* in garden seeds. It was those seed, as well as the subsoil plowing and manuring, that enabled me to take the premiums at the Fair. Seth Twiggs came along the day I was putting them into the cellar, and said: " Waal, Squire Bunker, I dew declare, I never saw such a sight of garden sass going into your cellar afore!"

Seth was right. I never had such roots or cabbage heads. It was fun to pull them. And I have pretty much made up my mind that seed is one of the chief points in good farming. I think there is a difference of one quarter in the crop between good seed and poor. So, when I went down to the city this spring, I took time by the forelock, and got another lot of seed at the same place. And I want to say to all your readers in Hookertown, and the rest of Connecticut, that if they expect to compete with me at the fair next fall, they must burn up the old seed, papers, basket and all, and get the best in the market. It is a penny wise business to use poor old seed in the spring, and mighty pound foolish in the fall.

NO. 13.—BOOK FARMING IN HOOKERTOWN.

Mr. Editor.—I suppose every man likes to know how the truck he sends to market suits his customers. At any rate that is the case at my house, where a good report of the butter and a call for more is certain to keep my wife good-natured for a week. As her butter is tip-top, and I bring home the news once a week, she passes for a very amiable woman the year round. Now I suppose an editor may have some human nature about him, and may like to know how his wares suit the market, and what sort of influence they have upon the world.

There has been a great change up here in Hookertown, and all through Connecticut, during the last four or five years. Since then we have got our State society a going, and new county societies have been started, and I guess I speak within bounds when I say that ten times as many agricultural papers are taken as there were five years ago. These things have had a mighty influence upon farming, and I should think in our town the garden crops had been doubled, and full twenty per cent. has been added to the crops in the field. Some folks have got to taking the papers, and reading them, that I should as soon have expected to see reading Latin. Seth Twiggs was in at our house last evening, and he was telling how he come to take the *Agriculturist.* I give you the story as he told it to me.

"I tell you what it is, Squire Bunker, that lot o' garden sass I see'd you putting into the cellar last fall did the work for me. You see, I'd always thought that this book-farming was the worst kind of humbug, leading folks to spend a heap of money, and to get nothing back agin. I'd heard the Parson and Deacon Smith, and the young Spouter from Shadtown, (there was a twinkle in Seth's eye here, and a very grave look at Sally,) talking about guano, and what tremendous crops it would fetch, and then agin about phosphates and superphosphates, which was all as dark as fate to me. You see I thought them big words was all nonsense, and the stuff itself no better than so much moonshine on the land. The Deacon's crops, you know, have been amazing for some years, and then the strawberries last spring, and that lot of sass, convinced me that there must be something about book-farming arter all. So I went home and talked the matter over with my woman, what the minister said, and how the crops came in where they used the sub-sile plow."

"Well," says she, "Seth, what is the use of your always standing by, and hearing things said that you don't understand, like a stupid calf? Why don't you 'scribe and take them books?"

"Cause why? How can I afford it? I haven't quite paid for my farm yet, and the baby was sick this winter, and the doctor's bill isn't paid. And you know, wife, we have always gone upon the principle that 'a penny saved is two-pence earned.' We can't spend a dollar for farming books."

"Well, Seth," said she, "never mind. I can raise the dollar. 'Where there is a will there is a way.' I can make the old shawl and bonnet do another year, and that will be ten dollars in your pocket. Everything that a farmer has to sell is high; at any rate, we should think so if we had to buy it. I can remember well enough when butter was only ten cents a pound, now it is thirty; and many a bushel of potatoes you have carried to market for twelve and a half cents, now they are one dollar and more. Seth, if you railly want them books, I'd have 'em any how. It wont take a great deal of land to raise an extra bushel of potatoes, and if you're put to it for help, I'll agree to hoe 'em."

"Enough said," says I. "Woman, I'm bound to have the books." So I sent a dollar down to Mr. Judd by the Parson, the last time he went down to the city, and it wa'n't long before the January number came, as full of good reading as an egg is of meat. I had a regular set-to a reading on't, the first night, and I declare if it wa'n't smack twelve o'clock before I gin it up. I'd got along to that phosphate factory, when wife spoke out—says she: "I thought them farming papers was all nonsense!"

"Don't talk," says I. "You see this paper, wife, is on my side. It is showing up the humbug, and no mistake. And there is more humbug in the world than I ever dreamed of."

Upon this, Seth lit his pipe and vanished in smoke.

NO. 14.—HIS VIEWS ON PASTURING CATTLE IN THE ROAD.

Mr. Editor.—You see, I was so busy last month, planting, and getting things started for the summer, that I didn't find a minute's time to write to anybody, and hardly to be polite to my neighbors. I wish all my neighbors had been as busy, and as slack on politeness as myself. But no sooner had the grass begun to start in the spring, than some of them began to send along their compliments by their cattle, as much as to say, "By your leave, Mr. Bunker, I will keep your lawn in front of the house well cut and shaven, and won't ask you anything for the job." I counted, on Saturday, at least a dozen animals in the road. There was Jake Frink's horse and colt, and Bill Bottom's drove of yearlings, and Uncle Jotham Sparrowgrass's two cows, besides two or three other folks' cows that I should not like to mention in the same company.

Now you see, Mr. Editor, if a man's going to be polite at all, it is always best to attend to it in person. This sending along civilities by stray cattle is rather doubtful courtesy. It might happen, you know, that the shaving of one's lawn down to the roots would not be acceptable, and if it were, a second civility in the shape of the hogs to turn the sod of the lawn bottom side up, might be a

STRAY COWS IN THE CORN. Page 41.

little too much of a good thing. (You see I have learned to say "*lawns*" since I commenced reading the papers.)

Now, I don't like to say a word against my neighbors in general, or the Hookertown people in particular. But this turning cattle into the street is a piece of bad morals that is a disgrace to any community. It is against the law, and every man has a right to put stray animals in the pound, and make the owners pay damages. But if one enforces the law, it always makes trouble, and the man who finds his cattle impounded, always feels aggrieved, and lays up a grudge against his complaining neighbor. He does not consider that he has himself been an offender first, and violated the law. It is a clear case, that when streets were laid out they ceased to be private property, and were henceforth to be held for the public good, to serve simply the purposes of travel. If a man turns his cattle into the highways to feed, he violates the rights of his neighbor as much as if he turned them into his neighbor's pasture. He appropriates to his own use what belongs to another. He not only trespasses upon the public domain, but his cattle become a nuisance to the whole neighborhood. They enter every open gate and yard, and frequently become unruly, leap fences, and destroy crops at this season of the year. The loss of temper from these constantly recurring provocations is very great. I think Job himself would have fretted some, to have waked up in the morning and found a dozen cows in *his* corn-field.

It is a barbarous practice, and costs the community a hundred-fold more than all the grass in the road is worth. We have to make a great deal more fence than we should need if everybody confined their cattle to their *own* pastures. Now, every man has to fence all his lands by the road, not for his own convenience, but to keep other folks' cattle from trespassing upon him. I have been in communities without fences by the road-side for miles, and rode through the standing corn, rye and oats. without seeing a cow or calf. When we reckon fence at a dollar a rod, we can see to what a large expense farmers are subjected, to give a few penurious people the privilege of pasturing their cattle in the road.

You see, Mr. Editor, I am not going to stand this nuisance any longer. I shall give Jake Frink and Bill Bottom one fair warning, and after that, if their cattle are found in the road, they will go to the pound. This kind of politeness costs too much entirely. What do you think of it?

[Esquire Bunker is right. Cattle running at large are a nuisance that should not be tolerated in any civilized community. The pound is a sure remedy. Let him try it.—Ed.]

NO. 15.—TIM BUNKER ON THE WEAKER BRETHREN.

Mr. Editor:—I see by a former number of the *Agriculturist* that you had your reporter up here, taking notes at our Farmers' Club. I had no idea that he was around, or I should have fixed up my remarks in a little better shape, and dove-tailed the argument on mixed papers a little tighter together. I hold that what a man sees fit to print, should be water-tight. I want you to understand, and the public also, that I am not responsible for anything the reporters say about me, and that none of Tim Bunker's sayings are the genuine article, unless they come direct from Hookertown, and are over my name. You see they have got to counterfeiting my name already, just as they have Perry Davis', the inventor of the pain killer, and old Dr. Townsend's sarsaparilla. It was only the other day, that I saw a lot of my sayings in the Times about bad butter, that were never designed for the public at all. It was a private talk between me and my old friend Jones, and who in the world put them things in that paper, is more than I can tell. It must be confessed, however, that he got the substance of what we said across the table, pretty near correct. I suspect Jones, the sly dog, knows more about it than he would like to tell.

I took my pen in hand to say a word about a class of farmers we have up here in our neighborhood. You see, in the church they have a kind of members that the minister calls "the weaker brethren." They don't seem to have faith enough in them to make their religion of any account. They are always at the tail end of the heap, and like the stragglers in a flock of sheep, under the wall, or stuck fast in the mud. They are a disgrace to the cause.

Now we have some Hookertown farmers, that make me think of these weaker brethren 'fore all the world. They don't read the papers, and don't believe in good farming any more than such disciples believe the gospel. You can not get them to take the agricultural journals, and they laugh at all the new tools that have been invented to help farmers in their work. Instead of cleaning up their fields so as to use a mowing machine, they sweat over the scythe at the rate of an acre a day. Instead of having a barn cellar to save manure, it is mostly wasted in the yards and highways. Instead of sheltering cattle, in the cold, snowy weather, they fodder them out at a stack all winter. I do not know but I am wicked, but I wish every one of them could have been out that cold night in January, when the mercury froze. I think they would have learned to pity dumb cattle. I find such farmers are always complaining of hard times, and are never able to pay their debts. They are always running down farming, and talking about emigrating to the West, just as if a change of place was a going to change their characters, and make such shiftless farmers thriving men.

Now I have been thinking that these weaker brethren were living on "Missionary ground" as the saying is, and that the farmers who read the papers ought to come over and help them. It is no use for you to advertise your paper on this account, for such people do not take any paper, either political or religious. If one of your agents were to come along, and ask them to subscribe, they would feel insulted, if they could get near enough to them to make their business known. I am going to propose to our Farmers' Club to go out among these weaker brethren and see if we can't get them to take the papers, and mend their ways. You see they can't say we are mere book-farmers, and that our notions are all moonshine, for they know that our farms look enough sight better than theirs, and that our farmimg pays, so that we have money to lend. After all, Mr. Editor, there is nothing like an argument with the hard coin at the end on't. It does weigh. They appreciate the farming that brings the clean cash. That is the kind of farming we find your paper recommends, and as it is a poor rule that don't work both ways, I send you the clean cash for a dozen subscribers gathered among these weaker brethren. Consider these as the first fruits.

Yours to command,

TIMOTHY BUNKER, ESQ.

NO. 16.—TIM BUNKER ON CURING A HORSE-POND.

MR. EDITOR.—Your readers have already heard something about Jake Frink, and how he took the Premium on carrots over me at the Hookertown Fair. Perhaps they would like to hear something about a horse-pond that Jake used to own, about half-way between my house and his. It was full a quarter of a mile from his house, but as it was the nearest water that Nature had provided, it had always been used to water Jake's horses and cattle, when they were not in the pasture. It lay by the road-side at the foot of a gentle hill, and the water for all the wet part of the year flowed off over the adjoining lot, making it a sort of quagmire, except in times of drouth. An animal would mire in any part of the lot up to its knees. It never occurred to him that he could bring water into his yard at a little expense, and save this daily journey of his cattle to the pond. He never thought how much manure was wasted along the road, and what a nuisance his cattle became to his neighbors, as they were often turned into the road, to get water, and to take care of themselves. He never thought that the horse-pond spoiled two acres of the best land on his farm, and that it cost him at least twenty dollars a year to keep up this watering place. The quagmire did not pay him the interest on twenty dollars a year. It ought to have paid him ten per cent on two hundred.

The horse-pond I did not care anything about, but Jake's cattle, geese, and pigs, always drawn up my way by this water, were a perpetual torment to me and to my neighbors. I thought I had a right to abate the nuisance. So I hailed neighbor Frink one day, last fall, about selling the two-acre lot near the horse-pond. It was before the fair, for since my remarks about stimulating the carrot crop with *horse manure* he has been rather offish. Ever since I put down the tile drain in my garden I have formed a great idea of curing wet land, and I thought this piece of sour, unprofitable pasture might easily be turned into a productive meadow.

Says I, "Mr. Frink, what will you take for that bit of swamp land at the foot of the hill?"

"It is worth about twenty dollars an acre, I suppose.

You hold a note against me for about what the land would come to. Give me the note, and I will give you a deed."

"That is rather a hard bargain, neighbor, the land does not pay you the interest on half that sum. But as I want the land, I will take it."

The deed was given, and I took possession last November. We had a wonderful mild fall and winter, and I went right to work upon the land. The old, broken-down wall by the road-side, that had always been an eyesore to me, I immediately dropped into a four-foot ditch, making a covered culvert of the stone. There was fall enough to take all the water clean from the bottom of the ditch, and carry it off at the lower side of the adjoining lot. I cut four ditches at right angles to the ditch by the road-side, and put in tile at the bottom. The depth to which they were laid varied from three to four feet, as the surface was not exactly even. I had no sooner cut the main drain than the horse-pond all ran away, leaving the bottom at least two feet above the water line in the adjoining drain. The change in the looks of the land this spring is astonishing even to myself. Here, where cattle have always mired as they went out to crop the first grass of May, there is now a firm foothold. I have already plowed the most of it, and have put in a crop of early potatoes. The drains are just thirty feet apart, and the tile at the lower end constantly discharge water, and will probably continue to do so, until midsummer.

But my astonishment was nothing compared to Jake Frink's, when he came along and saw his horse-pond entirely evaporated.

"My goodness, Squire Bunker, what does this mean! What am I going to do for a place to water my cattle in?"

"Hold, neighbor Frink. Did you sell me this piece of land?"

"I did."

"Did I promise you that I would not improve it?"

"No, you did not, but who'd have thought that you was going to knock a hole in the bottom of my horse-pond in this style?"

"Water will run down hill, neighbor Frink, and I can't help it. The same law that enables me to drain this swamp will bring water from the hill-side right into your yard and house. You then can save all your manure, just as I do, and your cattle will not have the trouble of going after water in the cold of winter, and you will not have the trouble of scouring all Hookertown, to look them up. Your cattle will no longer be a nuisance, and you will save yourself a world of fretting and scolding. I have really done you a kindness in drying up this pond-hole. But as you may not look upon it in this light, I will give you the muck that lies in the bottom, at least a hundred cords of the wash of the roads, and the droppings of your cattle for the last twenty years. It is better manure, to-day, than a great deal that you cart out of your yard."

Mr. Frink took my remarks in dudgeon at the time, and hardly spoke to me for a month. But this spring the lead pipe was laid, and he has now as good a watering trough, fed with living water, as any of his neighbors. The muck, too, is not despised, for as I write I see Jake's cart, well loaded, going up to the yard where muck has hitherto been a great stranger. In short, I have strong hopes of making something out of Jake yet, though he cheated me out of the Premium. But whatever may be true of his reform, the horse-pond is thoroughly cured, and if you will come up here on the glorious Fourth, to help us celebrate, I will show you as handsome a piece of potatoes as ever grew out of doors.

Yours to command,

TIMOTHY BUNKER, ESQ.

Hookertown, May 15, 1858.

NO. 17.—DOMESTICITIES AT TIM BUNKER'S.

Our readers have become so much interested in the affairs of Hookertown in general, and at Esquire Bunker's in particular, that we feel obliged to keep them "posted up" in current events thereabouts, even if not in all cases strictly agricultural. The Squire has been so busy with other engagements that he has failed to send us the usual letter for the month, but we chance to be prepared to fill the gap—not so well as he could do, of course. We had fully intended to celebrate Independence Day at Squire Bunker's, and since we have seen the bill of fare he had prepared, we regret more than ever that a pressure of business prevented our visit to Hookertown. Our German Edition, added to our other cares, has completely absorbed us, so that we have not had a moment to think of the clover fields and the hospitalities of old Connecticut. Esquire Bunker will please accept our apologies for this seeming neglect, and for anything defective he may find in the report of the occasion. The fact is, the young man we sent up there had his head turned, (or rather his heart) by the Hookertown damsels, and came back nearer addled than any fellow we have seen in a twelve-month. The whole report had such a tint of rose color, that we have reduced the tone full one-half, besides throwing out lots of poetry, that were more appropriate to the Knickerbocker than to our matter-of-fact journal. Well here is

"OUR OWN REPORTER'S" REPORT—SOMEWHAT GARBLED.

Hookertown, Ct., July 5th, 1858.

MARRIED.

SLOCUM—BUNKER.—At Hookertown, Ct., on Saturday, July 3rd, in the Congregational Meeting-house, by the Rev. Jacob Spooner, Rev. Josiah Slocum, of Shadtown, to Sally, eldest daughter of Timothy Bunker, Esq., of this place. A large loaf attests the fact to the printers.

The above slip from the Hookertown Gazette of this morning will indicate pretty clearly the character of the clover fields your reporter was called upon to inspect. I must say, Mr. Editor, that I never was quite so much taken aback as upon last Saturday. I had supposed, from your instructions, that I was simply to inspect Esquire Bunker's improvements, and to report to the public how much allowance was to be made for the enthusiasm of your Hookertown correspondent. For everybody understands, that these sober Connecticut people, when they are once waked up and take to riding hobbies, are as apt to ride fast as others. I had prepared myself to take notes upon extensive meadows, all blooming and ready for the scythe; upon under-draining, subsoil plowing, &c. I thought my Sunday dress was hardly needed in a short trip to the country, and so I came off in my every-day toggery. Young John Bunker met me at the cars, according to agreement, and away we went, up hill and down, for about six miles, after as handsome a pair of Black Hawk mares as you can scare up in the pastures of Vermont. Horse breeding has received a new impulse in the State within a few years, and the annual exhibitions at the State Fair are hard to beat in any part of the Union. Gentlemen of ample means have taken hold of the business, and they spare no pains or money to secure the very best stock. John has a passion for horse flesh, as the readers of the Bunker papers are well aware. Though a lad of fifteen, he is about as mature and well posted on farm matters as the old gentleman himself. This team, which belonged to himself and Sally, was well broken to the saddle, and with a good road could do a mile inside of four minutes. We were just thirty-five minutes coming over from the depot, and John said he "should have come much quicker but father told him not to drive fast."

When I reached here, I found the place all astir, and Esquire Bunker's lit up with such a glow of excitement as has not taken place since the horse-pond was cured. I supposed they were getting ready for the glorious Fourth, which has to be celebrated this year a day behind time. But I soon learned that Miss Sally was a bride, and that Rev. Mr. Slocum, of Shadtown, was the fortunate individual who was this day to lead her to the altar. The house and garden were full of the country lasses, the school-mates and more intimate friends of the bride, coming up to sympathize with her in her leave-taking of home, and in her departure for the parsonage of Shadtown. Wasn't your humble servant in a fix, to be caught in such a presence with his field dress of coarse linen on? Such a clover field as this was a good deal more than I had bargained for. I have seen something of beauty and womanly grace, as one has opportunity to see on the promenades and in the parlors of the metropolis, but I never met with a company so graceful and accomplished as were gathered to do honor to this occasion.

This country wedding has made clear to me, what I never understood before, the claim of this State to be called "*The land of Steady Habits.*" It was easy to see on very short acquaintance the home influences under which these daughters had come up—the thorough practical training they had received in the school-room, as well as in the kitchen and in the parlor. Probably the State is better furnished than any other with the means of education. In almost every important town, there is a good academy or high school, not only accessible to the daughters of farmers, but largely patronised by them. Here they go with their brothers, as soon as they leave the district school, to be drilled in many of the same studies with them—to emulate them in the natural sciences, in mathematics, and in the languages. The emulation is a healthful one, and the boys are generally put upon their mettle to keep out of the way of the girls. The embellishments of female education have this very substantial groundwork of *mental discipline*. It is claimed here, as sound doctrine, that a girl who studies geometry will make a better pudding and sing a better song than she possibly could if she knew nothing of Euclid; that Cicero and Sallust, German and Algebra, are only appropriate *discipline* for the wash-tub and for the cradle. Such a training gives breadth of mind to woman, and a strong, practical tendency to her maternal influence. Children brought up under such home influences, with the usual religious training, cannot be otherwise than well balanced and steady.

If you have imagined a company of simpering misses gathered at Sally Bunker's wedding, you are greatly mistaken. There was such a charm about their dress, that one hardly thought of it, and, for the life of me, I cannot tell now what any of them wore, save the fresh picked flowers, which so became them that they seemed always to have grown there. The conversation was intelligent and pleasing, like that of most well-bred people. They entered fully into the spirit of the occasion, and were determined to "see Sally off" in good style. Not only were the parlors at Esq. Bunker's appropriately ornamented, but the pulpit in the meeting-house had been festooned with white roses, as if the sanctuary, as well as the minister, was to receive a bride. That is the way they do things out here. The minister's wife is married to the parish as well as her husband, and is as legitimately a subject of criticism and jealousy. She must do duty, fill her place, conduct prayer meetings, and be an ensample to the flock, as much as the shepherd himself. No one can quarrel with this demand, for it is a legitimate fruit of the system of female education. Woman fills a large sphere out here. She is a man, and something more. The vocation of "the Women's Rights orators" would be gone in Hookertown, and they would be set down as vain babblers.

Now, I shall not tell you of the wedding ceremony, which came off in the crowded church at eleven, A. M.; of the entertainment at Esquire Bunker's, got up, I suspect, as much for your benefit as for his daughter's; of the notabilities of Hookertown there assembled; of the agreeable things there said and done, touching agriculture, and culture of other kinds; of the dance got up by a few of the young folks very slyly, on a green patch of turf in the garden—an affair that was not laid down in the programme; and of divers other matters that would be appropriate to a work of fiction.

Suffice it to say, that the whole thing went off in the happiest manner, and the jollification of to-day, the firing of cannon and the snapping of fire-crackers, the shouting of the boys and the gala dresses of the girls, the holiday aspect of old and young, might be taken as a little outbreak of Hookertown enthusiasm at the marriage of Sally Bunker. At the next country wedding, may I be there to see.

YOUR REPORTER.

NO. 18.—TIMOTHY BUNKER, ESQ., ON A JOURNEY.

HIS VIEWS OF RAILROADS—FARM IMPROVEMENTS—SAND BARRENS—SWAMPS—SORGHUM.

MR. EDITOR.—I do not know but you have thought that my letters to your paper have "gin out," seeing that I did not write anything the past two months. But the fact was, I have been off to see what was going on in the world, outside of my own farm. You see there are some people up here that think Hookertown is in the centre of the world exactly, and they haven't the least idea but what the whole world turns round on our axis. In fact they believe that the north pole runs straight through our meeting-house steeple, and what can't be learned in our parish is not worth knowing. Ned Bottom, a man of seventy, was never ten miles from home, and never saw a steamboat nor a locomotive. It was only last night that he was bragging about it, as if it was someting to be proud of. "He had never been caught in one of those man-traps. Not he!"

I suppose it is a fact, that a good many people get hurt on the railroads, but I guess not so many in proportion to the travel as are injured in the old-fashioned way of horse and carriage journeying. I cannot see what Providence has suffered such things to be invented for, unless He designs folks should use them to find out what the rest of the world is made of, and what other people are doing. Our minister preached a sermon a while ago about "Many shall run to and fro, and knowledge shall be increased," and he thought the day of the fulfillment of this prophecy had come. Now I suppose I don't hear any too much of sermons, and practice altogether too little. But I heard the whole of this, and thought I would fulfill my part of the prophecy, and started off in the cars, with my wife, the same week.

We first went up to Uncle Philip Scranton's, a brother of Sally's, who lives in Farmdale, over east of Hookertown. Connecticut, you know, is all cut up into railroads, and has more track to the square mile than any other State in the Union. It is wonderful to see the influence these railroads have had upon the farms, wherever I have traveled. Almost every farmer lives within sound of the whistle, and has a ready market for all he can raise, at the depot or nearest village. Instead of going off to Providence or Boston, a week's journey, to sell his cheese, butter, and poultry, an hour's ride in the morning brings him to a market. He loses little time and gets a higher price.

This stimulates production, and it is wonderful to see the rocky lands and the swamps that have been brought under cultivation to meet the increased demand for farm crops.

Uncle Philip is a farmer of the old school, but keeps up with the times better than a good many young men. He used to take the old New-England Farmer forty years ago, and got a good many ideas from Fessenden and others, who sought to improve farming in those days. You can see where those ideas have been bearing fruit on his farm ever since. He reclaimed a swamp by ditching, bogging, and covering with gravel, thirty years ago, and it bears near three tons of hay to the acre now.

He has found that it pays to clear up rocky fields, so rocky that most lazy men get discouraged. He has worked up these rocks into heavy stone walls, with a handsome face, and well capped. He finds these cleared rocky lands just the spot for orchards, and some of the finest trees he has are upon these reclaimed pastures. It is astonishing to see what a sight of work a man can do in a life-time, and what a beautiful homestead he can make of rough barren acres.

He has a nice garden full of fine vegetables, which are now in their glory. Up in one corner there is a lot of bee-hives, full of music and honey, setting the owner a good example in the way of industry, and rewarding him for his care with a bountiful supply of well-filled comb. All around the wall he has fruit trees and grape vines, which are now loaded with fruit.

I found a lot of your Sugar Cane up here, and indeed I have seen it all through the State where I have traveled. One farmer, who had a large lot, was going to run it through his cider mill to crush the canes, and thought it would answer all the purpose of a sugar-mill. Uncle Philip was trying his for soiling, and found it to work first-rate. He sowed sweet corn along side of it, both in drills, and found that the cane gave the most fodder, and that the cows would eat it the quickest. He says there is almost no end to the amount of stock a man can summer, if he will only sow corn or sorghum. He thinks he gets a quarter more milk from his cows for this daily fodder. He feeds only at noon, every day. He thinks this is the best time, because the cows have all the morning to eat grass, and then the new kind of food offered at noon induces them to eat more. The more food you can induce a cow to eat and digest, the more milk you will get, and the more profit you will find in keeping her. This is one of his maxims, and I guess he is right. His stock is a mixture of grade Devons and grade Durhams. He averages about three hundred pounds of cheese to the cow, every year.

Another of Uncle Philip's experiments is reclaiming a sand barren. He had about six acres of such poor sandy land that nothing would grow on it. It was not worth the taxes paid on it. He has put on muck and stable manure in such quantities that it will now yield forty bushels of corn to the acre. I find he has a great idea of muck, as all the farmers have in this region.

In-doors, Uncle Philip's wife manages things quite as well as he does upon the farm. The butter and cheese are well made, and the house is well kept. I wish the Tribune man, that told such stories about country cooking, could have set at her table for a week, as we did. The coffee and tea were enough sight better than I ever found in your city, and the bread, meat, and vegetables, were all that an epicure could desire.

I had no idea, when I stopped writing, that so many of your city folks was a going to follow my example, and *suspend.* I shall have to be more careful of my conduct.

Yours to command,

TIMOTHY BUNKER, ESQ.

Hookertown, October 15th, 1857.

NO. 19.—TIM BUNKER ON FARM ROADS.

Mr. Editor: I couldn't help thinking, when I was off on my journey, riding on the rails, what an awful waste of horse and ox power there was on our farms. On a railway they get rid of all the obstacles, make the path solid, and have the running gear as perfect as possible. The power has very little friction to overcome, and is all spent in drawing the load. On a plank road, they do a good deal to remove obstacles and make a solid road-bed, but plank-roads and railroads on our farms are out of the question for doing ordinary farm work. The next best thing is the common highway, in which there is some attention paid to the removal of rocks, to drainage, and to the making of a smooth firm road-bed. This kind of road is within the reach of all our farmers, and I think will pay a great deal better than the miserable cart paths that most of us are contented with. A farmer is just as well able to build what roads he needs to haul his wood, muck, manure, and crops, as a town is to build what roads it wants for the mill, the market, the meeting, and the common convenience. Roads leading to the fields and to the wood lot, that are a good deal used, ought to be worked every year as much as a common highway.

Only to think of the waste of time, of ox flesh, and of cart-tire, in hauling loads over such a road as Uncle Jotham Sparrowgrass has upon his place! It leads down to what he calls his Lower Place, about a half mile from his house. Though it has been used for fifty years or more, he has never spent a day's work in mending it. There are rocks in the rut a foot high or more, and holes where the wheel goes in up to the hub, in all wet weather. I suppose his team has been driven over this road two hundred times in a year, at least, with an average load of

A FARM ROAD. Page 56.

not more than three-fourths of what they would have drawn upon a good graveled path. In other words, if the cost of carting a load over this road is fifty cents, he has paid fifty dollars a year for the privilege of a rough road, to say nothing of the worrying of the teams, and the breaking down of the carts, and the swearing at the mud-holes. If any of the Hookertown people think that the swearing reflects at all upon Uncle Jotham, they can suppose that the hired man drives the team sometimes, though I don't say who drives. You see, when the teamster finds himself with a load of green hickory stuck fast in three feet of mud, it is rather a trying position for the temper.

A few days' labor spent in digging stones and hauling gravel, would make this road equal to a turnpike, and then it would not cost five dollars a year to keep it in repair. The teams would draw a full load instead of three-fourths, and the labor saved here could be devoted to other profitable work upon the farm. Now there are thousands of miles of just such miserable roads upon our farms, that ought to receive immediate attention. If there is any economy in having a good strong team, there is still more in having a good smooth road to work on.

Yours to command,

TIMOTHY BUNKER, ESQ.

Hookertown, Nov. 13, 1857.

NO. 20.—TIM BUNKER ON A NEW MANURE.

MR. EDITOR.—I ha'n't told you anything about my carrot crop, this year, and the way I astonished the natives, and myself about as much as any of them. It is seldom that a new idea gets into the heads of the people up here in Hookertown, but they all declared they got one, when they come to see my carrot crop. I guess I had one myself, but it was not exactly the same as my neighbors'.

You know, last year I told you about the subsoiling of my garden, and the lots of garden sauce I put into my cellar, in the fall of 1856. That waked up some folks considerable, and Seth Twiggs in particular. One day, last spring, he come down to our house—pipe in mouth, as usual. Says he, "Esquire Bunker, I am going in for some of them premiums, myself, this year, and I calculate to beat you on carrots, do your prettiest."

"Dew tell," says I, "and what are you going to manure with?"

"Pig manure and a subsile plow. You see I've got Deacon Smith to subsile my garden, and I've got manure enough to cover the ground an inch thick, all over. You're a gone coon, this time, Esq. Bunker, I shall beat you;" and the smoke rolled up in a cloud as he walked off, the picture of self-satisfaction.

Says I to myself, after Seth had gone, "a subsile plow is not the chief end of man. I'll try a few tile drains and a trenching spade."

The lower end of my garden, you know, is bounded by a ditch, and has always been too wet. I got sole tile enough to drain a quarter of an acre, putting them down three-and-a-half feet deep, and thirty feet apart. Thinks I to myself, "If Seth Twiggs gets the start of Tim Bunker on carrots, he'll have to manure with something deeper than subsile plows." After the tile were put down, I could see they were needed, because after every rain that came, they would discharge water into the ditch. Seth thought he was doing rather an extravagant thing, sir, putting on the manure an inch thick. It only showed what a fog his mind was in, about manures. I had a grand compost heap, that I had been making all winter—muck, night-soil, soap-suds, and a lot of bony fish—at least ten cords, and very strong. I had it all worked into that quarter of an acre with the trenching spades, full three feet deep. I then raked it all over with a steel-toothed garden rake, the teeth six inches long, making a seed bed about as soft as a bed of down. I sowed the carrots in drills, on the first day of June. The drills were fourteen inches apart, and I thinned them out to eight inches in the drill.

When I was digging them, the week before Thanksgiving, Deacon Smith, Seth Twiggs, and Uncle Jotham Sparrowgrass, came along. The heaps were laying on the ground, about as thick as haycocks, and nearly half as big.

"Quite a crop, Esq. Bunker," says the Deacon.

"Did you subsile this year?" inquired Seth, his countenance fallen and woe-begone, as he eyed the yellow boys lying around, many of them plump thirty inches long.

"Pray, what did you manure with?" inquired Jotham, as his eyes opened with astonishment.

"With brains," said I.

"Brains!" exclaimed Jotham. "I never heerd of that manure afore. Where upon earth could you get enough for a load?"

I could see that the Deacon enjoyed Jotham's innocence, and there was a sly twinkle in Seth's eye, which showed that the idea was crawling through his wool.

"If you do not believe me, gentlemen, if you will walk down to the lower part of the garden, I'll convince you of the fact."

"There," said I, pointing to the tile, which were then discharging water into the ditch, "I put the brains of ten thousand bony fish on top of that piece of land, and down below, there, you see some of my brains running out."

Uncle Jotham Sparrowgrass got a new idea upon brain manure then, and it is very well disseminated in this neighborhood now. My own new notion is, that we have a very imperfect idea of the productiveness of the soil, when worked and manured with brains. I measured up 403 bushels of carrots from that quarter of an acre, and I expect to beat it next year.

Yours to command,
TIMOTHY BUNKER, Esq.

Hookertown, Dec. 15, 1857.

NO. 21.—TIM BUNKER ON LOSING THE PREMIUM AT THE FAIR.

(WHEREIN ESQUIRE B. GIVES SOME BROAD HINTS ABOUT THE WAY PREMIUMS ARE NOT UNFREQUENTLY AWARDED.)

MR. EDITOR:—I told you in my last about raising a carrot crop with a new kind of manure. I did not tell you how I lost the premium on the same crop. It is an old saying, that "merit wins," but I think that must have been said in times when men were less tricky than they are now. I had always thought that the only thing necessary to get a premium was to raise the best crop; but I discovered at our last fair that there was a mighty difference between raising a premium crop and getting the premium for it.

You see, our County Fair was held at Hookertown, and the competition in the root crop was pretty sharp. The people of that town were up in force, and I guess, if there was one load of vegetables, there was twenty, heaped up with big cabbage heads and squashes, long turnips and beets, parsneps and carrots. The Rev. Mr. Slocum was up, and both his deacons, Fessenden and Foster, and Esquire Jenkins; and all brought along lots of garden produce. Smithville was well represented by the Lawsons, the Tabers, and the Wilcoxes.

Now, you see, it so happened that Tom Wilcox kept a livery stable, and had a mare that he thought might take a premium. He fed her high for a month beforehand, and got her into first-rate condition, and brought her on to the ground, without saying a word to the committee, or any body else, that she had the heaves. My neighbor, Jake Frink, was chairman of the Judges on roadsters, and must have known all about Wilcox's mare, as he sold her to him three years ago, and she was unsound then, and only brought seventy dollars.

But Jake had an ax to grind, and was mighty anxious to get a premium on carrots, so as to take the wind out of my sails. So he managed to get Tom Wilcox put down among the judges on vegetables. Jake thought the thing might be managed, and, sure enough, he did manage it considerable slick. As soon as the judges came on to the ground, Jake — accidentally, of course—met Tom, and says he:

"Mr. Wilcox, you are not a going to enter that old mare, are you? You know unsound horses are not allowed to compete."

"Dew tell, Mr. Frink, you don't say so. But look here, Jake, she is as fat as a porpus, and I have fed her on green stuffs so much, that she hasn't coughed for a week. Nobody 'll know anything about it, if you do not tell 'em of it. Ha'n't you got anything you want a premium on? 'One good turn deserves another.' I'm on the committee for garden sass, you know."

Upon this, you see, Mr. Frink took Tom around among the roots, and I had the curiosity to keep within hearing distance.

"Good carrots," said Tom, "but you see yourself, they a'n't so long or smooth as old Bunker's."

"I'll tell you what," said Jake, "I'll double my hill,

to make more of a show, and you can give the premium on that."

I did not hear any more; but I saw Jake's hired man unloading a cart about an hour after; and, I guess, if Jake's sample of carrots had a half bushel in it, as the rules required, it had six.

Some of the people opened their eyes, when it was read off at the close of the fair:

First Premium on Roadsters, Thomas Wilcox, of Smithville. $5.00

First Premium on Carrots, Jacob Frink, of Hookertown $2.00

But, you see, my eyes had been opened before. The only shadow of a claim these men had for a premium was, that the one had the fattest horse, and the other had the biggest heap of carrots.

At the last meeting of our Farmers' Club, we had up the subject of root crops for discussion. Of course, each man gave his experience, and among others, Jake Frink gave the details of his mode of raising carrots, for which he took a premium last fall.

When it came my turn to speak, I took occasion to congratulate my neighbor on his success, but was sorry that he had omitted to give one very essential item in his treatment of the crop, viz., a large application of *horse manure.*

Mr. Frink looked very red in the face, and pretty soon had occasion to go out and take the air. Whether he is troubled with apoplexy, I could not say.

Now, Mr. Editor, I think it is high time, that this business of giving premiums at the fairs had an overhauling. If we can't have premiums awarded according to the merits of the case, one very important end of the fairs is defeated. People will very soon lose their confidence in them, and will not bring out their products for exhibition. I hope you editors, who know how to write, will stir up your readers on this subject.

Yours to command,

TIMOTHY BUNKER, ESQ.

Hookertown, Jan. 16, 1858.

No. 22.—TIM BUNKER ON A NEW ENTERPRISE.

MR. EDITOR:—I never was more astonished in my life, than this morning, when on my way to mill down the Shadtown road. I have been thinking a good deal about miracles lately, and I declare they aren't a bit more strange than some things I have lived to see. Jake Frink with a watering trough in his barn-yard is a *poser*, and if you only knew the man as well as I do you would say so. But that aint a circumstance to what I am going to tell you now. You see, I hadn't got more than a mile down the Shadtown road, when I saw a lot of men looking over the wall. At first I thought there must be a fight, and that there would be occasion for me to exercise my office as Justice of the Peace. It would be almost a miracle if there should be such a thing in Hookertown, for we are an uncommonly peaceable community.

As I drove up, I saw Uncle Jotham Sparrowgrass, with a team and three hands, busy digging a ditch, and about a dozen Hookertown people looking on. There was Deacon Smith and Seth Twiggs, Jake Frink, Tucker, Dawson, Tinker, and Jones, and among the rest, the minister, Mr. Spooner. It seems Uncle Jotham had begun the job the day before, and the thing had made such a sensation, that a pretty strong delegation was out to see Jotham Sparrowgrass to work on an improvement.

There never was a prettier chance in the world to do a

nice thing for a bit of land. You see, he had a peat swamp of about three acres, lying in a hollow, mostly cleared of brush, and with a small pond-hole in the middle. The peat in some places was ten feet thick, and all the edge of the bog was wet and springy for at least two acres more. The whole was worthless as it lay, except for the muck which it afforded, of which Uncle Jotham never used a cart load in his life. The bog lay high, and by digging about ten rods, through the rim of the hollow, there was fall enough to drain the whole swamp, three feet deep or more. Here Uncle Jotham was at work with his men, like so many beavers.

The main drain had been cut, and one could see how these peat bogs had been formed. After the stones and surface mold had been removed, it was a solid light-colored clay, which would hold water tight as a basin. Everything that run into that hollow, and everything that grew, had to stay there. All the wood, brush, and mosses, that flourished there before the country was settled, had decayed, and made a vast bed of vegetable mold. The water, having no chance to get out, had operated as a great millstone to press it together very solid. It had now found an outlet and was making a straight wake toward the North Star, as if seeking liberty for the first time.

"You are just in time, Squire Bunker," said Deacon Smith.

"You have got another convert here," said the minister.

"Who would have tho't it?" exclaimed Seth Twiggs, as he took the pipe out of his mouth, and blew out a cloud of smoke, that made one think of a locomotive.

"Old Bunker will make fools of us all," soliloquized Jake Frink, as he thought of the horse-pond and the lead pipe leading to his barn.

"Good morning, Uncle Jotham," said I. "I thought you

didn't believe in doing anything with muck swamps, eh? What are you doing here?"

"Why, you see, Mr. Bunker, I've known this 'ere swamp for risin of thirty years, and have raised corn near it for about the same length of time; and I never had a piece of corn anywhere in this neighborhood that wa'n't badly eat with the muskrats. You see the scoundrels begin to work upon it early in July, and they keep at it until frost comes. I've sot traps for 'em, and shot 'em, and done every thing I could think of to kill 'em off, and I believe they are thicker than ever this spring. So you see, I was riding by your house last week, and seed where that horse-pond used to be, and I got to thinking, and this 'ere plan came to me, all at once, like a flash of lightning. Thinks I to myself, I've got them pesky animals in a tight place at last. I'll dry 'em up, and put 'em on the total abstinence principle, be hanged if I don't. You can't have a drunkard without bitters, nor a muskrat without water, can you? And you see, with one day's work I've took the water all down to the bottom of the pond, and I am bound to go three feet deeper, by the measure. Whether I make anything out of this bog or not, I'm bound to rid the rest of my farm of a great enemy."

It was a grand sight, Mr. Editor, you may depend upon it. I don't know as I bear any particular ill-will to the tadpoles and turtles, but somehow I kind o' like to see their confusion, when the water slopes off on a sudden, and they flop around in the mud, not knowing which way to emigrate. They lay there by the bushel, evidently very much troubled at the daylight. I would go further to see such a sight, than to see all the menageries ever exhibited. I have heard them tell about the fine points in a painting, the contrast of colors, &c. There is no contrast quite so satisfactory to my mind as this light-colored clay on *top* of a black muck soil. I am always certain of dark green to shade it pretty early in the season.

You see, full one-half of Uncle Jotham's talk about the muskrats is gammon. He don't like to own that he has learned anything from me, or any of his neighbors. But, you see, he has already made up his mind to plant that bog with potatoes this season, and substitute tubers for tadpoles and muskrats. The fact is, Mr. Editor, that horse-pond movement has done the business for quite a number of my neighbors, and is working better than physic. There are at least four of them started on a new track by that enterprise. Now, if you have the least spark of patriotism, come up and see us Independence day. If you expect to see anything of the Hookertown of the present generation, you must come quick, for I tell you now, this world moves, and no mistake. If you don't come and see what's going on, we shall get up a rebellion, we shall—do anything but stop the paper. That we are bound to have, whether you come or not.

Yours to comman

TIMOTHY BUNKER, ESQ.

Hookertown, June 5, 1858.

(It is put down in our note-book to visit Hookertown, July 4th—*if we can.*—ED.)

No. 23.—TIM BUNKER ON MAKING TILES.

MR. EDITOR.—I didn't like it a bit, that you did not come out to attend Sally's wedding. You must know that weddings do not come every day in a farm-house, and in mine they come only once in a generation, for Sally is my only daughter. She had got her heart very much set upon seeing you out here, for she and John have read the paper so much, that they think you sort o' belong to the family. John came back with that young buck of a reporter you sent, quite crestfallen—declared he wouldn't have gone to the depot if he had known you were going to disappoint him. He says he has made up his mind, since reading that account,that all the green things in the world are not in the country. Whether he means that some of the houses in the city are painted green, or the folks in them have that look, perhaps your reporter can tell. The girls, however, were amazingly tickled with the man's description of the Hookertown women, and are a good deal provoked that you didn't publish the poetry and all. They say if you will put in the part that you threw out, they will pay double price for it, as an advertisement. I suspect they have a great itching to know if he said anything more about them. You had better keep him at home in future, if you want him to do any thing more for the paper.

I told you, awhile ago, that if you wanted to see anything of the Hookertown of the present generation, you should come soon. I was a good deal more of a prophet than I thought of at the time, for the paper was not dry on which I wrote it, before I heard that a tile factory had been started in my own neighborhood.

"Who would have tho't it?" exclaimed Seth Twiggs, as he knocked the ashes out of his third pipe, and rose to go. "Why, Esq. Bunker, that is the strangest thing that has happened in my day. I should as soon expect to hear they were catching whale in the Connecticut River."

"And do you think there will be a call for the tiles?" inquired the minister, whose conservatism was a little disturbed by the advent of a tile factory in his parish.

"Trust Miles Standish for that," answered Deacon Smith. "The fact is, Standish never went into anything yet, that he did not see his way out of it before he started."

"Blamed if he hasn't got it all ciphered out," said

Twiggs. "Showed it me 'tother day when I was up there."

"And how many does he calculate to sell?" I inquired.

"A hundred thousand the first year, and half a million the second. Had the hundred thousand engaged before he started."

Miles Standish, you know, is a historic name, one of the first Puritan families that landed upon the shores of New England, and here is the family, in direct descent from the first Miles, in the seventh generation. The present Miles owns the ancestral farm; and on one corner of it is a clay bed, of unrivaled excellence. It has been used for some years as a brick-yard, and many a kiln has been sent off to the neighboring city, and down the river. But the reverses of last year stopped the demand for brick, and Miles has been in trouble ever since, until I hinted to him carelessly last spring, that he had better go to making tiles, and drain his farm.

I have since read somewhere, that this is the way they do so much draining in the old country. The tiles are made upon the farm where they are to be used, to a great extent, and there is very little paid out for freight. The owners of the large estates there have plenty of capital for the purpose, and tiles are made and put down by the million. But it will probably never be the best way with us for every man to try to make his own tile. Our farms are too small, and, as a rule, our farmers have not the necessary capital, even if they have clay beds. What we want is a tile factory in every neighborhood, or district of twenty miles diameter or less; so that a farmer with his surplus team can cart tiles to his farm in the leisure parts of the year. He can, in this way, make his team serviceable, which would otherwise lie idle. He will not feel the expense of freight at all.

As matters now are, freight is the great bugbear which prevents people from going to draining. The two-inch tile, which cost twelve dollars a thousand in Albany, about double the first cost by the time they get where an Eastern farmer wants to use them.

Hearing of the tile factory I went up to see it yesterday, and to have a talk with Standish about it. I found the hint I dropped in half joke last spring had fallen into good soil, and was bearing good fruit. He had got it all ciphered out, as Seth Twiggs said.

Said he, "Esq. Bunker, I've thought a heap on what you said about turning my brick-yard into a tile factory, and you see I've partly done it. The only thing that stumbled me was, whether I should have any market for the tile after I got them made. I looked over my farm, and found that I could use at least fifty thousand in draining some swales, and if these worked well, I should probably want more. I went round some into the neighboring towns, and found a good many who wanted to try the experiment, and were willing to engage from one to ten thousand apiece. I marketed a hundred thousand. You see I had a plenty of bricks to make a kiln of for burning, and this at the market price for bricks cost me about a thousand dollars. The iron machine for moulding tile that you see there, cost 150 dollars, and the drying-house perhaps 800 more. So that any man who owns a brick-yard with the usual fixtures for grinding clay, wants about two thousand dollars capital to start the tile business with, on a small scale. I can burn sixteen thousand tile in that kiln at once, and it takes about ten cords of wood to do it. The actual cost of moulding, not counting the clay anything, or the interest of the money, is about two dollars a thousand, and the burning, where wood is four dollars a cord, should not be over five dollars. This brings the actual cost of two-inch tiles not far from seven dollars a thousand. If I can sell them at twelve dollars a thousand, even though it costs me something to deliver them at the river landing, I can make a handsome profit.

If the thing works half as well as you claim, there can't fail to be a better demand for tile than there ever was for brick."

This Hookertown clay bed is one of the best you ever saw. You work right into a side hill, where the clay is fifty feet deep, or more. It lies in nice layers about the thickness of slate, and is entirely free from sand and gravel. It makes a very tough tile. There is clay enough right here in this valley, close to a navigable river, to make all the tiles the State will ever want.

The first tile factory in Connecticut is a great event, and will work as great changes among us as the first cotton factory did in Rhode Island. It will double the products of our farms in less than ten years, if the farmers will use them. It is wonderful to see the waking up on this subject. I don't know as I ought to speak in meeting, but I thought you would like to know that Jake Frink has engaged five thousand tiles, and is going to put them down this fall. It wont be a year before Jotham Sparrowgrass will have them down in his drained swamp; but he will never own that he is draining land. It will only be another contrivance to keep out the muskrats and the tadpoles. A very *curis* man is Uncle Jotham.

Yours to command,

TIMOTHY BUNKER, ESQ.

Hookertown, August 3d, 1858.

[REMARKS.—We are really sorry for the disappointment felt by our Hookertown friends, at our failure to appear at the wedding, but could not help it possibly, under the circumstances. We will do anything by way of atonement—attend Sally's second day wedding, or the next wedding that comes off in Hookertown, should any of the damsels see fit to get up one on our account. We shall not dare to send any more reporters.—ED.]

No. 24.—TIM BUNKER ON THE CLERGY AND FARMING.

Mr. Editor:—I supppose you and the rest of the folks have wondered some about Sally's marrying a minister. It does look a little queer, at first sight, that a smart, handy young woman, that knows all about the duties of the dairy and the kitchen, and takes premiums at the fairs, on bread and butter, should want to settle in a village. It is perhaps just as queer that the smartest preacher in the county should want to marry a farmer's daughter. But wedlock is an unaccountable affair any way you can fix it, and the particular attraction, I suppose, is in most cases as great a mystery to the interested parties as to people outside.

But this match, it strikes me, is not so much "out of sorts" as matches in general. Josiah Slocum, I guess, knows on which side his bread is buttered. It strikes my neighbors variously according to their characters. Uncle Jotham Sparrowgrass dropped in the week after the wedding, and says he:

"What a fool you have made of yourself, marrying your darter off to that Shadtown parson!"

"A thousand pities, she was so smart!" chimed in Seth Twiggs, as he knocked the ashes out of his pipe, and looked across the room to Sally's mother, who was busy with the needle.

"Why, what makes you think so?" inquired Mrs. Bunker, lifting the gold-bowed spectacles, given her by Josiah on her fiftieth birthday.

"Why," said Uncle Jotham, "did you ever know a bookish man that wa'n't lazy, and always running into all sorts of nonsense? And the clargy are ginerally the most moonshiny of all bookish people. There was Parson Tyler, of Mill Valley, over on the Island, when I was a boy, that put up a wind-mill on top of his corn crib, to turn the grindstone, churn butter, and chop the sassage meat, and do all kinds of things."

"Yes, and it worked mighty well, too," said Seth, who by this time had got his pipe charged again.

"And where was the folly of using wind power instead of elbow grease?" I asked.

"It is a fact, the thing worked well, and saved a heap of labor, but it always looked like laziness to see a man set still, while the wind turned his grindstone."

"And the whole neighborhood came in there to grind their axes rainy days, as I remember," said Seth.

"How long since you have been to meetin, Uncle Jotham, that you have got such notions of ministers?" inquired Mrs. Bunker, rather sharply.

Jotham Sparrowgrass, sinner that he is, had not been inside of a meetin-house, on Sunday, in twenty years, and it must be confessed was a little more offish toward ministers than he ever was toward book farming, and that is a pretty strong statement.

"That is the way with you wimmin folks," responded Uncle Jotham, "always twittin a feller upon facts."

"Sally might have done better," said Twiggs, as he tipped back his chair and puffed away. "You see she ought to have been a farmer's wife, she was so knowing about every thing indoors from garret to cellar."

"And she might have done a great deal worse," said Mrs. Bunker, who by this time had laid aside the sewing to take the young folks' case in hand. "It don't follow at all that Sally wont have any use for her training in the milk room and the kitchen, because she has gone to live in a parsonage. A girl that has been brought up to keep everything straight in the house, as well as to be a lady in the parlor, makes a good wife in any calling. I am quite sartain that her talents wont be buried in a napkin down in Shadtown; for the parsonage has ten acres of land with it, and Josiah is going to keep three cows and a horse, and grow stuff enough on the land to feed them and his family. His people say that he is not afraid of the plow tail, or the hoe handle; that he gets more stuff off of his ten acres, than many of them are able to get from their farms; that he is great on sermons, and just as great on cabbage, and it is difficult to tell whether he is a better farmer or minister; and his wife and the young folks are pleased with each other, and as long as the parties most consarned are suited, I don't see why other folks need to trouble themselves about it."

Mrs. Bunker resumed her spectacles and sewing, after freeing her mind, and Uncle Jotham found it convenient to leave on important business. Seth apologized handsomely, didn't mean any harm, and after finishing his pipe retired.

You see, a great many people have got very narrow views about their neighbors in general, and ministers in particular. They think no man can be more than one thing at a time, because they themselves have never done but one thing, and have not done that very well. If a man is good with a lapstone and an awl, they think he must be a poor hand with a hoe and a scythe. But I have traveled enough in Massachusetts to know that some of the best farmers and gardeners in that State are shoemakers, for a good part of the year. They have extra brains enough to plan farm work while they are driving the pegs, and keep two or three hands busy out doors while they have a shop full of hands. I have pretty much made up my mind, that that old saw about "sticking to the last" wants a new interpretation. If a man only sticks to the last, he may as well stick to two or three other things at the same time. The sticking to a thing is a matter of a good deal more importance than having only one thing to stick to. I take it, that brains are given to us in order to be used, and that if a man will only use them, he can do about as much as he wants to.

Folks especially think that a bookish man can not know any thing about practical matters, and that a minister is as likely to ride a horse with his face toward the tail, as any way. I am afraid that such people do not go to meeting as much as they ought to, and that they do not know enough about how ministers live. If there is any class of people that are not in danger of rusting out, that have a plenty to do indoors and out, and know how to do it in the best way, I am sure they'll be found among the clergy in this State.

And it has always been so in this region, from the first settlement of the country. In the country parishes, they thought they had not done the clean thing by the minister, until they had provided a small farm for him, and made it a part of the settlement. Shrewd men, those first settlers of Connecticut were. They knew that a man with his wits sharpened in college would beat them all hollow at farming, if they gave him any thing like a fair chance. They put them on small farms and small salaries, to keep them within bounds, and even then, they generally beat their parishioners, and raised the best crops, and brought up the likeliest families in their parishes. Only two per cent of their children turn out poorly, and if that don't vindicate their claim to good management and a fair share of common sense, then I am mistaken.

And I guess they haven't degenerated much in the present day. There is no set of men in the State that take any more interest in farming, and raising fruit than the ministers. They take hold of the societies, give addresses, and talk about as much to the point, as any orators we get on such occasions. And this is all orthodox doings out here, and I think they preach all the better for stirring around among folks, and knowing what they are thinking about. They were *men* before they began to preach, and I take it, there is no particular sin in their being men afterwards. At any rate they do common mortals a great deal of good, for entering into their labors and sympathies.

Yours to command,

TIMOTHY BUNKER, ESQ.

Hookertown, Sept. 4, 1858.

[A little allowance might be made for Squire Bunker's enthusiastic defense of the clergy, since his only daughter, Sally, has just been married to one of them, but with or without this allowance, we think the Squire brings out about the truth of the matter.—ED.]

NO. 25.—TIM BUNKER ON WOMEN FOLKS AND HORSE RACING.

HOOKERTOWN SCANDALIZED.

MR. EDITOR:—You never did see such exciting times as we have had up here at the County Fair. It has been the town talk ever since. Who would 'a thought it, that we should have a horse race in Hookertown, and a woman horse race, too! It is enough to make a man sick at the stomach to see what women folks are coming to. I thought it was bad enough when my John got caught down to Boston, two years ago, at one of those "fair" races, called an Agricultural Association. I never thought the business was coming home so quick.

But I'll tell you just how it happened, and you'll see that the Hookertown people are not so much to blame as they might be. You see, last winter, the members of the county agricultural society had to choose new officers. Dea. Smith had been president for some time, and wanted somebody else put in. So they chose Colonel Lawson, up to Smithville, and most of the managers were up in that neighborhood. The Colonel is a smart fellow, but ha'n't no more respect for public morals than a cow has for a milking stool. He goes in for making money by the shortest cut possible, keeps tavern, farms considerable, trades cattle, jockeys horses, and, they do say, attends the races in the neighborhood of your city, and has brought home considerable money that he don't like to tell exactly how he came by. What in the world folks were thinking of, when they put him into office, I don't see.

But they put him in, and the Colonel being a military character, and famous for riding a horse well on a general review day, was bound to make a sensation, and throw Deacon Smith's administration all into the shade. There was folks enough up in Smithville, just like him, that had just as lieves scandalize our place as not. You see, Smithville is a sort of Nazareth up here, in the land of steady habits, was settled in the beginning by the fag end of creation, and has always drawn that kind of people since. If a man got broken down in character, idle, or dissipated, he was pretty sure to fetch up in Smithville or vicinity. There he found congenial company, and could race horses, Sunday, to his heart's content. It is not until within ten years that they have had any meeting up there, and though they are somewhat reformed, the old odor sticks to them like pitch.

The great trouble with the Colonel was to find any decent woman that would put herself on exhibition before five thousand people, and make a fool of herself. He tried all the towns around, and everybody told him it would not do in Connecticut; that our young women were well educated and modest, and knew what belonged to their rights and to their sex as well as a militia colonel could

"A FEMALE EQUESTRIAN PERFORMANCE." Page 77.

tell them. We all thought he had given it up as a bad job.

But it seems the creature went home, and persuaded his oldest girl to show off on horseback. You see, Tom Wilcox, the same fellow that took the premium last year on a horse with the heaves, had a young horse that he wanted to sell for a big price. His daughter, Matilda Wilcox, offered to ride, if Tom would get her a new silk dress and a new bonnet with feathers—and get Letitia Lawson to ride in company with her. Nobody knew anything about it out of Smithville until all the arrangements were made, and the handbills were out, announcing "a grand female equestrian performance," to come off at Hookertown on the last day of the fair.

It made a sensation in these parts, you may depend. Every grog-shop in Smithville was emptied to the dregs, and I guess every gambler and blackleg in the County was on hand to see "Tish Lawson and Till Wilcox have a set-to." Every negro fiddler and ragamuffin in the neighborhood was drawn out to see the fun. There was a chance for betting, and a good deal of money changed hands on the occasion. I pitied the poor girls from the bottom of my heart, and I guess if they could hear the coarse, brutal remarks made by the crowd, they would never be caught in such a scrape again.

"A most scandalyous affair," said Seth Twiggs, as he stopped into our house next morning, the smoke rolling up in a cloud of excitement. "It beats the Dutch, Esq. Bunker. I wouldn't have my darter make a show of herself so for all outdoors."

"The thing is agin natur," responded Mrs. Bunker. "But it is just what their fathers might expect from their bringing up. They make tomboys of all their girls in Smithville."

You see, these girls, and Tom Wilcox's horse, that won the race, are the County talk, and will be for a month.

The grand object of the fair was lost sight of, and I don't suppose one person in ten took any notice of the fruit and vegetables that were on exhibition. They did not care a cent for porkers or calves. They had paid their quarter, "to see them galls run the hosses," and Tom Wilcox's horse was "the elephant of the day." I never heard so much swearing and blackguardism in all the fairs I ever attended. It was "cuss and discuss," as Deacon Smith said, from the beginning of the race to the end.

I rather think the scrape will do us good on the whole. There are some evils that cure themselves. Every decent man and woman that I have seen since is disgusted, and I guess the annual meeting of the County Society will be better attended next January, and Colonel Lawson will have liberty to attend to his military duties unmolested. We have seen enough of women folks riding at the fair.

It is all well enough for girls to learn to ride on horseback at home, or in a riding school, but it is agin natur for a woman to make a "show" of herself, any way. The business is just putting up a woman's modesty at auction, and it is because the thing is unwomanly that it draws such a crowd of low, indecent people to see it. Sure, it makes large receipts for a single fair; but the next time a good many respectable folks won't come. They don't want the modern Camillas held up before their families as models of female character. The whole is out of character, and demoralizing, and they won't support the Society, if the thing is kept up. It is clap-trap and humbug—a kind of chaff that don't catch old birds but once. It is a sneaking way of getting up a horse race, and imposing it upon a decent community. Let every tub stand upon its own bottom, and when it has none, let it cave in.

Yours agin horse racing in general
and women racing in particular,
TIMOTHY BUNKER, ESQ.

Hookertown, October 1st, 1858.

NO. 26.—TIM BUNKER ON BEGINNING LIFE.

A PEEP AT THE SHADTOWN PARSONAGE.

MR. EDITOR:—It is well that you are a good hundred miles out of Hookertown about these times. Since that picture on "gal horse-racin" come out, there has been a good deal of talk—and some swearing or more. Up in Smithville, I guess there has been more. I was up there last week, and fell in with Colonel Lawson, who got up the race. He come up to me in the street, looking as red in the face as a beet, and about as mad as a March hare, and says he,

"Old Bunker, did you write that mess of stuff in the paper about the Fair?"

"I did; them's my sentiments, and I can't back down on 'em any where."

"Wal, who got up that picter on the gals with their bonnets off, and myself holding the stakes? The piece was bad enough, but that picter was all-fired mean, and immodest. It wa'n't fit to be decent. I shall prosecute the publisher for libel."

"Libel, man! Why, wasn't the picter a true bill, according to facts?"

"A true bill! That's what I have to complain on. It was altogether too natural. There's Wilcox's gal, with her bonnet flyin, feathers and all, and a feller with his pocket-book out, that they say was meant for me. I can't go any where among decent folks, but what they are sticking Judd into my face, and inquiring with a smothered sort of grin, "Wall, Colonel, have you seen the last *Agriculturist?*" I'm gettin' tired on't, and if there's any law in the univarse I'm bound to prosecute."

"Keep cool, keep cool, Colonel. The least said is soonest mended. Folks that put their daughters up for a *show* have no right to complain if they are *showed up.* Folks whose pocket-books are emptied shouldn't go to law. Good morning, Colonel."

They say he lost a thousand dollars in bets at the Fair, and I guess you are about as much in danger of being prosecuted as you are of getting into the poor-house by publishing the paper. I am sorry for the girls that have made such a beginning of life. Caught by the tinsel of silk dresses and bonnets, they were drawn into a false position, that will very much damage their prospects for life.

And this, perhaps, is as common a failing among farmers as it is among city people. They begin life wrong, and start in business on a bigger scale than they can hold out. They buy a big farm, generally twice as much as they can pay for, and then they are always short on't for capital to work it with. It is pretty much like Deacon Smith's singing at the evening meetings; he pitches his tune so high at the outset that his voice breaks into a screech before he gets through, and nobody can follow him. His wind is all used up before the psalm is half sung. The farmer, instead of getting good, serviceable cattle, will often buy fancy animals, at a high price,—a yoke of cattle for two hundred dollars, and a fast horse for three or four hundred. He don't stop to think how he's coming out.

And then if his wife begins in the house in the same way, it makes a mighty uncomfortable concern. There was Tom Spalding and his wife began to keep house about the time I did. Tom was a little fast, and his wife was a little faster. She was handsome, fond of company, and must dress and live in tip top farmer's style. The farm Tom bought had an old house on it, but 'twas comfortable, and would have lasted ten years without laying out a dollar on it. But she must have it fixed up, inside and out, before they moved in. So Tom put on an addition, and new clap-boarded, and painted, and papered, and hard finished, and by the time he got through, it about finished him. She must have extravagant carpets and furniture, and a fine carriage to ride in, and everything to match the fine house.

When Tom got through with his fitting out, he found himself fifteen hundred dollars in debt. The farm was a good one, and produced grand crops, but with all he could do, the balance was on the wrong side at the close of every year, and at the end of a dozen years they had to sell out and emigrate. You see, the silk dresses and other women fixin' kept him in debt, and he had no chance to buy more stock, when he needed it, or to hire as much labor as he really needed, to carry on the farm to advantage. It is of no use to begin life in this way. If he had lived in the old house a few years, and waited for the finery until he had the cash in his pocket to pay for it, he might have been in Hookertown to this day, and as thriving a man as there is in it. "Pay as you go" is the true principle for everything that isn't *necessary*. A man may incur debt for a part of his land or stock, or for the tools of his trade. But he might as well go to the poor-house as to run in debt for fine clothes and a splendid house. Better sleep on a pine bedstead, till you are able to pay for mahogany.

I have talked this doctrine over so much in my family, that I guess the children have got it all by heart. Sally has, I am certain. I suppose your readers would like to hear how she is getting on, over to the parsonage. Most stories end with the wedding, as if folks were of no consequence at all, after they got married. But as I am only writing a statement of facts, about things in the land of steady habits, you must expect to hear of people after the honeymoon.

I felt bound to give Josiah and Sally a good setting out, for folks in their circumstances. There is some parsonage land, that Josiah knows how to make use of, and they have

4*

to live among farmers, and in plain farmer style. Now I hold, that a minister is bound to be an example to the flock, in his style of living, as well as in his morals, and in his religious duties. I have noticed, time and again, that example was a grand thing to put the nub on to a sermon. If a man preaches from the text, "Owe no man anything," and drives a fast horse that he hasn't paid for, somehow the two things don't seem to hitch together. I have known extravagant living to drive some ministers from their parishes. They got in debt, got discontented and soured, and were "not content with such things as they had," until they were able to get better. I didn't want any such trouble in Shadtown, and I knew a good deal depended upon beginning right. I gave Sally a piano, but I sent along a churn with it, to remind her that the cream of life was not all music. There was a lot of cane-bottom and mahogany chairs, but John slipped in a couple of milking stools, of his own make, as a sort of hint, I suppose, that all the sitting was not to be done in the parlor. On top of the dresses in the trunk, I noticed a pair of checked aprons. I guess Mrs. Bunker knew where they came from. I had to get a new carriage for Sally's Black Hawk horse, but I sent down the next day a horse cart, with a lot of farm and garden tools, as a sort of insinuatien that horse-flesh would sometimes be needed out of the carriage. The useful was pretty well mixed up with the sweet, in-doors and out. From all I can learn, the people are pretty well suited with the young folks, and with the arrangements I have made for them. They haven't got anything but what they can afford, and nothing that they do'nt want to use, and that, I take it, is about the whole pith of beginning life right.

Yours to command,

TIMOTHY BUNKER, ESQ.

Hookertown, Nov. 15th, 1858.

No. 27.—AN APOLOGY FOR TIM BUNKER.

LETTER FROM JAKE FRINK.

Mr. Editur:—Square Bunker went by our house this mornin jest arter sunrise on his way to the deepo. He sed he hadn't a bit of time to write, but he'd like to have me tell you, that he had been called out o' town, suddently on bizziness, and shouldn't be back in sum weeks. He axed me to write in his place this time, and I deklare I never felt so kuris in my life—I han't got much ederkashun, and never had, and I couldn't help thinkin' the Square was krackin one of his dry jokes on me, when he put me up to sich a thing—guess he'd be more astonished than the next man, if you should take it into yer head to print this ere riting. But you jest du it, and I'll give you a dollar out of my own pocket, for the sake of gitting the start on the Square for oncet. He is a hard man to beet i know, but Hookertown is a great country—and there is sum more peeple in it than you have heerd on. Them karrots, that Tim Bunker 's allers runnin me on, I wa'n't so much to blame about—I'd like to have my sa on that subjeckt. Ye see, I knew mi man jest as well as the Square did, and a leetle better. I allers understood trade, better than farmin, and I knew i culd git the premium by a leetle kalkulashun. Now kalkulashun I hold to be the cheef eend of man, that which distinguishes him above all kattle-kind, and so i used it in the kase of the karrots and carried my pint.

Sum folks perhaps thinks, that all Square Bunker rites abeout is made up eout of his hed, kind o' novil fashun. I tell you it's a mistake. The hull on't is a rekord of fax, and pretty much as they happened, so that up heer in Hookertown they look for the Square's letter in yeur paper, to see what has happened. That story about the hoss-pond is all true as preachin, and a great deel truer than sum on't, i guess. The bottom is all dry neow, and the lot is abeout the best one on the farm. That tile bridge was a kuris notion, and I must own beet on it. I might have thunk, and thunk, forever, and i should never have thunk that eout—but the watter rushes threw there, as if it had been shot eout of a kannon. I dew declare I bleeve he greesed the plank, it goes so slick.

I don't kno what the Square has gone off fur—but I guess its to bi kattle. Kattle have been mighty low all the fall, and the Square has plenty of hay, and fodder, and makes a considerable bizziness of fattin kattle in the winter, tho' he han't sed any thing on that pint yit in the paper. Indeed he han't told half he kno's, and i spect he wont if he rites a dozen years. I guess hee'l git a new idee when he sees this in print. I never had a letter printed, and indeed, folks in gineral have never dun much for me, but Jake Frink is a man of his wurd, and will pay, if you'll put it in.

Yourn furever

JACOB FRINK.

Hookertown, Dec. 30th, 1858.

NO. 28.—TIM BUNKER ON COUNTY FAIRS.

MR. EDITOR:—Jake Frink is a fool, as you might know by his letter. You see I was a joking him about the interest he and his neighbors have got to taking about my affairs, since I begun to lay tile and write for the paper. I can't stir, even early in the morning, but Jake'll poke his head out the window, nightcap and all, and want to know "where upon airth I'm gwine to neow," just as if I had never been off my farm before. But the thick-headed creatur never see the drift of my remark about sending an apology, and went and wrote that letter. Everybody that knows me knows well enough that I seldom do anything to my neighbors that I have to apologize for, and when I do I am apt to make it in person. Jake's letter looks curis up here, and I shan't hear the last of it in a year. All I have to say is that I'm glad it set him to thinking. Folks had better be thinking of something, even if they don't think straight, than to be as stupid as dolts. Jake may make something yet if he keeps thinking.

I went up that morning to the city to attend the annual meeting of our County Agricultural Society. You see, last year, they put in the Colonel president, and all the screws got loose, and we had that fuss of a "gal hoss race," as the boys used to call it. Now I have nothing to say agin womankind in general, or the girls in particular; but it does seem as if, when you got a woman out of her place, she made a good deal more of a smash-up than a man. Everything goes wrong. It is just like breaking down the hub of your cart wheel, when the frost is coming out of the ground in the spring. It is a mighty dirty job, and business has got to stop.

It was pretty much so with our County Society after the fair. It made a great deal of talk. Some very sensible men got disgusted, and declared they never would have anything to do with the Society agin, because it countenanced horse-racing. The Colonel's friends said the opposition was all a political move, agin their party. At one time it looked as if we should have to give up the Society, there was so much bitterness of feeling. It is surprising to see how far men will carry their political prejudices. Partisanship works into everything, controls men's votes for the officers, and committees of the Society, and sometimes determines the award of premiums. Democratic corn has to weigh a few more pounds in the bushel, and yield a few more bushels to the acre, in order to be equal to a competitor's of the opposite party. Black Republican butter, though up to the Orange County stamp, stands no sort of a chance beside an inferior article, if it was made from Democratic cream. And because a few men carry their prejudices to this extent, and try to buy votes to get themselves into the legislature, by this petty trade in premiums at the fall fairs, there are some addled enough to believe that all our Society affairs are managed upon this principle.

Our Hookertown folks did not go up to the annual meeting last year, thinking that the Society had got along where it would take care of itself. But things do not take care of themselves in this world. If you do not plant hoed crops, briars and thistles will grow. If the friends of an Agricultural Society do not follow it up and shape its policy, it will go wrong. We have no right to put our hand to the plow and look back. If we do, we are in very poor business to grumble that others stand at the plow tail in our place. About the meanest thing a man can do is to grumble. If he can't help it, grumbling will do no good. If he can, he ought to go to work and stop chafing.

I had to work about a month, before the meeting, riding round and talking with grumbling people, before I could get things into the right shape. I have always observed that there was great virtue in talking. If you have a good cause and keep it before the people perseveringly, you are certain to carry it in time. I knew if we could have a full meeting, from all parts of the County, and talk matters over, we could come to a good understanding, and make the Society efficient in doing its appropriate work, which I take to be horse *raising* and other kind of growth, and not horse *racing*, and *razing* of industry and good morals. The people who had the management last year, followed their own tastes without meaning any harm to the Society. They would have done better, if they had had better advisers. If the friends of good order wont take the pains to be in their places, and make their influence felt, they have no right to grumble when things go wrong.

The result was, that we had the largest annual meeting we have ever held, and a new board of officers was put in, without much division of sentiment. The Colonel's friends were so much ashamed of their own folly, that they did not make any show of opposition. These County Fairs are doing so much good that I think every good citizen ought to make sacrifices, if necessary, to sustain them. If they are attended with some evils, as much can be said against all other forms of associated effort. The millennium has not come yet, and no wheels move with so little friction that they do not need grease sometimes. Apply oil, and stop the squeaking. Our Society has done more to set folks to thinking about the principles of farming than any thing we ever had among us. There has been a steady gain every year in the variety and excellence of almost everything exhibited. The farmers see this and understand it, while city people and careless observers think every show is just alike, a chaotic mass of cabbages, turnips, and other roots; corn and other grains; horses, cows, pigs, and poultry. But the farmer recognizes at once the new Winningstadt or Enfield among the cabbages, the Ashcroft among the turnips, the Rhode Island Premium among corn, or any new comer among kine or swine. There is something to be learned every year. I have no doubt that Seth Twiggs, Jake Frink, and Uncle Jotham, have done more thinking about their business, the last two years, than in all the rest of their lives. And when folks begin to think about raising stock, and cultivating the best crops, they soon discover their own ignorance, and seek light. They want to talk and read. I guess there are ten agricultural papers taken in this town where there was one two years since. The Farmers' Club is well attended at the school-house every week, and the discussions are a good intellectual treat to everybody that has a rod of land to cultivate, and that is everybody here. The minister, the lawyer, and the doctor, the schoolmaster and the judge, are generally there, and the farmers come in from the whole neighborhood. Now all this has come of the County fairs. The Society has left its mark in everybody's yard or garden, dropping young shade trees, apples, pears, peaches, cherries, grape vines, and flower borders. The homesteads look more cheerful, and the people are more thriving in their business. This year the Society has offered a premium for every shade tree set out in the streets. We mean to line every roadside in the County, within five years. Even Jake Frink is beginning to dig holes to set out trees this spring. His old friends will hardly know Jake, or his establishment, in a few years more.

Yours to command,

TIMOTHY BUNKER, ESQ.

Hookertown, Feb. 8th, 1859.

No. 29.—TIM BUNKER AT HOME AGAIN.

MR. EDITOR:—I have been gone from home four whole months, and I do declare if they wa'n't the longest months I ever experienced. I haven't seen anything of your paper, and not much of any other, as to that matter, since I went off, and I've pretty much lost the run of things up here in Connecticut and out in your village. It was curis how it happened, so curis that I haven't got over my astonishment at the thought of my journey yet. I couldn't hardly believe I'd started, until I got home. I should have said, a year ago, that it would have taken six yoke of cattle, and a horse on ahead, to have drawn Tim Bunker out West or down South. But lo and behold! I've been on a journey of five thousand miles, and got back alive. I've seen the elephant from trunk to tail, and the next time I go on any such fool's errand you see I shall stay at home. They call it L. E. Fant, Esq., down South, and think it is a joke. I did not find it any joke at all.

The way it happened, you see, was this. Wife and I have always stayed at home—hardly ever venturing further away from Hookertown than down to your village, when I had cattle to sell, or something of that sort. We were a very quiet sort of people, and never had much company outside of our own circle of friends, until I got to writing for your paper, when the tide seemed to turn, and lots of strangers began to call on us. After that account of the wedding by your reporter, they come so plenty that my wife said she should have to go down to Shadtown, to live with Sally, in order to get rid of company. You see everybody that comes to Hookertown—and a good many come here in summer—has to look up Tim Bunker, and stare at him, jest as if he was a lion. They would go by, looking at our house as if it was haunted, or some man had committed murder there. One fellow come up here in the fall with a looking glass on three legs, and said he was going to take a picture of the house for some New York paper. I was called on before breakfast and after breakfast, in the field, and in the barn, early and late, until I was troubled to get time to attend to my own business. Now this would have been very pleasant to a politician, or a man born to fame, but it was mighty uncomfortable to plain country folks like Mrs. Bunker and I. There is nothing a man pays so dear for as for his honors. If he is wise, he will add another petition to the Lord's prayer,—"deliver us from evil and from fame." I don't know as this is quite orthodox, but wife and I have made up our minds on this point, and are too old to change.

Well, things come to such a pass that Mrs. Bunker declared she would not stand it any longer. She laid down her gold-bowed spectacles, the same that Josiah gave her, one evening last December, and says she: "Timothy, our house is getting to be a tavern, and I should like to go off and have a rest this winter."

"Well," says I, "where will you go?"

"Anywhere to get out of Hookertown, where you are not known."

"Very good, pack up the trunks, and we will be off down South next week."

I had no idea of her going, but I see in a day or two that she was in earnest, and when a Connecticut woman has made up her mind, you know there is no use in talking. So we started on our trip, and to make certain of getting into a place quiet enough for Mrs. Bunker, we fetched up on a cotton plantation. There was not any other house in sight, and no neighbors within a mile. It was mighty woodsy and lonesome, mail once a week, and preaching once in two weeks, and about eight miles off. Thinks I to myself "if Mrs. Bunker wants a quiet time I guess nothing will hinder her here." It was mighty nice for a week or two, and she was delighted with the woods and flowers, the dogs and pigs, the poultry and negroes. The third week she began to miss the papers, and to inquire about the mails. The fourth week she wondered why they did not have preaching every Sunday. The fifth week, she began to talk about John and Sally. By the time two months were up, she spoke of Hookertown, very peaceably. At the close of the third month it was a very handsome place, indeed the prettiest village she had seen in all her journeyings. Now that she has got home, she declares it is the centre of the world, and the tip-top of creation. That is rather a strong statement, but as I never dispute a woman's word, I shall have to let it go.

Now I can't tell you anything about what I see down South, 'cause, you see, folks that have not been there would not believe me, it is so unlike any thing at home. But I jest want to say, that if anybody or his wife gets restless and uneasy, that is the country to go to, to get cured up. It is better than Perry Davis's Pain Killer, or the Springs; I haven't seen so contented a woman in ten years as Mrs. Bunker, since she got home. She says she never will say another word about company as long as she lives; and as to her neighbors, they are the handsomest people in the country.

I guess she is about right. It does New England people good to go away from home once in a while, jest to see how the rest of the world live. They generally come home wiser and better. Every thing has gone on well in Hookertown, since I have been gone—just as well, for aught I can see, as if I had been at home. There are some people who think the world will come to an end when they die. Let them step out of the traces a few months, and then come back and see how smoothly the world spins on without them, and they will be cured of that folly.

There is only one thing that shocks me on coming home, and that is the blue window shutters of my neighbor Seth Twiggs. What upon earth possessed the man to have 'em painted that color, I don't see. Shutters, indigo blue, in this nineteenth century, and in Hookertown, too! It is an atrocity. Just as if there was not blue enough in the heavens without a man's putting patches of it on to his house! I asked Seth about this, the first thing when I got home. Says he, "Tim Bunker, you don't know every thing, tho' I admit you are a knowing man. You see I smoke a good deal, and blue is the handsomest color in the universe. It is blue inside very often, and I thought I might as well have it blue out of doors to keep the balance." I had nothing to say, and have only to add

Yours to command,

TIMOTHY BUNKER, ESQ.

Hookertown, May 1st, 1859.

No. 30.—TIM BUNKER ON RAISING BOYS.

MR. EDITOR:—As I was going down by the horse-pond lot, this morning, the same one that I drained last year, I found Seth Twiggs' horse, Jotham Sparrowgrass' cows, and Deacon Smith's flock of sheep, turned into my corn and oats. It looked as if they had been in the better part of the night; for the corn was pretty much all nipped off, or torn up by the roots, and the oats were badly trampled. The corn crop is of course ruined, as it is now too late to plant over. It so happened that I had fixed one of the gate posts yesterday and the dirt was all nicely smoothed off, and the enemy who had done this had left his footprints by the gate-way. I took the measure of the shoe print, and walked straight up to Jake Frink's, and inquired for his oldest boy Kier, a young fellow about eighteen, who is up to all manner of monkey shines, and has got a terrible bad name in Hookertown. Kier was called in, and it was found that the measure exactly fitted the shoes in which he stood, length and breadth of top and heel.

Jake Frink was a good deal astonished, when he see that his boy was caught in such an unneighborly trick, but I don't know why he need to be, for he has had no sort of control over his boys, and always let them choose their own company and pursuits. Kier has got a notion of drinking, the last few years, staying all night at the tavern, driving fast horses, unhinging gates, girdling young fruit trees, firing stacks, and turning cattle into corn fields. He seems to think it is very smart to destroy property in this way, and to make himself a nuisance in the neighborhood generally. He is caught now, and must walk up to the captain's office and settle. The next worst thing to a bad father is a bad public opinion that submits to vice and rowdyism. I am Justice of the Peace, and if I was not, I am a neighbor to Jake Frink, and bound to help him keep his boys in their place. I have a very poor opinion of that moral cowardice which gives up a civilized community to the depredations of a set of young Arabs, like Kier Frink. What is the use of having law, if you do not enforce it against the destroyers of property and the disturbers of the peace? If the young chaps want to cut up, and have music, it is fair that they should pay the fiddler. If they rob hen roosts, the hens should not be left to do all the squawking. It will do them good to look out of a roost, with iron grates to the windows.

Now I hold, that a man is a poor farmer, as well as a bad citizen, that raises such a boy as Kier Frink. The farm exists for the sake of the family that works it, and *its chief end is to make smart, useful men and women.* Your great crops and fine stock all go for nothing, unless you get the blossom of the farm—man. What is an apple tree good for, unless it raises apples? The shade is no better than that of any other tree, and the fire-wood does not amount to much. So the farm is not worth much, unless it blossoms out into good, nice housewives, and useful, upright men.

It is a good deal of a knack to raise a first-rate cow or steer, even after they are born right. There is many a full blood heifer, with first-rate milking qualities, spoiled by bad treatment. Keep her on bog hay winters, and let her run in the road summers, and I guess she would never amount to much. And you might have high grade Devons, with all the elements of splendid working cattle in them, that would bring three hundred dollars a yoke, and treat them so when they were calves and yearlings, that they would not bring a hundred. You might dwarf them or lame them, or injure their horns, or make them ugly and breachy by bad handling. An ox known to jump fences, or kick, or gore cattle, is very much depreciated in value.

It is just so with the human stock brought up on a farm. Almost every thing depends upon the bringing up —a great deal more than it does with the brutes, for the animal nature of man is only a small part of him, and his moral nature and habits are almost entirely shaped by those who have the care of him, while he is young. If this gets the right start, I have always noticed that it generally brings every thing else along right, with it. If a fruit tree gets to bearing when it is young, all the forces of the tree will run to fruit, and you will not be troubled with too much wood and foliage. And if a boy blossoms out into the virtues of industry, truthfulness, honesty, temperance, and purity, I think it is pretty certain we shall have that kind of fruit as long as he lives.

Now, to get this fruit early, we must prune both root and branch. The shoots that are running to wood must be shortened in, and a spade must sometimes be thrust down upon the roots, and cut them off. This seems harsh treatment, but every fruit grower knows that it is necessary. So we must shorten in the boys, when they run wild, nip off the blossom buds of vice, lying, stealing, swearing, drunkenness, and such like. There is an old article they used to do such things with, when I was a boy, —called Solomon's rod. The bark was very bitter, but wholesome, and it worked like a charm. I am afraid folks do not use it so much as they used to. At any rate Jake Frink has never used it at all. He was always scolding about the cruelty of whipping children, and if one of his ever got a little of the oil of birch in school, he was always ready to find fault with the teacher, and take the child's part. The youngsters very soon came to believe that their father had rather have them lie and make disturbance, than to speak the truth and behave well. His mode of bringing up boys has turned out upon society that promising lad, Kier Frink, a vagabond and loafer, at the age of eighteen! Solomon's rod, with steel at the end of it, was never half so cruel as the misplaced indulgence of his father. What sorrows are before the poor old man with such thorns in his pillow! I am glad to see that you keep up your chats with the boys and girls. Keep them straight a few years longer, and we shall have a generation of farmers worth looking at.

Yours to command,

TIMOTHY BUNKER, ESQ.

Hookertown, June 13th, 1859.

NO. 31.—TIM BUNKER ON RAISING GIRLS.

MR. EDITOR:—Ever since I sent you that account of the "gal hoss race" got up by Col. Lawson last fall, I have been thinking about the way girls are brought up in this country. Indeed, I have had considerable many ideas on that subject, ever since our Sally was born, and the matter has been brewing, as Mrs. Bunker says of her beer, for well-nigh twenty years. Last winter when I was down South, I got some more ideas, and I am now so full upon this topic, that I shall boil over, unless I dip out a little into your paper.

I count a well-grown, well-behaved, and well-educated woman, as the very blossom of creation. She was the last made,—reserved for the last, because best. As there is nothing so good and beautiful in the world as a good woman, so there is nothing so bad as a spoiled woman. And now I am sorry to say, that very many girls are utterly spoiled. They are not well balanced and well adapted to the work that woman has to do. The most are brought up with such notions that they go through life discontented and unhappy.

There is Deacon Smith's daughter Eliza—a fair sample of the kind of bringing up I mean. They are very good people over there, but they seem to forget that children have got to grow up, and can't be playthings forever. They did not teach her to do any thing, when she was a little girl. She pretended to go to school, but it was only when she took a notion to go. There was no habit of study fixed, and so she got discouraged, and disgusted with all kinds of books that required any thinking. She had as little discipline of body as of mind, could not sew well, did not know how to make up a bed, or to darn a stocking, could not broil a fish, or boil a pudding. Some how, her mother seemed to think these every-day matters were not worth attending to. She said she was going to make a lady of Eliza, and marry her off to some rich man, who would not want a wife that knew how to work. She was going to have her "larn the ornamentals," as she called them,—music, painting, embroidery, dancing, and such like. Sally used to say that she did not know enough about the lessons to last her over night, when she left the academy, and I do not think she has learned much more about the common branches since. She was sent off to a fashionable boarding school in your city, when she was fifteen, where they do nothing but put the polish on to young women. But I should like to know what is the use trying to polish a woman, before you have got a woman to polish. You can put the shine on to a leather boot, for there is some substance to it. But you might rub brown paper with the best of Day and Martin till doomsday, and not get a bit of gloss; there ain't substance enough to hold the blacking. And you can put the polish on to marble, and bring out leaves and flowers, and all sorts of ornamental things, upon the surface, but you might as well undertake to polish hasty pudding, as to do anything with soap-stone. It won't hold the stroke of the chisel, or respond to the touch of pumice stone.

And it is jest so with sending a woman in the gristle to a fashionable boarding school. A girl wants to be solidified by home duties, and solid studies, before she is fit to be sent away to take on polish. Something ought to be done for her physical education, to make her body fit for the responsibilities of house keeping, and I don't know of anything better than to have her help her mother. A woman has no business to be married until she has shown her capacity to keep house. She should know how to do every thing from washing dishes, emptying slops, making soap and yeast cakes, up to the nicest kind of cooking and needle-work.

If they are ignorant of these things, accomplishments won't save them from mortification and domestic unhappiness. They will be as bad off as poor Eliza was, at her first dinner party, after she got into her new house. She had not been married to Dr. Sturgis more than two months, before she invited a company of their friends to dine. The Deacon and his wife were there, and quite a number of middle-aged and elderly people, like Mrs. Bunker and myself. There was a great display of silver ware and fine linen upon the table, forks, castors, spoons, napkin rings, and fruit dishes, that you could see your face in, and china plates, platters, and vegetable dishes with gilt edges, and nosegays in the middle, so handsome and natural that you could almost smell the perfume of the flowers. There was an air of triumph upon the face of Mrs. Deacon Smith, as we sat down to dinner, as much as to say, "Now we shall see what it is to have a daughter educated at a fashionable French boarding school, and keep house in style." There was considerable unction about Mr. Spooner's grace before meat, as if he had got it up for the occasion. The company were in the best of spirits, and Dr. Sturgis was slicing away at the turkey's breast, when attention was suddenly arrested by sundry corn, oats, and buckwheat, slipping out of the undressed crop of the fowl. The women folks at that end of the table put their handkerchiefs to their noses, as if they had got wind of something that did not smell like the roses on the bottoms of their plates. Mrs. Deacon Smith fidgeted about in her chair, as if she was on pins. Eliza looked as crimson as a beet, clear to the roots of her hair. The Deacon was at the other end of the table, very busy discussing the last sermon or election with Mr. Spooner, and did not see the trouble. Our Sally looked wicked, and winked across the table to Josiah, and there was a twitching about Josiah's mouth, that I should say was wicked also, if he was not a minister. Dr. Sturgis got over the matter nicely, by remarking upon the undone condition of the turkey, and calling a servant to remove the dish. Fidelity to truth, I suppose, did not require him to tell whether the rawness pertained to the cooking, or the dressing of the fowl, or the housekeeper, that lay back of both. Fortunately a liberal allowance had been made for the dinner, and the boiled fowls, purchased of a farmer who married a housekeeper as well as a woman, did duty for the roast turkey cooked with his crop in.

Now I suppose a good many of your readers among women folks will hold up both their hands in astonishment, at my standard of a good housewife. I say it is a shame and a disgrace for an American woman not to know how to do every thing that is done, or ought to be done, in her kitchen. There is just as much merit and womanly worth in knowing how to bring a turkey upon the dinner table, so that it shall not be offensive to the smell and taste of her guests, as there is in singing a good song, or in dressing in good taste. It adds very much to the comfort of a woman to know how to do everything from garret to cellar. The polish is all well enough, but let there be something in the first place to put the polish on to. This doll-work, in the place of a good old-fashioned wife that knows what she is about, is poor business.

Now, what I want to say to all parents that are bringing up girls is just this. Do not be afraid of putting them into the kitchen—that school of womanly virtues—and keeping them there, till they can tell the difference between a churn and a tea kettle—till they know how to scour a skillet, black a stove, wash a floor, and cook a turkey.

Yours to command,

TIMOTHY BUNKER, ESQ.

Hookertown, July 1st, 1859.

NO. 32.—TIM BUNKER'S HAY CROP.

A NEW CASE OF THE BLACK ART.

MR. EDITOR:—"Eleven tun of hay on that mash! Who would have thought it three years ago!" exclaimed Seth Twiggs, as he knocked the ashes out of his second pipe, and proceeded to load again.

"Did you say eleven tun, Squire Bunker?" asked Deacon Little, as he leaned over his staff toward me, with his mouth open in astonishment, as if he thought somebody must have been lying.

"It beats my muskrat swamp all hollow, where I got two tun to the acre the first year after seeding down, and I thought that was enough to keep an extra thanksgiving on," chimed in Uncle Jotham Sparrowgrass.

"Eleven tun on four acres of barren salt mash, where grass tried to grow and couldn't three years ago, is a leetle miraculus, ain't it, Mr. Spooner?" asked Jake Frink, looking over to the minister, with as much deference as if he was a professor.

"The Bible says we are to have a new heavens and a new earth, and I think Esq. Bunker is probably fulfilling the latter part of the prophecy," replied the minister with a quiet sort of smile, that left one in doubt whether he was in earnest or not.

These remarks of my neighbors on my reclaimed salt marsh are a great contrast to the talk three years ago, when I first undertook that job. I have not said anything about this improvement yet, because I did not know exactly how it was coming out. You know the tide flows a long way up our great river, and all along the banks, at the mouth of creeks emptying into it, and along the Sound, we have marshes bearing a great abundance of salt hay—a poor article for fodder, but very good for litter, mulching, and manure. I had a few acres lying just below the lot I bought of Jake Frink, where I cured the horse-pond. There was not much to be done to it, but to put in a tide gate at the culvert, and to do some ditching, to shut off the sea-water. I thought if I could do this, I could bring it into good meadow with very little expense.

I talked the matter over with some of my neighbors, and they all said it was of no use. But I hold that man was born in the image of his Maker, and has a natural passion for creating new things. This shows itself in all children, as soon as they get out of the cradle. They begin to make hills in the dirt, to dig out small pond holes, and fill them with water, to build houses and mud forts, to whittle as soon as they can hold a jack-knife, and to exercise the creative art in general. I thought it was a very natural and human thing for me to undertake to create a piece of meadow. It was all the more natural for me, because I wanted a few more tons of hay to winter my cattle on, as I could pasture more in the summer than I could carry through the foddering season without buying hay.

But Deacon Little seemed to think it was a presumptuous thing, and a little nearer to sacrilege than anything should be up here "in the land of steady habits." The deacon, having passed his four score years some time ago, is one of the good old men, who belong to a former age, whom death seems to forget, they are so exemplary in all their deportment. The Bible is not only his authority in all religious matters, as it should be, but in every thing else. He at once brought my project to this test. Said he to me one day:

"It is of no use, Timothy—'a salt land and not inhabited,' is written in the Bible, and you might as well expect English hay on the plains of Sodom, as on that mash."

"But salt grass grows there now, and if you shut off the sea-water, why will not the fresh grasses grow?" I asked.

"Ah! Timothy, you forget that the Almighty made that a salt mash, and His works are perfect."

"Perfect for some uses, but not for ours. He has made me with brains to make new creations, and I shall try to make that piece of land over again."

"You are a sorry infidel, Tim Bunker, I am sorry to say it," and the old man left me, with a very poor opinion of my reverence for the Divine workmanship.

My other neighbors had as poor an opinion of my judgment and good sense, as the deacon had of my veneration for the Almighty. At the time the gate was put in, they were all on hand to see the new hobby.

"What new-fangled consarn's that?" asked Jake Frink.

"How is it going to work?" inquired Seth Twiggs.

"Ye don't expect that door will shet itself, and keep the water eout, dew ye?" wondered Tucker and Jones.

"A great piece of folly!" exclaimed Uncle Jotham. "Ye see, this thing has been tried time and agin, down on the Island, and allers failed. Ben Miller had jest sich a consarn, and tinkered away with it four or five years, and gin it up as a humbug."

"Yes," said I, "and Ben Miller tinkered with fish, and spiled his land, you said, but you see what whopping crops I get with fish, eighty bushels of corn to the acre, and forty of rye. You see, Jotham Sparrowgrass, it was never meant that one man should do everything."

"It is well Mr. Bunker has the money to lose on such an experiment," remarked Mr. Spooner, who evidently had as little faith in my success as our less intelligent neighbors.

Well, last year I got a good crop, but there was a considerable black marsh and onion grass left, and occasional weeds that rather spoiled the beauty of the meadow. But this year the herds-grass and red-top, that I sowed two years ago, got full possession, and a handsomer lot of grass you never saw out of doors. It was a grand sight on the morning of the 11th of July, when we cut it, the purple tassels of the herds-grass standing just about four feet high, and the red-top a little shorter, a thick mat of heavy grass, in many places good for three and a half tons to the acre. I tried to get my neighbors all out to see it, but it was hard work to get some of the sceptics along the road anywhere in sight of it, they were so determined that nothing but salt marsh grass should grow there forever.

I suppose I have ruined myself for life in the esteem of Deacon Little, who, having seen the hay, and heard the talk of the people, thinks I must have had resort to the black art to get the crop. The Deacon is about half right, for I did give about two acres of it a thorough top-dressing of black compost last winter, which started the grass as if there was something behind it. This is the only kind of black art I believe in, and this I am bound to practice and teach to my neighbors. I think it is not very dangerous.

Yours to command,

TIMOTHY BUNKER, ESQ.

Hookertown, July 25th, 1859.

NO. 33.—LETTER TO ESQ. BUNKER FROM HIS NEIGHBORS.

To TIMOTHY BUNKER ESQ.—You are getting people all by the hair, up here in Hookertown, which don't look well in a Justice. Them personalities must be stopped, or we shall have to put a stopper on your being justice of the pease, enny mower.

There is tew sides to all questions, and as many as tew to that *mash*. If taint a humbug, it's a grate hobby, and is bound to run itself strate intu the ground. Then, we guess, somebody else will be riting funny things in the papers, abeout their naburs, beside Square Bunker. One of 'em, a district Committee man, who knows all abeout skools, sez, that he never knew a mash yet that dident turn Injun, and he guesses Square Bunker cant work mirakles, to keep his'n from 'postatizing. He sez, that you've spent a deal of money, and it's nothing but money, that makes this mare go, as in other kases. Bimebye the tide gate will get broke, the ditches will fill up, the clover will die eout, and eel-grass begin to grow again—and some fine morning you'll be looking for that mash, and find it under water.

Jake Frink sez, that crabs, and salt water tadpoles, will be swimming all over it arter a little while. Jake feels as kross as Tophet, at being called nick-names, and we guess he ain't the only ones nuther. His son Hezekiah, that you have black-guarded so much, is gwine to marry a 'spectable widder, and he don't want to be nick-named, enny mower.

There's tew of your naburs, at least, who take the paper, that want this business stopped. When we inquire abeout tide gates, or enny sich like konsarns, we don't want to be maid fun of, and shan't.—How would you like it yer self, Square Bunker, to have your naburs twit you abeout them long-legged boots, or that old hat, that come deown from Noah's ark, and them other klothes, that aint exactly the rig for a justice; or abeout Kier Frink's beating you at shooting muskrats, and he has done it menny a time. Don't you kno' yer self, that twitting on facts, riles up people dreddfully, and is like fire and brimstone on the raw flesh? Neow, ye see, Square, folks as lives in glass houses should not throw stuns. We jest want to let you kno', that we've got stuns to throw, and shal sartintly throw 'em if you don't stop them personalities.

Very Detarminedly, Your Naburs,
GEO. WASHINGTON TUCKER,
BENJ. FRANKLIN JONES.

Hookertown, Sept. 10th, 1859.

NO. 34.—TIM BUNKER ON THE SHADTOWN PARSONAGE—AND A GRANDSON.

MR. EDITOR:—I told you at the time we fixed Sally out for housekeeping, that I should probably have something to say about the young folks after the wedding, when the writers of stories generally say goodbye to their heroes. I did not think then, that I should have anything special to say so soon, but this is a fast age of the world, and any writer who keeps up with the times will not have a chance for his ink to get dry in his quill.

Mrs. Bunker and I were sent for last week, to come down to Shadtown and make a visit, not thinking at all what honors awaited us. Shadtown lies on the river, a few miles from here, and is one of those homely names that stick to a place forever. They have a good many such names up here in Connecticut, and the folks, or at least a part of them, seem to glory in them, as if they were the right things in the right place. They were suggested by the character of the country, or by some incident in their early history, and the necessity of a change has never been felt. Break-neck Hill took its name from its dangerous character, and from the fact that a man was once thrown from his wagon, and killed there. Hard-Scrabble is a very poor, rough region, and both men and animals have to scrabble to get a living. Bean Hill was so called from the fact that that esculent grew in great perfection in the vicinity, and was greatly delighted in by the inhabitants. It was the invariable Sunday morning breakfast, the year round, and to professors even, was a reliable indication of the day. Tradition relates that the Deacon was once sadly misled by the failure of his usual dish, the bean bag having been exhausted unexpectedly. He had already ground his scythe, and would have gone to mowing but for the timely remonstrance of his good wife. This may have been a scandal, but the bean-eating is still kept up by the people, in all its early vigor.

They undertook to alter the name of the place some years ago, and call it Myrtleville, but they could not make it go. The old inhabitants said that "beans grew there, and myrtles did not; and they could not see the use of putting a name to a place that did not belong to it." Bean

5*

Hill they could see the reason of, for everybody in the place ate baked beans, and the crop was natural to the soil.

Shadtown was so called from the abundance of that fish caught at the landing—a name handed down from the first settlement. It is a staid parish, and the people boast that they have never dismissed a minister. A few have filled up their half century of service, and all have died among them. They are about as proud of this as they are of the name of their place. Shadtown was the name given by the fathers, is honorable, and is therefore to be honored and had in reverence for all coming time. The man that should propose to change it to Tivoli, Arno, or any other euphonious name, would be mobbed, if that thing were possible in this Commonwealth.

At the time Josiah was settled here, a couple of years ago, the people made a stir, and built a new parsonage. The old building had stood over a hundred years, and had accommodated their last three ministers. The good old practice of furnishing the pastor with a parsonage and glebe has always been kept up here. As the country filled up with people, and land became more valuable, they sold off a part of it, but there are still ten acres left of this fat valley land, and I guess better soil does not lie out of doors.

They built the new parsonage a little nearer to the meeting-house, setting it back further from the road, and throwing a part of the fruit trees into the front yard. They made the house every way convenient, put in a furnace, a range, a bathing-room, and all the fixings that a woman needs to keep house easy with. They enclosed a large yard, nearly an acre, with a nice fence, and planted it with evergreens and shrubs, so that it looked about as inviting as any house in the village.

It was curious to see what a great variety of fruits had been planted in the garden and orchard by the good men who had lived and died upon this spot. There is about an acre devoted to apples, and some of the trees, I guess, are a hundred years old, for they have been old trees ever since I can remember. Then there are perhaps twenty old pear trees, and a good many younger ones, just beginning to bear, to say nothing of the dwarfs that Josiah has just put out. All the small fruits, currants, gooseberries, strawberries, raspberries, and blackberries, have their appropriate place. Grape vines run along the sides of the barn, and on arbors built on purpose for them. Plums seem to flourish here, the soil being a little clayey. The peaches have declined, though there are the remains of famous trees, at least forty years old. There are cherries and quinces in abundance, and along under the wall, pie plant and asparagus enough to stock the neighborhood.

I learned, from Josiah, that his predecessors had been in the habit of doing this, the parsonage garden being a sort of free nursery for the parish. Seeds of flowers and vegetables, and grafts, and young plants of the smaller fruits were freely distributed every spring; so that almost every garden in the parish had its mementos from the parsonage. It was a literal sowing of good seed on good ground, for it almost always bore fruit to the minister's advantage, as well as to the people's. The whole region is noted for its good fruit, mainly originating from the parsonage. The finest peaches I have ever seen in any of the markets came from Shadtown. The parish has always been remarkable for its peaceful character, and for its religious prosperity. The unselfish example of the minister seemed to be contagious, and there was a "provoking to love and good works," not always manifest among good people. The minister took an interest in the bodies of his people as well as their souls, and diligently looked after their temporal prosperity. All appreciated these labors, and somehow, what he said on Sunday struck in all the deeper for what he did on week days. The children might not understand his theology, but they did understand his strawberries, and thought that the doctrines that kept such company were good enough for them. The hardest points in the catechism were taken on faith, and Shadtown has always been as orthodox as it has been peaceable and united.

Now, I am not much of a philosopher, but I guess the characters of the past ministers, being lovers of good fruit, as well as of good men, have had something to do with the prosperity of the parish. Their theology grew where their fruit did, in the open air and sunshine; and I guess light and air are about as necessary for sermons as they are for strawberries. Bad digestion makes a man's thoughts about as sour as his stomach, and the acidity of the pulpit often leavens the whole parish.

The folks in Shadtown say that Josiah is walking in the footsteps of his predecessors, only a little more so, that he gets all the new pears and strawberries, and as soon as he finds they are worth cultivating, he sends them out to his neighbors. I found John's milking stools had come in play, and the butter and cheese which Sally had made with her own hands, were about equal to anything we have in Hookertown. Mrs. Bunker says, that she will have to own beat on housekeeping and butter-making, but it is much safer for her to say that than it would be for any body else—in my hearing. She was very much pleased with her visit, but most pleased with her first grandson, whom they have named "Timothy Bunker Slocum." Whether the child, or its name, made her absent-minded, I am unable to say, but I noticed her spectacles on wrong side up, twice in one morning, and that the knitting was entirely forgotten.

Yours to command,

TIMOTHY BUNKER, ESQ.

Hookertown, Sept. 1st, 1859.

NO. 35.—TIM BUNKER ON DRESS—IN REPLY TO HIS NEIGHBORS.

Mr. Editor:—I was considerably astonished to see the letter from Tucker and Jones in your last paper. I did not suppose that I had said anything to break the peace, or to stir up my neighbors, and even that letter don't fairly convince me. You see it is a great country, where it takes two folks to write a letter—and such a letter! Anybody that knows those two men knows that they did not write that letter. It is not in them, and what is not in a man can't come out of him any way. I took the paper right to Tucker, as soon as it come, and says I to him, says I,

"Tucker, do you know who wrote that letter?"

"No, I don't, Square," says he, "blam'd if I do."

And neighbor Jones said the same thing. If they told a whopper, it probably is not the first one they have told, for though I say it, that should not, their reputation don't stand any the highest for speaking the truth.

I suspect they either got somebody to write the letter for them, or some envious person who wants to get hold of my piece of reclaimed marsh, wrote it in their name, meaning to run it down, so as to get it as cheap as possible. That is about the drift of the letter, as far as I can see any in it. But I may as well say, first as last, that that piece of land is not in the market. Land that will cut three tun of hay to the acre, or pasture a cow through the whole season, is about good enough to keep. The marsh has turned the heads of some people, and I have had a lot of folks from abroad to see it, and to learn how the trick was done. A fellow called the other day from way down beyond Boston. He had a project in his head, to reclaim three thousand acres, and make a mint of money out of it.

It can be done just as easy as to flip a cent, if he has the money to do it with.

That letter tried to make it out that I had spent a great deal of money on my marsh. This shows how little the writer knows about it. I have got more than muck enough out of the ditches to pay for all the improvements and top-dressings applied to it; so that I am a good deal in debt to that land to-day. The principal part of the expense of such an improvement is in the embankment, and that was all made in this case.

As to this marsh ever going back again, of course it will, if it is not taken care of. Any fool can see that if the tide gate is not kept in order, the sea water will come in, and the salt grasses will grow again. But any fool in Hookertown will tell you that Tim Bunker knows enough to keep a tide gate in order, and to shut out "crabs" and "eel-grass."

The letter tries to make a handle out of my *dress*, and on this subject I guess I am posted about as well as some of my neighbors. I believe in people's dressing according to their characters and their business. If there is anything better than rubber boots for a ditch half full of water, I should like to see it. I have not got above my business of farming yet, and don't expect to very soon. Some folks, I suppose, like Tucker and Jones, if they should be made a Justice, or elected to any high office, would not wear anything but calf-skin, for the rest of their lives. And thereby I think they would show that the calf was a little more than skin deep.

You see, Mr. Editor, this matter of dress is of more importance than most people think. It makes or ruins a multitude of people, and has a great deal to do with these crashes that you have in the city, every few years. And to begin with, as Mr. Spooner would say, there is a great deal in dressing folks up with the right kind of names, when they start in life. I don't think your correspondents were as lucky in their names as they might have been. George Washington Tucker and Benjamin Franklin Jones sound considerable grand and fixed up, as if a man would have to stoop some when he come into the room where such people lived. But I guess if you knew the folks that wear them as well as I do, you would not think there was much call for manners. You see, Tucker's father was never worth a red cent in the world, above the clothes he had upon his back, and his mother had more pretensions than any woman of her size I ever knew. He was a tailor by trade, and spent all his earnings upon broadcloth and silk, for himself and wife. I remember when parasols first came round, Tucker got one for his wife, and she was so anxious to show it, that she carried it to meeting with her, and hoisted it in meeting time, just as Mr. Spooner begun his sermon, as much as to say, "Tucker's wife is some pumkins arter all." The way the minister looked at her was a caution to all peacocks, dogs, and other vermin. Deacon Smith had to come over and tell her to take down that windmill, for he hadn't seen one before, and he did not know what to call it. Mrs. Bunker said, "she thought she would have sunk into the earth."

Well, you see, when their first child was born, thinking, I suppose, that they would not have much else to give, they gave him the name of Geo. Washington Tucker. Now, what's the use of dressing up a poor boy with such a big sounding name? You see, it makes too heavy a load for an ordinary mortal to carry through life. If he ever makes anything, becomes a business man, it is a great waste of paper and ink to have to write so long a name. And if he don't make anything, he becomes a standing joke like the present George Washington Tucker. He has always lived in a hired house, and worked hired land, when he worked any. To tell the plain truth, he has never hurt himself with work of any kind, and though a farmer, has been about as shy of the dirt as his father was before him.

I suppose it's wicked, but I never see him in meeting without thinking of that parasol forty years ago. The green of that silk went as straight into that boy as if he had grown on a mulberry tree, instead of being born like other mortals.

Jones came of a better family. His father, Gen'l Jones, was flourishing forty years ago. He had a good deal of money left him by his father, and married rich. The General was mighty fond of cocked hats, epaulets, and other military fixings, and his wife was fond of French fashions and extravagant dress. They used to drive through the street in Hookertown, in a splendid carriage, drawn by a pair of black horses, with harness glittering with silver buckles and mountings. Nobody held their heads higher than the Joneses of the last generation. The General's house was crowded with gay company from the city, his wife and daughters dressed splendidly, and gave brilliant parties, where the wine flowed like water, and the dance and song lasted till morning.

The Gen'l died a bankrupt when the present Benjamin Franklin Jones was a boy of ten. Of course the property had to be sold, and Ben had to go to work for a living, which was the best thing that ever happened to him, or any other man, according to my notion. He, however, had got some high notions in his childhood, that have prevented him from succeeding in life. He has never loved work, like one who has grubbed in the dirt from the time he could grasp a hoe handle. You must begin early with the boys, if you want to make them love work. Rub their noses in it as soon as they can run, and they will always love the smell of mother earth, as long as they live. But if you dress them in fine clothes until they are ten and twelve, and then try to break them in, it is just like breaking in a six year old pair of cattle—mighty hard work.

To state the case just as it is, Benjamin Franklin Jones is too much afraid of dirtying his clothes, to get along in life. And these are the kind of folks, you see, that are laughing at Tim Bunker's old hat and long-legged boots, and talking of throwing stones because I live in a glass house. They have the advantage of me in flinging stones, for they haven't got any houses at all, of their own, if I should want to throw back again. My hat is old, as they say, but it is paid for, which is more than can be said of the hats of my illustrious neighbors, George Washington Tucker and Benjamin Franklin Jones. One was won in a bet at the last presidential election, and the other has been charged in the merchant's book for more than three years.

Yours to command,

TIMOTHY BUNKER, ESQ.

Hookertown, Oct. 12th, 1859.

NO. 36.—A WEDDING AMONG TIM BUNKER'S NEIGHBORS.

The connection between city and country is getting to be so intimate, by means of railways and steamers, that the change of customs is almost as complete in the rural districts, as in the metropolis. All along the great thoroughfares, the Paris fashions are as omnipotent as in this goodly city of Gotham. Marriage ceremonies are celebrated with about as much pomp and show, and as little good sense, as in the higher circles of city life. There are, however, quiet nooks in the older States, remote from the sound of steamer and locomotive, where the stream of life flows on with hardly a ripple upon its surface. There, people by scores boast that they have never seen a steamer, and have never been inside of a rail car. They have come little in contact with the outside world, and maintain a freshness and individuality of character, rarely met with in our times. There, the social parties all have utility as their basis, and the flowers of the heart come up blooming around the edges of quiltings, apple-parings, and Dorcas sewing societies. There, the "meeting-house" is the orthodox name for the church edifice, and the social as well as the religious centre of the parish. There, the rural population gather on Sundays, in costume not squared to the fashionable cut, and hats and bonnets of the venerable age of ten years and upwards are still visible. There, sparks lit up between services, or even during sermon, are prolonged into Sunday night sparking, and the nine o'clock bell reminds lovers, as well as more sleepy people, that it is time to be at home. There, courtship makes haste slowly, and a love affair is not suffered to blossom into marriage, until it is fully discussed by all the gossips in town.

Hookertown is on the borders of such a quiet region, and there may be seen occasionally in the street of that somewhat noted village, natives of the unsophisticated rural districts—men and women who preserve the freshness and simplicity of fifty years ago, who insist upon marrying their daughters very much as themselves were wedded in the good old times. Esquire Bunker has given us occasional glimpses of this past age, in his letters, and it is with a view to furnish us another sample of this Arcadian life, we presume, that he sent us the following note a few days ago.

Hookertown, Nov. 10th, 1859.

Mr. Editor:—When your reporter was up here in Hookertown, last year, to take notes on clover fields, and stumbled on a wedding at my house, he was considerable tickled with the way they do up such things in the country, and thought he should like to come again. Now, if that fellow has any kind of hankering to see a real country wedding, let him come up and see Kier Frink married next week. Hookertown has got a good deal corrupted by city folks coming in among us, especially since I begun to write for the paper, and I guess half of the people dress about as smart as the common run of folks in the city. But there is a region up around Smithville, where they do up things just as they did when I was a boy. Kier has been a courting ever since the eighteen-year-old-fever came on him, and they say he had been out a sparking when he let the cattle into my corn field last summer. At any rate, things have come to a crisis, and he has just told John that he was "going to be tied next week," and given him an invite to the wedding. John will take your man over if he comes.

Yours to command,

TIMOTHY BUNKER, ESQ.

We looked after the matter, and here follows a

CONDENSED REPORT OF "OUR OWN REPORTER."

"FRINK, FAGINS.—At the Whiteoaks, Ct., on Thursday, Nov. 17th, by the Rev. Jacob Spooner, Hezekiah Frink, of Hookertown, to Widow Jerusha Fagins, of the former place."

The above announcement in the Hookertown Gazette, of this week, will attest that the joyful event, which called your reporter away from the city, has transpired. The "Whiteoaks," you must know, is not a distinct township, but a neighborhood name, attached to one of the school districts in Smithtown, whereof Smithville is the commercial centre—the grocery being located there, where the good housewives barter butter and eggs, for sugar, tea, and molasses. The Whiteoaks being remote from the social centre of the town, and without religious privileges, has always been a hard neighborhood, and never seemed to belong to Connecticut. Men of broken down fortune, and men who never had any fortune of any kind, gravitated thither as naturally as crows toward a dead carcass. It was the paradise of horse jockeys, loafers, gamblers, and drunkards. The people lived partly by farming, partly by burning charcoal, and partly by their wits. They were always ready to swap horses and oxen, when they had any, and the juvenility of the breed of cattle raised in these parts was always a marvel. A horse was never owned among the Whiteoakers, acknowledged to be over eight years of age, but always sound and well broken to both harness and saddle, whether he had ever been inside of thills or not. In this interesting region, where law and morals take care of themselves, lived, a year since, Theophilus Fagins and his wife Jerusha, with about a fair average of the happiness allotted to the Whiteoak community. Between coaling, horse trading, and drinking in the neighboring village, Theophilus came to an untimely end last winter, leaving a disconsolate widow and six children. She had reached the mature age of fifty, but had not outlived the tender passion, as the sequel shows.

While her love lay a bleeding, in the susceptible days of spring, Kier Frink was introduced to her by one of the coal-men returning from Hookertown. Kier was charmed with Whiteoak society, and particularly with the blandishments of the widow, who did everything to make his visits agreeable. There was no rigid Sabbath keeping, and not much going to meeting, but plenty of tobacco and cheap rum, with an occasional shooting match, or horse race, in the neighborhood. The widow had a house and small farm left her, and it seemed to Kier that his fortune would be easily made, if he could step into the shoes of the departed Theophilus.

This he essayed to do, and notwithstanding his youth and bashfulness, he was accepted by the widow, and the nuptials were appointed at an early day. I learned from John Bunker, who took me over to the Whiteoaks, that Jake Frink had no objections to the match, though the woman was old enough to be Kier's mother. Jake was accustomed to say, "Taint every young man that can marry a 'spectable widder, with a farm of 50 acres, well watered and timbered. I allers knew Kier would come to suthing, and now ye see."

A short horse is soon curried, and this wedding being the briefest we ever attended, is soon despatched. It appeared to excite about as much attention in the neighborhood as a horse trade, and the parties themselves manifestly looked upon it as an every-day business. We shall leave to your imagination, to picture Kier, with the down of youth upon his chin, leading the widow with her blooming charms to the altar, clasping of ungloved hands after a ludicrous fumbling for the dexter digits, the few words of the minister that made the twain one, the snickering of the young ones, to whom the sight of a marriage ceremony was a novelty, the awful pause that followed the prayer, and the final dispersion of the company. The most impressive part of the proceedings was the distribution of molasses gingerbread, which answered for the bridal loaf, and the manifest appetite of the groom for that admirable confection. The widow Fagins had learned the special weakness of her betrothed, and provided for the occasion. In this instance, a wedding is about as nearly stripped of its poetry as we ever remember to have seen it. Connecticut is a great country, containing a good many types of people. The Whiteoakers are a nation by themselves. I had to tell Esq. Bunker that my hankering to see a Simon Pure country wedding was cured up. The minister's fee was seventy-five cents, *all in quarters.*

YOUR REPORTER.

REMARKS.—We suspect Squire Bunker must have influenced our reporter somewhat, for he, (our reporter,) generally looks upon the bright side of every occurrence. A "Simon Pure country wedding" always has its pleasant features—though in this case it is but just to say, in excuse of our reporter, that we should have found it rather difficult to keep out of our thoughts the character of Kier Frink, his bringing up, etc. The history of this young man and its *finale* is instructive to parents, and on this account we have given it a prominence which would otherwise be questionable.—Ed.

NO. 37.—TIM BUNKER ON SAVING A SIXPENCE.

HOW HE BEAT JAKE FRINK.

Mr. Editor:—I hadn't calculated to write at all this month, until I got your letter. I never was much of a hand for indoor work, and could always use a crowbar enough sight better than a goose quill. I must say I like to make tracks upon the soil a great deal better than upon paper. When you have turned over an acre of sod a day, with a deep tiller, it kind o' looks as if you had done something. I have a natural affection for such furrows; but these scratches upon paper are rather small potatoes, and few in the hill. If it wa'n't that I had got interested in the farmers who read your paper, and could sort of feel their hands in mine, I would never touch a quill again.

Your letter found me down on that bit of swamp pasture, that I bought of Jake Frink, and underdrained last year—where I cured the horse-pond. I was just putting down a new bridge across the ditch, that I had left open on the back side of the lot. There was an old bridge a dozen rods above, going into another lot, that Jake had built when he owned it, several years ago. Neighbor

Frink, you will remember, beat me on carrots at the fair, in a way that was not fair. I have always felt bound to keep up a decent kind of resentment ever since, and to beat him in as many honorable ways as possible.

Well now, there was that old bridge, the work of Jake Frink, and looking just like him in a good many respects. It answered its purpose well enough, but it cost just about four times as much as it need to. A four-inch pipe would carry all the water that ever run in the ditch, even in time of a spring thaw. But Jake had built a stone culvert two feet square, and covered it with heavy stone slabs, as if a large brook was always running through. It must have cost him twelve or fifteen dollars, reckoning labor at any thing like a fair price.

And here is a point I think of a good deal of importance to farmers. There are not more than half of them that do a thing in the best and cheapest way. They don't save a sixpence where they might just as well as not. What is the use of walling off land into two-acre lots, when ten and twenty-acre lots are a good deal more convenient? Why, some men up here in Connecticut have kept themselves cramped for money all their days, by building stone-fences where they were not wanted. What is the use of burning out twenty cords of wood to keep warm, when you can do it a great deal better with half the quantity? *Good* stoves in a house save fifty dollars a year mighty easy. What is the use of taking four acres to grow a hundred bushels of corn, when you can grow it cheaper upon one? What is the use of paying fifteen dollars for a bridge across a ditch, when you can have one just as good and durable for three?

It was curious to hear my neighbors speculate, when I got the things together to make the bridge.

"Going to set up a crockery-shop, Esq. Bunker?" said Uncle Jotham, as he struck the tiles with his staff.

"What new tricks you got in your head neow?" asked Seth Twiggs, as he thought of the tiles and the brain manure in the garden.

"Going to dig a grave, and brick it up?" asked Jake Frink, as he looked over the fence.

"Nothing of the kind, Mr. Frink—you made a grave for ten or twelve dollars in your bridge up yonder, and I think there has been grave-digging enough of that kind in this bit of land."

I had got a dozen horse-shoe tile of seven-inch size, costing, all told, just one dollar; and a white oak plank two inches thick, twelve feet long, and about a foot wide, sound as a nut—cost, fifty cents. I laid the plank upon the mud in the bottom of the ditch, about three inches under the water. I then put the tile upon the plank, covering them with a lot of old straw, and then packed in the turf, grass side down, over them, and filled up with gravel from a neighboring hill. There was about a half-day's work carting dirt, and the whole was finished. That oak plank, I calculate, will last a good deal longer than I shall, and I shouldn't wonder if my grandchildren found it as sound as it is to-day. The tile will last as long as brick in a chimney. The whole cost of the bridge is not over three dollars, and it is quite as durable, and a good deal more ornamental, than that rough stone affair that cost fifteen. The fact is, I am getting sick of the sight of stone above ground, except in line walls, since I have begun to drain, and to use a horse-mower. I can't help thinking, how much better they would pay in a good stone culvert under the sod, or even in raising up the land in swampy places. On the surface they are unsightly, they take up a good deal of room, and are always in the way of the plow and the mower. Beneath the sod, they are out of the way, and are saving the sixpences in carrying off the excess of water. There is nothing on the farm so handsome as a clean green meadow, just ready for the scythe.

I guess I have beat Jake Frink twelve dollars on the bridge, and that will do to set over agin the carrots.

Yours to command,

TIMOTHY BUNKER.

Hookertown, Dec. 15, 1859.

NO. 38.—TIM BUNKER ON GIVING LAND A START.

MR. EDITOR:—"What are ye gwine to du with that 'ere bag of Scotch Snuff?" asked Jake Frink one morning, as he looked at a lot of Peruvian No. 1, just landed at my barn door.

"Who has a better right to have a quilting than Mrs. Bunker, and to entertain the old ladies with a pinch of the Scotch dust?" I asked by way of rejoinder, and to stimulate Jake's curiosity, which was already wide awake.

"I thought snuff allers come in bladders," suggested Seth Twiggs, as he blew out a column of smoke, that would have done credit to a locomotive.

"How du ye know but what it is a whale's bladder!" inquired Tucker, who had been to sea, and was anxious to show off his nautical knowledge to Mr. Twiggs.

"That's guanner, ye fools!" remarked Uncle Jotham Sparrowgrass, with a very emphatic blow of his cane upon the ground. "Haven't ye never seen any guanner? I've seen it a dozen year ago, over on the Island—Judge Randall tried it time and agin.—Never could make much out of it. He got one or tu decent crops, and then the land fell off, worse than ever. The Judge said it was a great humbug. Guess he's right."

"Ye aint a gwine to put that on tu the land, be ye, Squire Bunker?" inquired Jake with an astonished look.

"I shouldn't wonder if I did."

This conversation with my neighbors, two years ago, shows the general impression about guano in any community, when it is first introduced. I had got it to try an experiment on some poor land, that lay off a couple of miles from my house. I suppose a man ought to apologize for owning land so far from home, for it is certainly very bad husbandry. The expense of cultivating it is nearly double that of a home lot, and manuring with stable dung at that distance is out of the question. The fact is, the land belongs to Mrs. Bunker, and, as it came from her father, she never felt like selling it. It has been used for pasture ever since I can remember. For the last ten years I have not been very particular about pasturing it, for there was not much grass there to be eaten. It was miserable old plain land, and had once been a light sandy loam, before the loam was carried off in crops. It bore five-fingers and moss pretty well, was fair for pennyroyal, and famous for mulleins and sweet fern. The sheep had worn little paths around among these brush, and if sheep have any virtue to restore exhausted land, that field never found it out. I suppose all the vegetable matter that grew upon an acre, if it could have been gathered, would not have weighed two hundred pounds. It used to be said of it, that it was too poor to bear worms and insects, so that skunks had to starve or emigrate.

We have a great deal of such land in all the old States, thoroughly worn out, and not paying the interest on three dollars an acre, to their present owners. They are generally farmers in moderate circumstances, and have no spare capital to give such land a start, and it lies idle and worthless. I thought it was worth trying to give this out-lot a chance to do a little better by itself and its owner. My plan was to turn in green crops, a process in husbandry that no body practices in this neighborhood. I had read of it in my *Agriculturist*, and thought it was just the thing for lots too far off from the barn to be manured from the stable. The trouble was to get the green crop to turn under.

I thought the guano would probably start rye, and with this I could make a beginning. I plowed up five acres two years ago in October, and put on five bags of guano, or about one hundred and fifty pounds to the acre. The rye came up well, and looked a remarkably dark green, and by the time snow fell, the ground was well covered with a thick mat of rye. That rye made a good deal of talk, and even on Sunday it used to be discussed between meetings, when folks ought to have been thinking on other matters. It passed the winter well, got a good start in the spring, and by the middle of May, the heads began to appear. It stood thick, and was thought to be one of the best looking pieces of rye in town. It went against the grain amazingly to turn it under, for according to the look, I should have had fifteen bushels to the acre.

About the middle of June, John and I went into it, with two teams, to plow it under; for I had made my plan, and was not to be turned aside by the talk of my neighbors. Tucker and Jones said it was a great shame to spoil such a field of grain, and even Mr. Spooner remarked, that making manure of bread stuff did not seem to be very good economy. Now, you see, I did not care so much what George Washington Tucker and Benjamin Franklin Jones said, but I did not like to be undervalued by the minister. So said I to Mr. Spooner: "A thing always looks homely until it's finished; and you just wait till I get through with this field, before you make up your mind."

The rye was plowed under, and the ground turned up about two inches deeper than ever before. In about a fortnight I sowed buckwheat, harrowing it in with about the same quantity of guano that I had used in the rye. The buckwheat came up and grew more rankly than any thing I ever saw before. All the neighbors were astonished at the monstrous growth, and most astonished when I brought out the teams, the last of August, to turn it under. They said Tim Bunker must be crazy to make manure of the heaviest crop of buckwheat in town. But the buckwheat went under, notwithstanding. The last of September, I sowed with rye again, and as I had put two green crops under the sod, I thought the land had got start enough to take care of itself. I sowed with the rye, clover and herds-grass seed, calculating that these would take the ground, when the rye came off. Last July I harvested from that five-acre field, one hundred and twenty-five bushels of rye, worth as many dollars. They have got to making paper out of the straw, so that I got ten dollars a tun for that, or about seventy-five dollars.

Now, every man who is used to ciphering can tell whether the operation paid or not. The crop, I consider worth two hundred dollars, to say nothing of the fine catch of grass, which now promises at least a tun and a half of hay to the acre. The cost of the manure was about forty-five dollars. The labor of plowing, sowing, harvesting, and the grass seed would, perhaps, swell the cost of the improvement to one hundred and fifty dollars. This leaves a handsome sum on the right side of the balance sheet, and the land in much better condition. The old plain would have been well sold at five dollars an acre, for it did not pay the interest on half that sum. I should not want to sell now at ten dollars an acre. The experiment has worked much better than I thought it would.

Now, I think we have here a hint as to the economical way of giving land a start. If it lies near the barn, where manure can be carted cheaply, the stable manure is the best renovator. If it lies at a distance, it can be done with

Peruvian No. 1 and green crops, and it is much better to do it with this than to have it lie idle. Mrs. Bunker is as much pleased with the result as any body, for she says "it has always distressed her to have any thing belonging to the Bunker family lying idle."

Yours to command,

TIMOTHY BUNKER, ESQ.,

Hookertown, Dec. 10th, 1859.

NO. 39.—TIM BUNKER ON GIVING BOYS A START.

MR. EDITOR:—"Be sure you're right then go ahead." Davy Crockett got out considerable truth when he started that proverb. I guess it is about as applicable to starting boys in life, as it is to starting land on a right course to make it profitable. Now you may take poor, run-down land, and plow it, and crop it, as much as you have a mind to, and you can't make it pay for the labor of working. It needs the right start to begin with, and then you can go ahead and get pay for cultivating.

Now a great many folks make the same mistake with their boys that I did in working Mrs. Bunker's dowry lots, until I begun to turn in green crops. They don't give 'em the right start. A good many work their boys till they are twenty-one, and then send them off to shift for themselves, without capital, and without any experience in the earning and use of money. They stint them on schooling in the latter part of their minority, because their work is worth as much as a man's. They seem to have as little regard for the future welfare of the boy as they do for their land when they get all they can out of it without putting on any manure. They pay very little attention to their morals, and before they know it, the boy has learned to chew tobacco, smoke, drink, and swear, and perhaps to rob water-melon patches, and hen-roosts. He comes up to manhood a Kier Frink, fond of low company, and ready for any mischief that offers. They do not see their mistake until it is too late to mend it.

Now, you see, to give boys the right start, you must begin early with them. If you don't get right notions into their heads before they are twenty-one, I guess you might as well give them up. You can't begin too soon to cultivate their hearts, and to teach them to respect the rights of their Maker and the rights of their fellow-men. Some seem to think it makes no difference what sort of principles a young man adopts, or what habits he forms. I have lived long enough to see that there is nothing pays so well in the long run as correct moral habits. These make a young man entirely reliable, and his friends can trust him in any business. Any one of the vices to which so many boys are addicted is a great pecuniary damage. It is just like contracting a heavy debt at the beginning of life, and having to pay interest all through. You may safely put down the use of tobacco as a debt of five thousand dollars, the use of intoxicating drinks as five thousand more, and swearing, lying, and theft, at about the same figures. A young man wants nothing so much, when starting in business, as the confidence of his fellows. This must be based upon his character.

But when we have got a boy's heart and morals all right, there is something else to be done for him. A man, however upright, will not succeed without industrious habits, and a knowledge of the value of money, which is one of the best incentives to industry. There is only one way in which we can estimate money at its proper value, and that is to earn it. A silver dollar represents a day's work of the laborer. If it is given to a boy, he has no idea of what it has cost, or of what it is worth. He would be as likely to give a dollar as a dime for a top, or any other toy. But if the boy has learned to earn his dimes and dollars by the sweat of his face, he knows the difference. The painful stretch of his muscles through the long rows of corn, or at the plow tail, is to him a measure of values, that can never be rubbed out of his mind. A hundred dollars represents a hundred weary days, and it seems a great sum of money. A thousand dollars is a fortune, and ten thousand is almost inconceivable, for it is far more than he ever expects to possess. When he has earned a dollar, he thinks twice before he spends it. He wants to invest it so as to get the full value of a day's work for it.

It is a great wrong to society and to a boy to bring him up to a man's estate without this knowledge. A fortune at twenty-one, without it, is almost inevitably thrown away. With it, and a little capital to start on, he will make his own fortune better than any one can make it for him. The most of the capital they need to start with, they might earn in their minority. It is better for farmers to pay their boys regular wages, beginning, say, when they are fourteen, and teaching them how to take care of it, than to give them a much larger sum when they are of age. The seven years' wages, if put in the Saving's Bank, in annual investments, would come to over a thousand dollars, and with this, and a good character, and industrious habits, a young farmer's fortune is secure. That is double the capital I had to start with; but then I had Sally Bunker for a wife, and the like of her is better luck than common mortals can expect.

Yours to command,

TIMOTHY BUNKER, ESQ.,

Hookertown, Jan. 15th, 1860.

NO. 40.—JOTHAM SPARROWGRASS WITH A TILE IN HIS HEAD.

Mr. Editor:—"What's comin next!" exclaimed Tucker, as he saw Jotham Sparrowgrass' team drive up the road with a load of tiles, Uncle Jotham following after as fast as his cane could carry him.

"Should sooner have thought to see old Sparrowgrass on a tin peddler's cart, sellin wash basens and byin rags," responded Jones.

"Guess he's gwine tu set up a krokery shop to supply the Whiteoakers with sass-pans and sich like," answered Seth Twiggs with a side-long glance at Kier Frink, as he stood leaning against the wall.

"Sass-pans, you fool! The coal-men have got beyond that, I ken tell yew, and use tin like other folks. Guess ye better smoke less and see clearer, Seth Twiggs," responded Kier Frink, who was tender of the reputation of the Whiteoakers, and felt his toes trodden upon a little.

"He aint a gwine to du nuthin of the kind," added Jake Frink. "Ye see, Uncle Jotham has caught Tim Bunker's disease, and is gwine to finish up that land round the muskrat pond. He pretends that he don't believe any thing in the Squire's notions, but the fact is, there aint a bigger Bunkerite in town. You see, old Sparrowgrass was born when the sign was in the crab, and he gets at every thing sideways, jest like one of them 'ere fish."

Jake Frink was not very wide of the mark in regard to Uncle Jotham's disposition. Ever since he made an open drain through the rim of his pond, and drained three acres, summer before last, he has talked against new-fangled notions and fancy farming a little louder than before. He seemed to have a natural amount of satisfaction in his victory over the muskrats and the tadpoles, but no particular delight in the dry land. But I could see all the while, that he was getting up to a new effort, sideways, as Jake Frink says. I loaned him the paper, and found he always had some inquiries to make about draining, how they made tiles, how the water got into them, how deep they had to be laid, and how they worked. I have frequently found him down at my horse-pond lot, running his cane into the ends of the tiles, where they empty into the ditch, as if to make sure that it was real water that was discharging from the hole. He evidently thought there must be some trick about it, that the water could not get into tiles after they were laid. But there was proof in that horse-pond lot that he could not very well get away from.

I have been studying that lot some myself, this winter. It is only two seasons since the tiles were laid there, and you would be surprised to see what a change the surface of the land has undergone. The light bluish clay that I threw out from the bottoms of the drains and spread around upon the surface, has all crumbled to pieces, and got to be about as dark as the rest of the soil. I have noticed all along over the drains, and for a considerable distance upon each side, the ground becomes dry very soon after a rain, and little cracks are visible. The land used to be so full of water that no air got into it, from November to May. Now the air follows every rain, and every freezing and thawing disturbs the whole mass of the soil several inches deep. The mechanical improvement of the soil seems to go on quite as rapidly in the winter as in the summer. Jack Frost, I guess, is about as good a friend as the farmer has, if he would only give him a chance to work. The tiles make a path for him, and he uses up the coarse lumps and clods a little better than any harrow I ever tried.

Uncle Jotham has doubtless seen these things, though he has said nothing, and would have probably declared any time within the last three months, that tiles were the greatest humbug out, in his candid opinion.

The conversation I have reported among the wiseacres of Hookertown, occurred last fall. A few days after I had occasion to go upon the Shadtown road to see what had become of the load of tiles. I found Uncle Jotham with three hands and a team, busy making ditches on the side hills around the drained pond.

"Good morning, Uncle Jotham. I thought you didn't believe in crockery—rather pizen to the land."

"Wal, now, Squire Bunker, to tell the plain truth, this 'ere business has been brewin in my mind ever since that horse-pond of yourn was dreened off. And when I come to let the water off here, and got my first crop on land that was once under water, I had to cave in myself, worse than the tadpoles, when the water left them. You see, the taters I raised here on these three acres the first season, brought me five hundred dollars delivered at the landing, and that amount of money, ye see, would make tearin work with almost any man's prejudices. I found I could get the Hartford tile down there pretty reasonable, and I jest made up my mind to finish the job. Am I duin it right, Squire Bunker?"

I found he had determined to put in drains upon all the side hills sloping down to the reclaimed meadow, leaving the drains there still open. These hill sides embraced four or five acres, and were naturally a heavy clay soil, always wet, until midsummer. The drains were about three feet deep, and I found he had got a man used to the business, to do the work in the best manner. I have frequently looked over the ground this winter, and it is a charming sight to see the various colored clays and rough clods gradually breaking down under the action of frost and rain. The results, of course, remain to be seen, but nobody who has seen the working of tiles can doubt what they will be.

Thus the leaven of new ideas is working all through this region. When one man gets a tile in his field, another is certain to get one in his head, and after carrying it a spell, it is in due time laid, and carries water. When Jotham Sparrowgrass tile-drains, you may know the world moves.

Yours to command,

TIMOTHY BUNKER, ESQ.,

Hookertown, Feb. 15th, 1860.

NO. 41.—LETTER FROM TIMOTHY BUNKER, ESQ.

JAKE FRINK SOLD.

MR. EDITOR:—The spring work came on so sudden, that I didn't get time to say any thing about Hookertown folks, last month, and now I would'nt say a word, if it were not for fear that other folks would get taken in just as bad as neighbor Frink. You needn't think that Jake's body has been put up at auction; but, what is about as bad, his wits have been in the market, and gone to the highest bidder. Now, you see, we have got our full share of poor land up here in Connecticut, and of all the land in these parts, Jake Frink's is about the poorest. He has a lot of twenty acres, lying up towards the Whiteoaks, of poor worn-out sheep pasture, not worth to exceed five dollars an acre. He bought it a dozen years ago, and gave a hundred dollars for the lot, and it has not improved any under his cultivation. All he has ever done for it has been to plow up occasionally a patch of it for buckwheat, or for rye. The rest of the time it has been pastured with sheep.

It is a light, sandy loam, bearing a plenty of five-fingers, and mullein, and a little red-top, with other wild grasses. Jake was upon this piece of land last summer, plowing for buckwheat, when a fellow came along in a fine carriage, with a span, and inquired for Mr. Frink — Jacob Frink, Esq., he called him. As Jake tells the story, he was considerably elevated, to hear a well-dressed city gentleman calling him "Esq."

"So I holler'd whoa to old Buck and Bright, and axed him what his name might be, and where he was from. And he said:"

"I'm Mr. Smith, the senior partner in the firm of Smith, Stubbs, Darby & Co., of Philadelphia, proprietors of the patent for the improved, imperial, nitrogenized Tafeu."

"Wall, now, I'm Jake Frink, and nothing else, and don't know enny thing but English, and not much of that. I don't know what Tafeu is, never heard of it."

"Just so, Esq. Frink. I should think from the looks of this field, that you were a stranger to the most remarkable manure ever invented for the improvement of the soil."

"Oh! it's a manure, is it!"

"Yes, sir-ee, a wonderful fertilizer, that will grow forty bushels of wheat to the acre, one hundred of corn, and from three to four hundred of potatoes. It is great on grass, bringing up such poor, sandy land as this to a production of four tuns of hay to the acre. It has the happiest influence upon fruit trees, making the wood grow rapidly, and adding four-fold to the fruit. By the use of this Tafeu, the produce of a farm may be doubled the first year, and quadrupled the second. Every man who purchases the article is sure to get rich."

"You're jest the man I've been wanting to see this many a year. You see I've been farming on't, this well-nigh thirty year, and I ha'n't got all my land paid for yit. I am all the time cramp'd to git along, and if you've got a resate for making folks rich, ye see I shall go in."

"But I have not got the Tafeu along with me, to sell this morning, I am securing agents to dispose of it. I sell rights to towns, and to counties, and the man who gets the right to sell the article makes his fortune, the first season, while the man who buys will have to wait a little. For instance, if Esq. Frink buys the right for Hookertown, and sells a thousand tuns, he makes five thousand dollars, for we allow our agents five dollars a tun on the sales. You have in town at least two hundred farmers, and they will want, on a safe calculation, five tuns of Tafeu, each."

"Yes, we've got more'n four hundred farmers in town, and I'm the chap that can sell the stuff tu 'em, if there is any vartu in talk."

"You see," continued the fluent Mr. Smith, "I sold the right to Col. Babcock, of Spruce Hill, last year, and he told me he made over ten thousand dollars, and there are hundreds more I could mention in other States, that have made handsome fortunes out of our fertilizer, the first season."

"And how much are you going to ax for the right to sell in Hookertown?"

"Well, we generally sell county rights for fifty dollars, and town rights for about ten, a little more or less according to size. But seeing it is you, Esq. Frink, we will let you have the Hookertown right for nine dollars."

Jake Frink is not a monied man, but he happened to have just that amount in bills in his wallet, and he handed it over to the oily-tongued Mr. Smith, who delivered him his right to sell Tafeu in Hookertown, duly signed and dated. He told Jake as he drove off, that a cargo would be in from Philadelphia, and delivered at the landing next Saturday.

Saturday came, and Jake went down with his old bob-tailed mare, bright and early, expecting to see a schooner discharging Tafeu. But he found nothing but a coal vessel at the dock, and the captain had never heard of "Smith, Stubbs, Darby & Co.," and doubted very much whether there was any such firm in Philadelphia. The next Saturday came, and Jake, thinking he might have misunderstood the day, went down again, but no Tafeu vessel had arrived. Jake now began to suspect he was sold, and scolded some, if not more. His golden visions became dim, as the weeks wore away, and no news came from Mr. Smith and the cargo of patent fertilizers. He has not heard from him since. Jake is particularly sore about this Tafeu business, and his neighbors, especially Jones and Tucker, when they wish to touch him on the raw, inquire for the price of the Philadelphia fertilizer.

Now, I suppose there are thousands of dollars taken out of the pockets of farmers in just this way every year. Some of these concentrated fertilizers I suppose are worth the money paid for them, but the chances are, that a man gets cheated when he buys them. This is pretty certain to be the case when they are bought of traveling agents like Mr. Smith. It is worse than highway robbery, for you do not know that you are robbed until the thief is out of your reach.

However, "there is no great loss but what there is some small gain," and Jake Frink claims that he has got his money's worth in experience. He says he "should jest like to see a man come along and undertake to sell him patent manure agin. Wouldn't he catch it!" Jake put into his yard last fall double the quantity of muck I ever knew him to cart before, and, judging from the quantity of manure he has spread this spring and plowed in, he will be a gainer by his experience. Beware of Patent Manures.

Yours to command,

Timothy Bunker, Esq.,

Hookertown, April, 1860.

NO. 42.—TIMOTHY BUNKER, ESQ., AT THE NEW YORK CENTRAL PARK.

Mr. Editor:—I have heern tell a great deal about your Park, that Mr. Olmstead is fixing up for your city folks, on the upper end of your island. Every body that went down to the city from our place had a good deal to say about it, and the lots of money they was laying out there in making hills higher, and hollows hollower, building bridges where there wa'n't any brooks, and putting pond holes where there used to be dry land, making a clearing where there was a forest, and putting trees where there was cleared land. I expect they talked all the more about it, because Mr. Olmstead was a Connecticut man, and used to live close by us up here in Hookertown.

Mrs. Bunker was a good deal stirred up about these accounts, and thought she should like to see the thing for herself. Sally hasn't said a word about visiting since she got back from down South. She thought then, she said, she should never care to get out of sight of Connecticut again as long as she lived. She has held of that mind until this spring, and has hardly been out of Hookertown street, except to go down to Shadtown to see the baby. I have stuck pretty close to home myself, thinking that Hookertown was about as nigh the hub of the universe, as any other spot in this country. So, one day last week, Mrs. Bunker says to me, "Timothy, have you read in the papers what Fred Olmstead is doing down there in the city?"

"Well, yes, I have read some things, and heern a good deal more."

"They say the city is fixing up a sort of country place, to walk and ride in, and Fred is telling 'em how to spend several millions on brush pasture, and sheep walks, and tadpole ponds!"

"Suppose you go down and see, Sally; I have a little business in the city, and shall be glad of your company."

Mrs. Bunker's trunk was packed next day, and we took the boat for the city. At first, she was inclined to think the whole story was a hoax, for she did not see, where houses were so plenty, how folks could find any room for pastures and woodlands. But after riding up on a railroad that went by horses, six or seven miles, with houses and stores on both sides, considerable thicker than they are on Hookertown street, and we began to get sight of some vacant lots and trees, she thought there might be something in it.

The city pretty much faded out after a while, and we came to a place they told us was the Park. We found some very wide roads, they called avenues, about as smooth as a barn floor, and wide enough for six loads of hay to drive along abreast. "Now," exclaims Mrs. Bunker, "what are these people thinking of? Don't they expect to leave the road behind them when they ride out? Fred ought to have told them better than that." I should think there were more people at work there, than we have got on all the farms in Hookertown, some drilling rocks, some carting stone, some setting out trees, and some moving dirt from one place to another, without any particular object in view. I could n't help thinking what lots of corn and potatoes they would raise this summer, if they were only working on farms.

They called one place a Ramble, and had guide-boards put up, all round, pointing that way, as if it was something remarkable. Mrs. Bunker said "it reminded her, for all the world, of Uncle Jotham Sparrowgrass's cow pasture, before he drained the muskrat pond, and she didn't think the lay of the land was a bit handsomer."

It is curious to see how folks' minds work. Here in the country, the great object seems to be to get rid of water, rocks, and brush. You see, I spent considerable in draining the horse-pond, and Uncle Jotham made dry land where the muskrats built their nests. But Fred Olmstead has got things turned tother end foremost, and gone and filled up a valley of well-nigh twenty acres with water, and made all the shores of the pond as crooked as a ram's horn. I should n't think there was a rod of it any where in a straight line. Then, in the country, we plow up huckleberry brush, sweet fern, alders, hardhack, and all such stuff, glad enough to get rid of them. But down there, we saw lots of huckleberries, blackberries, brakes, and things of that kind, put round into the shy places, as if they were something very nice.

In one spot, I remember, we came upon a sluggish little pond hole, with rushes, lily pads, pickerel weed, and other water plants, and on the banks a rank patch of skunk cabbage. At the sight of this last plant, Mrs. Bunker put on her spectacles to see if she wa'n't mistaken, and then burst into such a fit of laughter, that, one spell, I thought I should have to call a policeman to stop her. The idea of cultivating that savory article in a flower garden seemed to upset all her notions of propriety.

Up here, in the country, we take a great deal of pains to bury the rocks, and get them out of sight. In the Park, we saw a good many places where the dirt had been removed to bring the rocks into view, and in one place they had dug a great ditch, clear from the pond away under a great boulder, as big as a small meeting-house. They were fixing it up for a grotto, I believe they called it, and they said it would cost five thousand dollars. It looked pretty much like Dick Sanders' saw-mill flume, or Mrs. Bunker said she thought it would, when the moss got grown upon the rocks around. I thought it was a smashing price for a big rock. In another place they had tumbled a great lot of smaller rocks into a swale, and turned on a spout of Croton water to make it look like a brook. Now it run down under the stones out of sight, and again it run over one long flat rock, and fell down six or eight feet into the pool. This they called a cascade, but it looked to me just like a water-fall in a trout brook, only it wa'n't half so handsome. They said this concern cost over eight thousand dollars, and that is mor'n Dick Sanders' whole farm is worth, saw-mill, trout brook, and all. The little walks around the place they called the Ramble, Mrs. Bunker said, made her think, for all the world, of a huckleberry pasture full of rabbit paths, and she didn't believe but Fred Olmstead had just made a map of some place up here on our hills, and told his hired men to mark it out accordingly. It was a pretty woodsy place, she admitted, but thought the city folks were paying pretty dear for their whistle.

That may be so, but I suppose they have earned their money, and can spend it as they please. I couln't help thinking that it was enough sight cheaper for a man, if he has a longing for such things, to export himself into the country, than to try and import the country into the city, where, at best, he only got a small sample, and not a very perfect specimen at that. I have n't a doubt that Mr. Olmstead has done his work as well as any body could, but it seems to me that we who till the soil, get rather better looking trout brooks, water-falls, and bush pastures at a more reasonable rate. We came home thinking that we were about as well off as our neighbors, content to live in a region where trout brooks run naturally, and where brakes and ferns, bulrushes and pond lilies are the portion of every man's farm. It is a great country where skunk cabbage is grown in the flower gardens.

Yours to command,

TIMOTHY BUNKER, ESQ.

Hookertown, June, 1860.

[We generally let Squire Bunker have his say in his own words, for he utters a good many solid truths in his way. His intended criticisms upon *our* Central Park we think are about the best puff it has had—it looks so country like, so "woodsy," that it seemed just like the country to our rural visitors, and that is exactly what is aimed at. Ed.]

NO. 43.—TIM BUNKER ON IRRIGATION AND INVISIBLE TOLL GATES.

"What next!" exclaimed my neighbor Tucker one morning, as he poked his head over the wall of the lot where the horse-pond used to be, and which is now known in all Hookertown as the Horse-Pond lot.

"What are you turnin up that furrow for?" asked Jones, with his mouth agape, as if he saw an elephant.

"You ain't a gwine to plow this field, be you, Squire?" asked Seth Twiggs, as he blew an extra long whiff out of his mouth, and leaned his elbow on the wall.

"Plow it, you fool!" exclaimed Jake Frink, "that 'ere field cut four tun of hay to the acre this season, and you don't think Tim Bunker is gwine to take up such a sod as that, do you?"

"'Tarnally tinkering with the land," added Uncle Jotham Sparrowgrass, as he looked in astonishment at a new adventure upon a piece of land, that he thought was finished.

"You don't expect to get any more grass off of this lot than you cut this year, do you?" inquired Mr. Spooner, as he came to join that portion of his flock who keep a sharp lookout on all my movements.

The Horse-Pond lot is admitted to be a great success, and Jake Frink grits his teeth every time he goes by it, and wonders he was such a fool as to sell it, though it would have laid there unimproved to this day, if he had kept it. A part of it I have in sugar beets and mangolds, and though I have seen some beets in my day, I must say these are the beaters of all that tribe of plants. You see I fell in with a lot of old lime plaster from a house they took down in the village this spring, and carted on perhaps a dozen loads. The lime was just what the soil needed to decompose its excess of vegetable matter, and, judging from the growth of these beets, they have had about as much plant-food as they could take care of. They have three months to grow yet, and they already cover the ground, though they are planted two feet apart. The crop will not be short of two thousand bushels to the acre.

But the larger part of the lot has been in grass, and according to the estimate of my neighbors, the yield was four tuns to the acre, though I guess they overstate the matter a little. It was tall herds-grass and lodged in spots, but it takes a great deal of hay to make four tuns to the acre. But good as it was, I am not quite satisfied with it. You know it is not in human nature to let well enough alone, or to think that we are on top of the ladder, while there is a single round above us.

I was just laying out the ground for watering it, when my neighbors gave me a call yesterday. You see, the land slopes away from the road, and water can be run all over it by making shallow channels upon the surface with a plow, and mending them a little with the hoe and spade. I have a first-rate chance to turn water on, and as the ground is now all drained, I claim that the more water on top, the better, as long as it can get out at the bottom.

Almost all water has more or less sediment in it, even when it seems to be clear, and the land is just like a strainer to take all this floating matter out. There is a good deal of nourishment for plants in this sediment. The soup is rather thin, I admit, but I suppose some things may suit plants that would be rather spare diet for man or beast. When I get my channels properly constructed, I can irrigate this lot from two sources—the wash of the road, and a brook that I can turn from its course at a cost of not over twenty dollars. You see, the lot lies right in a hollow between my house and Jake Frink's, and can now be made to catch all the water from the two hills, a distance of at least a mile, which used to go into the pond before it was drained. The wash of a road is good any where, I suppose partly from the manure that drops from passing animals, and partly from the soil, which is ground up very fine by the continual tramping of iron-shod feet, and the crushing of wheels. I have noticed that where-ever any of this dirt is run on to a mowing field, even where there is hardly a trace of manure, it makes the grass much stouter, and you will see the effects of it for several rods from the fence. I have sometimes thought it would pay to have a machine for grinding up soil very fine for top-dressing. At any rate, there can be no doubt that all the wash of roads ought to be saved, wherever it can be turned on to grass land.

In the roads that lead into villages and cities this wash is particularly valuable, because there is more travel to grind up the soil, and more manure dropped. Hooker-town is a place of considerable trade, and I suppose on an average there are fifty carriages and teams that go by this lot every day. I calculate to make them all pay toll, and contribute to the growth of my grass without knowing it. Suppose I get from each passing team only five mills; this amounts to twenty-five cents a day, or over ninety dollars a year. I think the wash that comes into this hollow, when spread over five acres, will make more than ninety dollars difference in the yield of the hay. Every farmer who owns a lot similarly located, can erect an invisible toll gate, and collect the tolls without robbing his neighbors.

The water from the brook I can turn on, in dry times

in the fall or summer, after the hay is taken off. This brook comes from a swamp covered with timber and brush, principally maple and huckleberry and other hard woods, and every fall brings down a great quantity of leaves and vegetable matter. It also flows through meadows and cultivated fields, and after heavy rains carries a good deal of mud and sediment. This, I think, can not fail to benefit vegetation, though it is not so rich as the road wash.

The arrangement of the channels is a matter of considerable importance. It is found from experiment that the grass gets all the more valuable parts of the water and sediment in running six or eight rods, so that the main channels should be about that distance apart over the whole field. If the lot lies like mine in the form of a parallelogram, sloping to the south, the channels may be arranged as in the cut. The road runs parallel with the north side of the lot. The water comes in through the wall at *A*, and follows the main channel until it discharges at *B*. This channel is made about eighteen inches broad at the top, and about a foot deep. It is kept nearly level where it runs east and west, so that small notches in the brim will pass the water off in nearly equal streams. These small streams are partly absorbed by the soil, in running eight rods to the channel below, where they are caught and mingled with the muddy water again, and again passed off through small cuts in the brim, and so on until the whole field is irrigated. The fall is about two feet in the eight rods, but the channels could be easily worked with much more fall, as the water would only run a little faster from *C* to *D* and in the parallel courses.

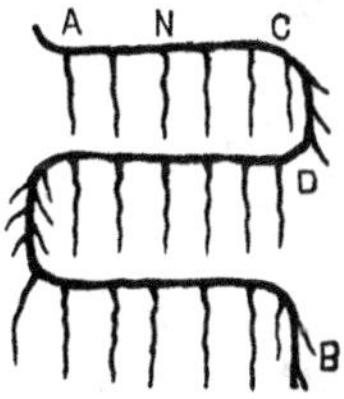

"Irritation of the land!" exclaimed Kier Frink, as he looked out of his coal cart, where he has stopped to hear what was said by the company. "What does he mean by that? I never heern of that even in the Whiteoaks, where they irritate almost every thing from cats up to old hosses."

"He is gwine to turn a brook on here and git six tun of hay to the acre," answered Tucker.

"If he can," added Jones.

"And blame him, he'll du it neow, ye see, for he's a master hand to carry his pint," said Seth Twiggs.

"Neow du tell," responded Kier, hitting his horse a smart lick, "Tim Bunker waterin a swamp! git up old hoss, this aint a safe place for yew."

And the old coal cart vanished up the hill as if the driver had seen a ghost. But I am not quite crazy yet, though some of my neighbors think I am leaning that way. I shall keep you posted on "the irritation of the soil."

Yours to command,

TIMOTHY BUNKER, ESQ.

Hookertown, Aug., 1860.

NO. 44.—TIM BUNKER ON FEEDING WITH OIL MEAL.

"It's no use to try it," said Jotham Sparrowgrass, as he poked his cane into the tub where I was preparing a mess for my fattening cattle.

"No use to try what?" said I.

"Why, to fat cattle with iled meal. You see the thing has been tried, time and agin, over on the Island, and failed. Never could make the cattle eat the stinking stuff. Job Woodhull and Zophar Mills both tried it one summer. You see they had heern a great deal about feeding animals with ile meal, and they took it into their heads to make a lot out of fish ile and Indian meal. They had a plenty of ile from their fish works, and they put in about five gallons to a barrel of meal, and mixed it up well. They tried to get oxen to eat it, but it was no go. They kept trying every thing with it for a week or more, and by that time it was about the stinkenest mess that was ever got up on the Island, where they are famous for smells, especially in the fish season. I guess they have'nt heerd the last of that ile meal yet."

"The oxen were sensible brutes for not touching such stuff," said I. "But you see, Uncle Jotham, this is not that kind of oil meal."

"Du tell!"

"You know there are certain kinds of plants that produce oil-bearing seeds, and when they are pressed for the sake of the oil, a cake remains, which is good for manure or for provender. They press rape seed and the castor oil bean, and the refuse cake makes a very good manure. They press flax-seed to get linseed oil for painting, and cotton seed to get oil for burning, for making soap, and other purposes. The cake that remains is ground up into meal, and is fed to cattle."

"Well, I never paid much attention to it, but I allers tho't oil meal was such as they made on the Island."

This talk with Uncle Jotham occurred more than a year ago, when I first begun to use the meal made from linseed and cotton seed cake. I had not much faith in it myself, when I begun to use it, though I ought to have had; for linseed cake has been used for fattening cattle, and various feeding purposes, for several generations. It is astonishing to see how little faith people have in any thing they have not seen and tried.

In England, if a farmer has got to purchase feeding stuff, he is certain to invest in oil-cake. In this country, it is pretty certain to be corn or oats. Almost all the oil-cake made in this country is sent to a foreign market, because very few of our farmers have tried it. Once in a while we find an imported farmer like John Johnston of

FEEDING WITH OIL-MEAL. Page 145.

Geneva, or the dairy farmers, using oil-cake for feeding. But not one farmer in a hundred has ever seen it or tried it. As a rule, they have no faith in buying any thing to keep up their cattle in high condition. They sell grain, and feed out hay and grass. These, no doubt, are the staple articles of fodder, but all cattle will do better to have some addition to hay and grass. I have always fed every thing I could raise on my farm—oats, buckwheat, rye, and roots—and have no doubt it pays. If any body can use grain to a profit, the farmer can. The man who buys his grain expects to make a profit on it, and in most cases, does so. Why should not the farmer feed his grain and make the profit himself? If there is a profit in feeding twenty bushels of corn to a bullock, of say, three dollars, the farmer, especially if he live near a good market, can make the profit a little better than any body else. He wants the manure for his land, and the manure is on the soil where it will be plowed in. There is no expense for carting it three or four miles from the village, or of shipping it fifty miles, or more, from the city.

I always liked to feed grain, corn meal, oats, etc., but I think now the oil meal pays better than even the grains. The linseed meal comes pretty high, and that is one great objection to its use. But the cotton seed meal comes even cheaper than corn meal, and I think does better than linseed, pound for pound.

I had not used it a month, before Jake Frink came along one morning and hailed me.

"What ye ben duin to yer cattle lately, Mr. Bunker? I see the hair looks mighty sleek and shiny, as ef it had been combed with a fine tooth comb, and had some intment on tu it."

"You are right, neighbor, but the ointment was applied on the inside. I have been feeding with oil meal."

"What upon airth is ile meal? Never heern of sich stuff."

"Well, there is a fellow up here in Shadtown has started the business of pressing cotton seed oil, and sells the meal from the ground cake to the farmers."

Jake Frink was about right in describing the glossy coat of my yoke of oxen, though, perhaps, I did not do full credit to John's curry-comb, and wisp of straw. They are Devons, and John takes a good deal of pride in polishing them down, especially when he drives a load of wood to market in Shadtown. Whether any body looks out of the window at the young farmer's team, or at his wood, I am not able to say. He is uncommon fond of going to see Sally at the parsonage, I have noticed lately, and the span of Black Hawks are quite as shiny as the oxen. Probably he don't want to disgrace his sister, when he is in town.

I have been trying this feed for a year or more, and think I get more for my money than in any kind of feed that I buy. It comes considerable cheaper than corn meal, and goes further in making milk, butter, cheese, beef, mutton, pork, etc. It is excellent for working cattle, making them shed their coats early in the spring, and keeping them in good flesh. It increases the product of milk from twenty to thirty per cent, depending, somewhat, upon the condition of the cow. I have found about two quarts a day enough for a single animal. If fed too liberally, it gives the milk an unpleasant flavor. It keeps the cattle in good thriving condition. In making beef, a larger quantity should be used; there is no bad taste imparted to the meat.

Almost all cattle are a little shy in eating it at first, and, in this respect they are pretty much like their owners in buying it. But if a small quantity is mixed with some palatable food, they will eat it, and soon become very fond of it. One great advantage in using this and the linseed cake meal is the excellent quality of the manure. It seems to do execution on the land like hog manure. I have never had such a yard of manure as I carted out this last spring, and I think it must be owing, in part, to the two tuns of cotton seed meal used by my cattle last winter. It would have made a great difference in the looks of my farm, if I had begun to use this article ten years ago. But we must all live to learn.

Yours to command,

TIMOTHY BUNKER, ESQ.

Hookertown, Sept., 1860.

NO. 45.—TIM BUNKER ON THE FARMERS' CLUB.

HOW TO GET RICH BY FARMING.

[Perhaps it might be more modest to omit the following letter from the Squire, but it contains some good hints. And here allow us to remark, that these letters, which have been continued so long, and we expect will be continued hereafter, are none of them 'got up' in our office, as some have supposed, but they are veritable letters, sent to us from Connecticut. We are happy to know, that the plain, homespun truths here told have been of great value to thousands who have read them, not only in this journal, but in many others, into which they have been copied.—ED.]

MR. EDITOR:—I have not had much to say lately about our farmers' club, that our minister, Mr. Spooner, and a few of us started in Hookertown, a few years ago. Well, you see, at first the thing didn't take very well. It looked kind of bookish, and men accustomed to the plow handle didn't exactly like to come to the school-house, where we generally hold our meetings in the winter, to learn farming. Some of them called it Mr. Spooner's school, and some Tim Bunker's pew. Jake Frink, who has never forgiven me for buying that horse-pond lot, and draining it, called it the Horse-Pond Convention. In the summer time we meet around at the farmers' houses, generally once a month, some Saturday afternoon, so as to look at the crops and stock, as well as to discuss questions. Well, by a little coaxing and management, we have got most of the young farmers in the neighborhood of the village interested, so that we frequently have twenty at the meeting, and that makes about as large a company as a plain farmer cares to talk to. My immediate circle of friends are among the most punctual members. Mr. Spooner and Deacon Smith are always on hand to keep things straight; Seth Twiggs comes up to see what he can through his clouds of smoke; Uncle Jotham Sparrowgrass limps around with his invaluable scraps of experience from Long Island; and Tucker, Jones, and Jake Frink, drop in to see what new exercise is going on in Tim Bunker's pew.

The club is getting to be a good deal of an institution, if not a great one, in Hookertown. The last topic talked up was "How to Make Farming Profitable." We had a stranger into the meeting from Massachusetts, Mr. Pinkham; and he took the ground that it was not profitable, and for his part he did not believe it could be made to pay. He said "he had got a little property together, but he did not make it by cultivating the soil, though he had worked at it thirty years steady. He had a farm given to him to start with, and if he had done nothing else but farm it, he believed he should have run in debt every year. He had worked in the winter and on rainy days at shoe making, and all that he was worth, over and above what he inherited, was owing to his trade."

Uncle Jotham guessed Mr. Pinkham was about right, if men managed their farms in the old way. He had known a hundred farmers or more, on the Island, and there wa'n't a half dozen of them that got ahead any, until they begun to catch bony fish. This made manure mighty cheap and plenty, and a man must be a fool that couldn't get big crops with manure a plenty. But to have nothing but barn-yard manure, and next to none of that, he didn't think a farmer could more'n make the ends of the year meet.

"I don't believe he can du that," said Jake Frink, "unless he has better luck than I have had. I've worked hard as an Injun on my land, for well-nigh forty year, and I hain't got so much land as when I started. I hev ben allers comin short at the eend of the year, and every now and then, have had to sell off a chunk of land to some lucky naber. And it allers happened, that I sold jest the best lot I had, but didn't see it till arter it was gone. That horse-pond lot, that didn't use to raise any thing but sour grass, bulrushes, and hardhack, now bears three tun to the acre of first-rate herds-grass. Some folks make farming pay, but I never could. Some how it don't run in the blood."

Mr. Spooner said farmers did not have capital enough to carry on their farming profitably. No man can be successful in business without capital. The merchant has his years of discipline as a clerk, and earns a small capital before he sets up for himself. But the farmer often runs in debt for his farm, and has hardly money enough to buy his stock and tools. This keeps him troubled all the time. He is afraid to hire help, to purchase such new machines as he needs, and to make those improvements in his land which are essential to profitable husbandry.

George Washington Tucker thought there was a good deal of truth in Mr. Spooner's doctrine. "I don't know zactly what the parson means by capital, but if he means money, he's jest right. I never had a red cent tu begin with, and that's the reason I haint got along no better. As they used to say in sifering, 0 from 0, and 0 remains. It's jest so in farming."

"Them's my sentiments," said Jones. Now the fact is, both Tucker and Jones are lazy, and never did a good day's work in one day, in their whole lives. The cipher lies in the persons of those two individuals, and not in their purses. I didn't say that in the club; if I had, I guess I should have spoke in meeting.

I did have to say, however, that I thought the trouble about bad farming lay a little deeper than the want of capital or the want of labor. "The want of *brains*, I guess, lies at the bottom of all the unprofitable farming. What is the use of a man's having money, if he does not know how to apply it to his business? What is the use of a man's having labor, if he does not know how to direct it, so as to make it pay? Farmers do not read enough about their business, and reflect upon it. I know of a dozen farmers who have from one to five thousand dollars in the bank, and they have occasion for the use of twice that sum in order to make their farms productive. Capital in the bank only pays six or seven per cent. In the bank of earth, if wisely invested, it will pay ten per cent. I have got fifteen per cent on what I have laid out on the horse-pond lot."

"Above all expenses?" asked Mr. Spooner.

"Yes, above all expenses, and I expect to get it for years to come. I do not find it difficult to make land pay the interest on three hundred dollars an acre, and any man who will read and digest the *American Agriculturist* can do the same thing."

"Where is that paper printed?" inquired Pinkham. "I've heard tell so much about that paper, and about improvements Squire Bunker has made since he began reading it, that I've a notion to take it myself a year, and see what it is, any way."

"At 41 Park Row, N. Y., by O. Judd, and it only costs a dollar a year, and often you get a dollar's worth of seeds thrown into the bargain."

"You say that 'cause you rite for it, Squire," said Seth Twiggs; to poke fun at me.

"It's true I write some about Hookertown, but what I get out of it that I don't write, is worth about five hundred dollars a year to me; and I guess this town is worth ten thousand dollars more in solid cash for the ideas they have got out of the *Agriculturist.*

"Judd's a hull team!" ejaculated Twiggs, as he knocked his pipe on the round of his chair, with an emphasis that sent the bowl spinning half way across the room, "and if that paper hasn't got a half a dozen big horses hitched on to it, as strong as Pennsylvania roadsters, and as fast as yer Morgans, then I'm no judge of what's in it. You're a bennyfacter, Squire Bunker, for getting me and so many to read that paper."

Well, I guess they'll all find it out by and by. Just look at Dea. Smith's new underdrained ten-acre field, where he harvested forty bushels of wheat to the acre this summer. Look at Seth Twiggs' garden with the tile in, and subsoiled. He raises a hundred dollars' worth of stuff where he used to raise less than twenty. Look at Jake Frink's new watering trough in his yard, and Uncle Jotham's drained muskrat swamp, and new barn cellar; and, to cap all, my reclaimed salt marsh, cutting three tun of hay to the acre. I made two thousand dollars by that operation, and I might have thunk and thunk my brains out, and I never should have thought of that, if it had not been for the paper. Improvements are going on all over the town, and it is because they read the *Agriculturist.* All the way up to Shadtown, I can tell just what farmers read it by the looks of the farms and buildings. You see then, my recipe for getting rich by farming is, to take the paper, read and digest inwardly, and apply outwardly.

Yours to command,

TIMOTHY BUNKER, ESQ.

Hookertown, Oct., 1860.

NO. 46.—TIM BUNKER ON BAD WATER.

A STIR IN HOOKERTOWN.

"What upon airth do you s'pose is the matter with my well?" said Uncle Jotham Sparrowgrass, one morning in August. "We hain't been able to drink it for more than a month."

"Guess there's a cat in it," responded Benjamin Franklin Jones, who is always at leisure to attend to any business of his neighbors. "I found one in mine, last week. Shouldn't have found it out if I hadn't seen some of the hair in the bucket. Smelt like pizen though, depend on't."

"No, there ain't any cat or rat in it. The water is as clear as a crystal, and I had it cleared out last week, but it didn't help it a bit."

"Shouldn't wonder ef it had been pizened," suggested Seth Twiggs, with a slight twinkle in his eye, and a puff of smoke that made the kitchen blue. He loves to play upon the fears of Uncle Jotham, and knows his weak spot. "Kier Frink was round all last month, you know."

"You don't say that creetur is at hum agin! I thought we'd got rid of him when he married the widder," responded Jotham, with a faint feeling at the stomach.

"Ye needn't lay it to Kier," said Jake Frink, "for my well has been out of fix all summer, and the boy wouldn't pizen our well. I know 'taint any thing uncommon to have the water taste bad in summer at our house. Water gets low, smells a leetle like the bottom of a ditch, and I s'pose it's for the same reason. It draws the smell out of the dirt."

"Our well used to taste bad in summer until I put them tile into the garden, and made the surface water run off through them into the brook," remarked Twiggs.

"Ye don't s'pose the bad smells come from the top of the ground, do ye?" asked Jake.

"That's a new idee," said Uncle Jotham, "but there must be something in it, for my sink drain ain't more than ten feet from the mouth of my well."

This talk of my neighbors gives a clue to an evil that prevails in other communities besides Hookertown. It has prevailed here more than usual this summer, because the fore part of the summer was dry, and the springs and wells got low. You have pure water down in your city, for it is brought to you in iron pipes, that guard it against all the foul dirt and smells through which it has to pass. But out here in the country, where we brag about having every thing sweet and clean, we are often troubled with bad water, especially in the summer time. A good many of my neighbors have had to apologize a little for their water, though some of them got so used to it, that they didn't know but 'twas the natural taste of all water. Somehow, there was a good deal that needed an apology that didn't get it. Even Dea. Smith, who is pretty particular about most things, had a well this summer, that gave out an "ancient and fish-like smell." Folks that are afflicted in this way all wonder what's the matter with the water, when the matter is about as plain as the sun in the heavens.

I suppose nobody thinks the water gets bad without some cause, and yet they talk just as if they believed so. Seth Twiggs has the right of it—this bad taste and smell almost invariably come from the surface. Now, Mr. Editor, I don't want to disturb the stomachs of your readers, and prevent them from drinking water any more, for I am a teetotaller and believe that Adam's ale is about the best article of drink that was ever put into a tumbler. But I must say that I prefer a pure article.

It stands to reason that water will run down hill, whether it is pure or foul, and will keep running till it finds the lowest place, whether it's the bottom of the well or the lower end of a brook. We see this when we dig a ditch, or lay down a tile. If it is put down four feet in the earth, it will draw the water on each side, for a rod or more, right into it. If the soil is very compact, or made up mainly of black earth, it would probably absorb all offensive matters in the water, until it became saturated or charged with the foul gases, when a good deal of filthy water would go down into the drain and be carried off. Now I do not want to disgust any of your readers, by telling them that the contents of their sinks, vaults, and stables, drain into their wells. They might take it as an insult. But let them just look at the location of their sinks and vaults. If a drain four feet deep will draw water say twenty-five feet distant, how far will a well of thirty or forty feet draw it?

Seth Twiggs thinks he cured his well by putting tile into his garden. That is only a part of the story, for the next season, he cemented his privy vault, and its contents now go regularly to the compost heap. The sink drain, too, that used to empty within ten feet of the mouth of the well, is now intercepted by a row of tiles, carrying the water after it leaches through the soil, off into the brook. The soil about his well is loose gravel, after you get down some four or five feet, and this has been made still more loose by the digging and stoning of the well. The water would go through the whole circumference back of the stones four or five feet, about as readily as through a sieve. There is a great absorbing power in soils, but after a while they will not take up any more of the foul gases, and the sink water and other offensive matters must go down to the level of the water in the well, with very little filtering.

How far a well must be removed from the sink and other offensive places, to keep the water pure, will depend somewhat upon the circumstances, as the depth of the well, and the character of the soil. A deep well, of course, would drain the surface much further than a shallow one. Dea. Smith's well is thirty-five feet deep, and there is nothing offensive upon the surface nearer than three rods. I have no doubt that there is a connection between the sink drain and the well, and that this is the source, in most cases, of bad water in wells.

But it will be asked, probably, by some wiseacre like Jake Frink, why then don't the water taste as bad in winter as in summer? Jake don't see that it makes a mighty difference whether he have five pounds of good beef in his soup, or barely a knuckle of mutton. In winter, the soup is diluted. Rains fall abundantly, and not unfrequently the wells are raised ten feet or more, so that they do not draw water from so great a distance. The water, too, is generally much colder, as it comes to the table, and the bad taste, if there be any, is not so perceptible, as in warm weather.

Seth Twiggs has hit upon the remedy. If a garden is not tile drained, the sink receptacle should be a cemented cistern. You can only keep foul matters out of your well by taking care of them. Worked into the compost heap, and then applied to the lands, they will give you nice vegetables and health. In the wells, they will give you bad smells and disease.

Yours to command,

TIMOTHY BUNKER, ESQ.

Hookertown, Nov., 1860.

NO. 47.—TIM BUNKER ON CATTLE DISEASE.

"Guess she's got the cattle disease, by the looks on her," said Uncle Jotham Sparrowgrass, as he looked into Jake Frink's yard last April, at one of the sorriest cows ever seen in Hookertown. She was down and unable to get up, had lost her calf, and was very much down in the mouth.

"What kind of disease is that?" asked Jake, solemnly, evidently prepared to hear the worst.

"Cattle disease! you fool," exclaimed Ben Jones. "She is *one of the cattle*, and, of course, if anything ails her, she's got the cattle disease."

"I rather think it's the crow ail," suggested George Washington Tucker, as he joined his neighbors in the cow yard, to sympathize with Jake in his affliction. "At any rate, the crows will have a meeting on her case 'fore long, see if they don't."

"Dreadful cavin in for'ard of the hips," remarked Seth Twiggs, as he scratched a Lucifer on the wall, and lit his second pipe. "I shouldn't wonder if it was *the cave*, a disease they've had in Hookertown this twenty year."

"It looks to me like the cattle disease they are having up in Massachusetts. The eyes are glassy, the hair stands on end, and the breathing is fast," remarked Dea. Smith.

"They call it the pleuro-pneumonia, I believe," added Mr. Spooner, who reads agricultural papers as well as theology.

"Has it killed many cattle?" asked Jake with a troubled countenance.

"It has taken off a good many hundreds, and is spreading into this State," said the pastor.

"Then she's got it," said Jake, "and I shall lose her in spite of all doctorin. Salt won't save her."

"The crows will, though," said Wash. Tucker, who clung to the crow ail, as the only theory that cleared up the mysteries of her case.

"I guess she's got the slink-fever," suggested Kier Frink, who had stopped his coal cart, to see what the trouble was. "They have had it a good deal on father's

CATTLE DISEASE.—"SALT WONT SAVE HER." Page 156.

farm ever since I can remember. Cows lose their calves, grow thin with a cough, and die."

"Now, jest tell us, neighbor Frink, what that 'ere cow has been fed on, for I don't want to feed mine the same way," said Seth Twiggs.

"Well, she haint been fed high at all. She aint pizened with oil meal, or any of them feeding stuffs they bring up from the city. You see, I'm rather short on't for fodder and stable room, and I kept the ole cow on butts and swale hay all the fore part of winter, and foddered her at the stack. She'd allers wintered eout well enuf, and I thought she was so tuff, she wouldn't mind it. I put her on to oat straw about the middle of the winter, and have kept her in the yard ever since, but nussin don't seem to agree with the ole critter. She allers was kontrary, blame her. Guess she'll die jest eout of spite."

"Rather high feed," suggested Twiggs, looking across that pile of skin and bones at me, as if I was authority in the matter.

"Now," said I, "the difficulty with this cow is starvation and exposure. If I was here sitting upon a *crowner's quest*, I should find under oath, that this animal died of hunger and cruelty, administered by Jacob Frink, of Hookertown."

This conversation of my neighbors last spring shows the secret of a great deal of the disease among cattle in all the Northern States. I have no doubt that they had something a little extra up in Massachusetts, perhaps an imported disease, that was wisely checked by stringent legislation in that and other States. The stock interest is so great in this country, that we can not well be too vigilant in guarding it. But I think starvation and exposure kill more cattle every year, than the lung murrain did. This disease is around in almost every neighborhood, and thousands are slain by it, and other thousands are so damaged that they are of little or no profit to their owners.

It is not thought contagious, and yet it is wonderful, how it goes through a whole herd, and spreads from farm to farm. Yet nobody is alarmed, because he is familiar with the disease, and knows the remedy is of easy application.

Now, Mr. Editor, I want to have my say on this subject, and you musn't put the stopper on till I have it out. You see, now is the time to prevent this disease. If you neglect cattle till they get down in the yard, like Jake Frink's cow, it is too late, or if it isn't too late, it will cost all they are worth to get them up into good flesh again. You see, folks are greatly mistaken about what constitutes the value of an ox or cow. I take it, it isn't the breath of life in the carcass that makes a cow or ox worth having. But this seems to be the popular notion, that a cow is a cow, whether she have five hundred pounds of good wholesome flesh between her skin and bones, or the skin and bones have come together pretty much like a collapsed steam boiler. Men calling themselves farmers, and living in a farming community like Hookertown, seem to think that a poor, half-starved cow in the spring is in just as good condition to give milk, and make butter and cheese, as one well fed. They think all the hay and meal they can cheat their cattle out of in the winter, is so much clear gain. They keep animals out of doors, at the stack-yard, through all this cold, stormy weather, that are expected to bring calves next April. They lie upon the frozen earth, and often upon the snow, with the thermometer at zero or below. They are fed upon corn-stalks, and often upon poor hay, without meal or roots. Now I am not particularly savage in my disposition, but I should like to have these improvident stock owners spend just one night, at the stack-yard, with their poor shivering cattle. I rather guess they would build barns or sheds, and make them comfortable.

A cow kept in this way, comes out in the spring in poor flesh, too weak to bear a good calf, or to make good veal, if the calf is doomed for the butcher. Half the summer is spent in recovering the flesh she has lost during winter. A few years of such treatment weakens her vital force so that she is liable to die a hardening, long before she becomes an old cow. Is it any wonder that cattle become diseased under such treatment, that the ribs stick out, and the hair sticks up, and the crows scent their prey? We have got laws that fine men heavily for abusing dumb animals with the whip. We ought to have others that will prevent them from torturing their animals with frost and hunger.

My remedy for cattle disease is, first, good warm stables. They can be made tight, and at the same time be well ventilated, so that the thermometer will not sink much below the freezing point. Without good stables, no amount of feeding can keep the animal comfortable, or make it profitable to the owner.

And secondly, good feed, and plenty of it, good timothy or clover hay well cured—corn meal, oat meal, linseed oil cake meal, or cotton seed meal, with the roots—carrots, beets and turnips—are articles that should enter into the bill of fare. As a rule, the more a cow eats, the more profitable she is to her owner. You might as well think of having meal when you don't put corn into the hopper, as milk and butter without plenty of fodder. There is nothing like having a good lot of flesh and fat to start upon in the spring, if you want to make a good dairy, and keep your cattle clear of disease.

Yours to command,

TIMOTHY BUNKER, ESQ.

Hookertown, Dec., 1860.

NO. 48.—TIM BUNKER ON SEED.

"Where you get de seed of dem big beets you raise last year, Massa Bunker?" said Jim Baker to me this morning. "Never seed sich beets down South in all my life. Reckon dey come from Africa, or somewhere dey git up airly in de morning."

"No, Jim, I got them from New York, where they lie abed badly in the morning, I am sorry to say. Half of them don't get their breakfast till nine o'clock."

"Can't be, Massa. Must have come from some place close by sunrise, or dey never growed so big. I watch 'em last summer, and I declare fur sartin, I th'ot dey never would stop growin."

Jim Baker, though he has been with us but two or three years, is one of the institutions of Hookertown, as much so as Mr. Spooner, or the school-master. He was liberated by his master, a few years ago, with all the rest of the negroes upon the estate, and sent out to Liberia. He had made himself useful upon the plantation as cooper, in preparing sugar and molasses casks. He went out to Liberia, with rather elevated notions of that land of promise, and of the freedom he was there to enjoy. Feeling rather above digging for a living, and not finding much demand for a cooper's labors in that new country, he became homesick, and took the first vessel bound for the States. Some of his shipmates hailed from this place, and Jim brought up here, and considers himself settled for life. He takes naturally to gardening, and often excites the envy of Jake Frink, by beating him on garden *sauce*, and a rude kind of joking, which Jake calls "*sassy*." Jim takes note of all the best gardens, as he goes round doing odd jobs among the villagers, and is an appreciative beggar of good seeds. He turns up the white of his eyes at an extra sized patch of onions, and if he can not get a dozen of the bulbs to set out, he wants just a pinch of the seed to plant. With his hat under his arm, and that deferential air which marks the well-bred servant, he is pretty sure to get what he wants. "Nebber could see, Massa Bunker, what's the use planting poor seed. Sartin to git jest what you plant."

Jim's philosophy and Jake Frink's do not belong to the same school. Jake thinks a seed is a seed, just as a cow is a cow, whether she is a skeleton, or has five hundred weight of beef laid in between her skin and bones. Jake has no idea but what old seeds are just as good as any, and so he keeps his old stock on hand from year to year. He has an old basket in his pantry for this purpose, and there you will find seeds of the cucumber, squash, pepper, corn, beans, onion, cabbage, turnip, nasturtium, and a little of every thing else that ever grew in his garden. They have no labels, and there is no means of ascertaining the age of any package in the basket. Some he has begged, a few he has bought, but the most he has raised upon his own premises in that slipshod way that marks every thing about the establishment, and which has long since passed into a proverb. If you were to say a thing looked *frinky*, every man in Hookertown would know just what you meant.

The last three or four cabbage stumps, or turnips, he happens to have left in the spring, are set out without any regard to quality or variety. So his cabbage is neither Early York, nor Drumhead, Red Dutch, nor Savoy, but a mongrel stock, showing streaks of every thing he has raised. His turnips and other tap-roots follow the same law, for they have all been cultivated upon the same system. Jake has no idea of the mixing of varieties in the blossom, or of their running down by bad cultivation.

With Jim Baker, a seed is not a seed. "Tell you what, Massa Bunker, every ting 'pends on what you plant. Iniquities of de faders visited on de children, and no mistake." Jim lives up to his philosophy, as a good many people who talk more do not. The best beets are selected, and planted in good rich soil, and the seeds are carefully labeled and put away where they can be found in planting time. Dinah cleans out the old basket every fall, and nothing but the seeds of the squashes, and other vines, are allowed to remain over a second year.

I raise but few seeds myself, because I have found it better economy to buy such as I want at the large agricultural warehouses in the city. As a rule, the men who devote their time to raising seeds will get a better article than those who have other business constantly upon their hands. Their success in business depends upon their fidelity, and they are generally careful to give the public a good article. Well-established firms in the city have extensive arrangements with seed growers in all parts of this country and of Europe, to furnish the best articles in their respective lines of business. If I want twenty varieties of garden seeds, it is much less trouble to send an order for them by express, than it is to try to raise them, and take care of them.

This month I always lay in my stock of seeds, the best varieties, and enough of them. I know just how much ground I am going to plant in each crop, and can tell within a few ounces of the quantity I shall need of each variety. If it is put off till planting time, when every thing is in a hurry, the best time for planting often goes by before you are ready, and you get only a partial crop. The best investments I have ever made in a small way have been in this article. Take particular notice. Never buy cheap seed.

Yours to command,

TIMOTHY BUNKER, ESQ.

Hookertown, Feb., 1861.

NO. 49.—TIM BUNKER ON BREASTWORKS.

Mr. Editor:—There never was such a stir in Hookertown before, since the days of the Revolution, and I doubt if the fathers were any more lively than our folks are. I never shall forget the Sunday when the news came that Fort Sumter was on fire. I shouldn't felt worse if Connecticut River had sunk, or Hookertown been destroyed by an earthquake, and since that Sunday we haven't talked about much else but the war. The next Sunday, Mr. Spooner preached a sermon from the text, "He that hath no sword, let him sell his garment and buy one," that made every man's heart go like a trip-hammer. The next day, we had a liberty pole raised a hundred feet high, and a flag hung out, that went through the last war, with several shot holes through it. We have raised a company of eighty men, and money enough to support them for a year. Almost every family that had any grown-up boys has sent one or more to the war. The middle-aged men and old ones have formed themselves into a Home Guard, and if the boys don't put things through in good shape, we are going ourselves to straighten them out.

John came home from meeting after Mr. Spooner's sermon, and says he:

"Mother, I am going to enlist."

Mrs. Bunker raised her spectacles from Scott's Bible, which she happened to be reading just then, and said she:

"I can't make any objections, John. Your grandfather fought at Bunker Hill, and Mr. Spooner says this is a continuation of the same war, a war for the life of the nation. I hope you will show that the Bunker family has not degenerated."

John being our only boy brings the thing pretty close home to us, but now that the ministers and women are raised, there can't be any backing down. There is no trouble about getting troops, and money enough to support them. They all want to go. You see, a man might as well emigrate at once, as to have the women agin him.

But I have been thinking that we are in danger of leaving an enemy in the rear, that we have not been calculating upon. I have always noticed that excited people are not the best judges of expediency. Many a brave general has been conquered by an enemy in the rear. In going to war, you see, quite as much depends upon having the inner man fortified, as upon having breastworks between us and the enemy. You see, a soldier is a sort of engine, that won't go without fire any more than a locomotive. And you have to supply the fire, wood, and water, three times a day pretty regular, or your army of soldiers is no better than a flock of sheep. Men can't fight on an empty stomach. You see, this fighting is a good deal like mowing, or rather like pitching on a load of hay when a thunder shower is coming up, and you have only twenty minutes to get the load on, and to get it into the barn. There is nothing like a well-fed stomach to do sharp work on; even a good conscience and a good cause don't amount to much without it.

Now, you see, the enemy we are like to leave in the rear, is short crops. There may be no danger of famine in this country, where land is so cheap, and where so large a part of the people are farmers. But there is danger of short crops, and a very high price for all kinds of provisions and breadstuffs, which occasions a great deal of suffering among the poor in the cities and villages, and throws everything into confusion. And it seems to me that this is the enemy that farmers are particularly called upon to guard against.

We have got material enough for soldiers in our cities and villages, merchants and mechanics who are thrown out of employment, or whose profits are very much reduced by the disordered state of business. While they are rearing the breastworks outside, we must take care of the breastworks within, and see that they are well fortified with beef, pork, mutton, bread, potatoes, etc. There isn't quite so much glory attached to this kind of fortification, as there is to gunpowder and musketry, but there is quite as much virtue in it. You see, powder and ball are not worth much after the pork and beef fail. Many more forts have had to surrender for want of provisions than for want of powder.

Now, the women and young folks don't see this so clearly as men who have smelt the smoke of battle. They go in for the fuss and feathers, and worship the epaulets and military caps, and think these are going to save the country. The real battle-field will be in the rear of the armies, away down in the Gulf States, and north of the Ohio and the Potomac, and the steel that will do most execution is that which furrows the bosom of the peaceful earth, rather than human bosoms. In modern times, the plowshare is the most potent of all military weapons, for it supplies gold to the military chest, powder to cannon, and rears those inward fortifications, without which earth works, fosses, and granite-walls are useless. Every wheat field with its plumed heads is a regiment of soldiers, and every stalk of corn, with its golden ears upon the field of peace, is a sentinel doing duty for the country.

This is about the pith of public sentiment up here among the old folks, and I send it down for what it is worth. It struck me that there was something in it worth considering, when every man is anxious to get off to the war. It will never do to have an enemy in the rear. You see, I go in for breastworks and fortifications, especially for the inner man.

Yours to command,

TIMOTHY BUNKER, ESQ.

Hookertown, June, 1861.

NO. 50.—TIM BUNKER ON LIGHTNING RODS.

Mr. Editor:—"What are you putting up that iron thing on your barn for?" asked Jake Frink, as we were at work upon the last job about the barn, which I have not yet said anything about in the *American Agriculturist.*

"I am going to have the barn finished," I said. "We want a rod just as much as we want windows in the frames, or shingles on the roof."

"I guess the litenin 'll go where it is sent, rod or no rod," observed Tucker, as he thrust a new piece of pig-tail into his cheek.

"Wasn't Squire Rodman's house struck with lightnin last week, though it had a rod on it?" asked Jones, triumphantly.

"Yes, but the rod was joined with hooks and eyes, and the connection was not perfect," observed Mr. Spooner, who was one of the group.

"Don't you think you're provokin the Almighty by puttin up that rod?" asked Deacon Little, who has never forgiven me for turning salt marsh into meadow, and raising three tuns of herds-grass to the acre. "You see," continued the Deacon, in his favorite style of argument, "that what is to be, will be, and you can't help it by lightnin rods or any other instrumentality. If it is decreed that your barn is to be struck with lightnin, I guess iron rods ain't goin' to save it. A man better not tamper with thunderbolts."

"Now," said I, "Tucker, what have you got a chimney to your house for?"

"Why, to carry the smoke off, to be sure, and to keep the house from burning up when we make a fire."

"Well," said I, "won't the smoke go where it is sent, just as much as the lightning? And yet you don't find any difficulty in making the smoke follow the inside of the chimney, until it gets up in the air out of your way. Now, I admit that lightning is a little more dangerous to handle than smoke, but it follows certain laws, just as straight as smoke does. You see, lightning has what the philosophers call an affinity for iron, and it follows the outside of a rod, just as smoke does the inside of a chimney. Some say it goes down, and others say it goes up. At any rate, it sticks to the rod, and so passes off without doing any damage, just as smoke sticks to the chimney. If you want to know why it does that, I will tell you when you can tell why smoke goes up chimney. It follows the road that is built for it, just as regularly as a locomotive follows the railroad."

"An engine would go rather promiscuous, Squire, if't wa'nt for them 'ere rails," said Seth Twiggs, as he blew an extra puff from his pipe, illustrating that smoke would go where it was sent, when it did not follow a chimney.

"But that ain't a fair argument," said Deacon Little, "you know it ain't, Tim Bunker, you infidel. We make smoke and can control it, but the Almighty makes the lightning."

"Well, Deacon," I asked, "What have you put shingles upon your house for?"

"Why, to shed rain, of course."

"Very well," said I, "and the Almighty makes the rain, if he don't make smoke; and if a man is to be wet, he will be, and you can't help it by putting shingles over his head, or by any other instrumentality. It is no use tampering with what Noah's deluge was made of."

The Deacon saw he was caught, and looked over to Mr. Spooner for help. He always believes in Mr. Spooner's orthodoxy, when he sides with himself, otherwise he is heretical.

"I do not see how you can get round the Squire's argument against shingles," remarked Mr. Spooner, rather dryly.

"It stands to reason," I continued, by way of clinching the argument, "that rain is just as much a Heaven-sent article as lightning. If a man is wise in turning off the rain, by a shingle, he cannot be a fool, or an infidel, in turning off the lightning by an iron rod." It is surprising, Mr. Editor, to find so much ignorance and prejudice in the community against the use of lightning rods. It is just as well settled, in the minds of all intelligent people, that these conductors are a complete protection against lightning, as it is that roofs are a complete protection against the storm. Roofs sometimes leak, and the rods sometimes do not connect. In either case, the fault is not in the theory, but in the imperfect realization of it. A whole roof is a complete protection against rain. A good rod is a complete safeguard against lightning. And yet we find a hundred roofs where we find one rod. A house or barn is considered finished when the roof is on, and the glass is in the windows. I don't consider it finished until the lightning rod is on.

Most people consider it pretty good policy to get insured against fire, though there are some who seem to think it a sort of gambling to do that. A man builds a barn, worth $3,000, and when his stock and hay and grain are in, it is worth not less than $5,000. He gets it insured, at a cost, say of $10 a year, and thinks it good economy. Upon the same principle that a man gets insured against fire, I think he had better get insured against lightning. It is much cheaper, and he has the advantage of being his own insurance company. All the rods that protect my barn, with the expense of putting them up, cost only $33, the interest on which is only $2 a year. The protection is perfect, and the rods will last as long as the barn does. Here is $5,000 worth of property made sure against lightning, for $2 a year.

It is very common to read in the papers of lightning striking barns—setting them on fire, or killing oxen and horses sheltered in them. I consider that there is more danger to buildings in the country from this source than there is from fire. In the city it is different. The lightning rod is a very cheap insurance company. It never proves bankrupt and fails to pay. Dishonest clerks will not run away with the capital. Scamps and scoundrels can't steal the fluid, and fire the barn with it. It will follow the rod with a good deal more certainty than smoke follows the chimney.

The pecuniary advantage of this protection is clear enough, and I guess Deacon Little will begin to see it pretty soon. But this is only one item. You see, it is a great satisfaction to know that your stock and your family, as well as your buildings, are all safe when a thunder shower comes up. I am not more scary than most people, but it is a mighty uncomfortable sensation, when the thunder is crashing around your dwelling, to think that the next bolt may find its way to the earth, through your body, or through one of your family. As our bodies are very good conductors, and we are not born with lightning rods on us, I think we had better put them on our houses, and then the lightning will go just where we send it.

I always noticed, before I put up the rod, that Mrs. Bunker took to the bed as regular as a thunder gust came up in the summer. She has got considerable courage, but she said "no woman could be expected to stand lightning." But since we have had the rod, she sits by the window reading, with her spectacles on, just as calmly as if the lightning never killed folks. I don't know how two or three dollars a year could purchase so much comfort in any other article. People's tastes differ, you see, about comfort. Mine runs towards lightning rods.

Yours to command,

TIMOTHY BUNKER, ESQ.

Hookertown, July 15th, 1861.

NO. 51.—TIM BUNKER ON BUYING A FARM.

Mr. Editor:—Deacon Smith has just been in to talk over the matter of buying a farm for his son David. You see, I have lots of neighbors that come to me regularly for advice, since I took to writing for the papers. I expect I have about as much business of this kind on my hands as if I had advertised, "Timothy Bunker, Esq., Consulting Agriculturist." How that card would look in the papers! If a neighbor wants to buy a horse, I am expected to tell him whether he is sound, just as if I could read his in'ards like a book. If another wants to sow wheat, he seems to think it won't grow, until I have told what lot to sow it on. I declare I believe some of them think water wont run in a tile, unless I have squinted along the bore, and told them just how much fall they must have to the 100 feet.

You see, the farming business has not caved in yet, notwithstanding the hard times. A good many of the factories have stopped, and some mechanics that have been doing pretty well, are now idle. Nobody now wants to buy a fine carriage, or to build a splendid house. People who have money do not like to spend it for articles of luxury, and people who have got their living by making these things, have been thrown out of employment. But the oldest of all employments is yet a thriving business, though the profits are not quite equal to what they have been. We must have breastworks for the war, and when the war is over, there will still be a demand for the fortifications *inside.* We buy and sell farms out here, and expect to for some time to come. I rather think farming will be the best business going for some years ahead. As a people, we have been living altogether too fast, for the last twenty years. The change in the style of living would make the bones of our fathers rattle in their graves. We have got to come back to a more simple mode of life, and spend less on our stomachs, and a good deal less on our backs, especially our women. Only to think of a thousand dollar shawl on one woman—a whole farm with its fifty acres of soil on the shoulders of one individual? They do say the like of it might be seen in your city less than a year ago. I rather guess some of them fast men with their fast women are wishing they had some of their scattered coin back again in their tills. Why, my mother, bless her memory, never spent a thousand dollars for dress in her whole life, and she lived to be eighty. Now, there is reason in all things, as she used to say, and we have got to be a good deal more reasonable in our family expenses, or slump through. This war will bring all our people to their bearings, and make us spend our money for something worth having—for a principle, and not for pudding and pomatum. There will be some satisfaction in knowing that we have maintained the liberties and the blessed institutions handed down from our fathers, at any cost. I have given my boy to this cause, and if I have to give my farm, I think I shall grow rich by the operation. What is property worth to Tim Bunker when his country is lost? I have thought a good deal about this war, especially since John enlisted, and I have made up my mind that it will have a great many advantages as well as evils. It will stop this fast living and extravagance, and bring back a great many to the simple habits and sterling virtues of our fathers. It is better to make sacrifices for a noble cause, than to make money.

A good many, like Deacon Smith's son David, are beginning to see a comfortable, honest, happy life on a farm, who would otherwise have been tempted to try their fortunes in the city, and gone to ruin like the thousands before them. I have thought a good many would be looking toward the farm this fall, and the substance of my talk with the Deacon might be useful.

I lay it down as a principle, that a man ought to own at least half the capital he means to invest in farming. If a man has nothing but labor to dispose of, he should sell his labor to the best advantage, until he accumulates sufficient capital to set him up in business. Not one man in a hundred will succeed, who runs in debt for his farm and stock. There must be several hundred dollars of interest money to pay every year, and this will be a heavy load to carry, with all the other expenses. But if he have money enough to buy a hundred acres of land, he may safely run in debt for the tools and stock. We must have some floating capital always on hand, to take advantage of the times, and buy cheap when we can. If a man wants more stock, it is better to buy it when stock is low, than when it is very high. Sometimes a little extra manure will help out a crop wonderfully, and fifty dollars spent in guano or bone-dust will bring back a hundred in less than six months. It is very important to have the fifty dollars where you can lay your hand on it.

Then a man ought to consider his own habits and tastes, in the location of his farm. This is especially important to men who have lived in the city, and enjoyed its advantages. Society is much more a necessity to them than to a man who has always lived in the country. He will feel uneasy without the daily mail, and a little of the stir to which he has been accustomed. He should by all means locate near a village, or on the line of some railroad. The farm, good as it is, will not be a substitute for every thing he has been accustomed to. And if a man have been bred to this business, he should consider what particular department of husbandry he likes best. A man bred to the routine of a grain farm would probably do better with this than with a stock farm. It is less important that a grain farm should be near a village, or city, than a farm where a mixed husbandry prevails, and where a near market is essential. A man with a genius for trade should locate near a good market, and raise everything that sells well, both animal and vegetable products.

If one has a fancy for stock, cheap land and a wide range of pasturage are essential to success. A valuable horse or yoke of cattle may as well be marketed a hundred miles off, as sold upon the farm. Most of the horses and beef cattle sold in your city are raised from a thousand to fifteen hundred miles away. Land worth a hundred dollars and upward an acre, as many of the farms are near cities, cannot be devoted profitably to pastures. They are worth more for something else.

It is always well to remember, in making a purchase of so much importance, that farms, as well as men, have a good or bad reputation, that is generally deserved. Some farms are so fertile, so well proportioned, or so convenient to market, that they have always kept their owners in thriving circumstances. Trace their history clear back to the first settlement of the country, and you will find every owner what the world calls a lucky fellow. Other farms have the name of always keeping their owners poor. Sometimes they are in an unhealthy district, and much sickness has made large doctor's bills. Now unless you know just what the secret of an unlucky farm is, and can remedy it, avoid such a spot as you would the poor-house. You cannot afford to try many experiments in a matter of so much importance. Is it a swamp that needs draining? You may safely venture, for there is wealth as well as health in knocking the bottom out of it. But as a rule, it is better to buy a farm that has a good reputation. If it has made others prosperous, with better husbandry it may make you rich.

Yours to command,

TIMOTHY BUNKER, ESQ.

Hookertown, Aug. 7th, 1861.

NO. 52.—TIM BUNKER ON TOP-DRESSING AND FEEDING AFTERMATH.

A SECOND LOOK AT HOOKERTOWN IMPROVEMENTS.

"Bigger than 'twas last year," said Seth Twiggs, as he looked over into the horse-pond lot where I was mowing this morning.

"I declare it looks like a rye field," said Mr. Spooner, as he measured a head of herds-grass, ten inches long, by a small rule that he carries in his pocket. A mighty accurate man is Mr. Spooner. I expect he gets in the way of exact speech, studying his sermons, for he makes the joints fit so close, that they won't leak water. When he says ten inches, you may know it ain't a sixteenth short. I should expect to find it a quarter over.

"You see it is up to the Squire's breast, plump four foot high," exclaimed Jake Frink, as he leaned over the wall. "Guess I was the biggest fool in town when I sold that piece of land for a song."

"Not half so big a fool then as you are now, for keeping the better half of your farm as starved as this was three years ago," I replied.

It is curious to see how the minds of some people work. They see no beauty or value in anything until it has passed out of their hands, and begins to show its good points under different treatment. This two-acre lot, that was always a quagmire and an eye-sore to the neighborhood, when Jake owned it, is now a very charming spot, as the grass turns out three tuns to the acre. It never paid him the interest on ten dollars an acre. It pays me ten per cent on three hundred, to say nothing of the satisfaction of turning a swamp into a meadow.

Seth Twiggs is right about the size of the grass, and yet

I have done nothing extra for it this year. To be sure, the season has been more moist, but that hardly accounts for the difference. You see, in draining a piece of wet land two or more feet deep, you bring a large quantity of surface soil gradually to the action of the atmosphere, and of the rains and frosts. It undergoes a curing process, and the soil improves, year by year, until the water line is reached. This is the third crop I have got off of this lot since I put the drain down, and each year has been a marked improvement upon the last. I suppose I might cut a second crop if the lot was not so handy for pasturing.

And then I have noticed that it is a good plan to feed and mow alternately. I much prefer to mow a common meadow one year, and pasture the next, than to mow straight along for four or five years, as most farmers do. If a meadow is very rich, like this drained lot, I think it does better to feed the second crop, than to mow it. If it produces a tun and a half at the second growth, as I think it will, of course so much is returned to the soil in the manure of the cattle. And then I have another important advantage in the seeds of the clover that are scattered by the cattle. I have noticed that the second growth of clover starts immediately, and as I do not turn in until the last of August, many of the plants, both of the white and red, go to seed, and are scattered before the cattle eat them. I do not believe in feeding late, but leave time for the grass to make a good covering for the roots. As a result of this treatment, I find that clover does not die out the first year, as is usual. I have a good deal of clover in fields sown three years ago. Other grasses are benefited in the same way, and the sod remains thick and strong. I have sometimes thought that the feet of the cattle acted like a roller, pressing the seed into the soil. At any rate, the fact is as stated, and I do not mow any second crop, where I can pasture it. I don't think second mowing pays best.

"Have you got rid of 'em?" asked Jake Frink, as he looked over into Uncle Jotham Sparrowgrass' reclaimed bog.

"Rid of what?" asked Jotham, with feigned astonishment.

"Why, them pesky muskrats, that used to eat up all the outside rows of corn in your field and mine."

"Haven't seen a muskrat in these parts for well-nigh two year. Have seen some corn, though, and occasionally a potato!" said Jotham, with a swing of his cane that showed he felt as if he was lord of all he surveyed.

He dug over three hundred bushels to the acre there last fall, and the part now planted to that crop is as handsome as anything I have seen this season. Uncle Jotham manages pretty well for an old-style farmer, catching at any improvement with a good deal of eagerness, but stoutly denying that it is new. He has always seen something like it over on the Island, thirty years ago. He has had, this year, in about equal patches, potatoes, corn, oats, and clover, upon this deserted domain of frogs and muskrats. The clover was quite too large for good fodder, or would have been, if he had let it grow till the usual time of cutting. But it was cut in June, a thing he would not have thought of, three years ago, and he will have at least two tuns at the second cutting, if he does not steal my thunder, and feed it off. But if he does that, he will be sure to state positively that he knew Ben Woodhull, on Long Island, to do the same thing as long ago as when he was a boy.

Coming back to my horse-pond lot, Mr. Spooner had to ask, "What makes that grass so much heavier on the back part of the lot? It is almost another story high."

"Well, you see, thereby hangs a tale. Last year, as soon as I got through mowing that part of the field, say about the tenth of July, I spread on a few loads of compost there, and you can see just where it stopped. The compost was made of pig-pen manure, with muck rather fresh dug. I had a good deal of query in my own mind about the best time of spreading manure on mowing land, and had pretty serious doubts about midsummer, and feared the loss of ammonia, etc. This don't look as if the manure lost much of its strength. The rest of the piece was top-dressed in March, and it is not near as heavy. I am not prepared to say, exactly, that I think midsummer is the best time, for I suppose the grass has not got all the strength of the manure put on this spring, and another season, or the after-feed this year, may make the case look different. I have no doubt the manure put on last summer acted as a mulch, sheltering the roots of the herdsgrass, which suffer extremely, and are often killed by too close cutting. The roots got strong and vigorous during the fall, made a good math for protection during the winter, and started early this spring.

As advised at present, I should *put manure upon any level piece of land, whenever I happened to have it.* I think it will pay better interest on the meadow than in the yard, and accordingly I shall clean up this month, and spread every spare load I have upon the meadows. Cutting a tun of hay to the acre don't liquidate, when you can get three, just as easy, with more manure. Things are looking up, notwithstanding the war. Breastworks will be plenty.

Yours to command,

TIMOTHY BUNKER, ESQ.

Hookertown, Sept. 15th, 1861.

NO. 53.—TIM BUNKER ON PAINTING BUILDINGS.

COST OF PAINTING—HINTS ON COLOR, ETC.—STONE HOUSES—NEW ARGUMENT FOR SHADE TREES.

Mr. Editor: Cleanliness is said to be next to godliness. It certainly looks better to see a farmer's house and barn all nicely painted, and it makes the paying of the bills rather easier, to know that paint is the cheapest outside covering for all wooden buildings. So I am going to paint up, this fall, notwithstanding the war. I rather guess I shall have something left to pay the bills, after the war taxes are paid. It is only five years ago that I painted up every thing I had upon the farm, even to the ice house, and the pig sty, and I suppose they might now stand another year without much damage. But as I was coming home from Shadtown last week, Mrs. Bunker took occasion to remark that she thought the gable end of the house looked a little dingy and bare. At any rate, it did not look so well as Mr. Slocum's house, and she thought if a poor minister could afford to keep the parsonage in so neat a trim, that Timothy Bunker could afford a new coat of paint.

Now I half expect she was joking, for she knew well enough that *I* had paid the bills for painting the Shadtown parsonage, because Josiah and Sally, being young folks, had enough other use for their money. I didn't say much, but I rather thought to myself, "guess Mrs. Bunker's getting jealous of her daughter."

But, you see, she is not going to have any occasion to think that an old bride is not just as good as a young one, though it is her own daughter, and all in the family.

What made me more ready for painting was the fact that Jo Dennis, the painter, was out of a job, complaining of the war, hard times, and nothing to do in his line. Now I like to see industrious people busy, earning money, and so I set Jo at work.

I find I learn something about painting every time I do the job. *It requires from five to ten per cent of the first cost of a building every fifth or sixth year to keep it painted.* This amounts to a heavy tax, such as we should think oppressive if it was imposed upon us by the Government. I have been thinking that a great many could save this expense by building with stone. In most parts of the country stones are plenty—granite, sandstone, marble—that split easy, and are of handsome color. In many places, near good quarries, it would not cost any more to build of stone than of wood. Barns, and outhouses especially, might be made of stone, wholly or in part, to great advantage. Deacon Smith built a stone barn, ten years ago, and it keeps hay just as well as his old one, and has some advantages over wood. He claims that it is a great deal warmer in winter, and of course it takes less fodder to carry his cattle through. It is cooler in summer, and more comfortable for such animals as he keeps in the stable. It is more easily made rat-proof. The walls are made of split granite laid in mortar, and will never need any repair or paint in his day, or in that of his grandchildren. The first cost was only a third more than wood, and he thinks the interest on this difference is more than made up in the saving of fodder, repairs, and paint.

We have a few stone houses in Hookertown, some of them the natural color of the granite, and some whitewashed, and they are the warmest and most comfortable houses among us. If I were going to build again, I should certainly use stone, for both house and barn.

But most of us have built of wood, and we must do

the best we can with the houses we have. There is one good thing about it, we can change the color of our houses as often as we please, and come out in a new fashion, while the stone house maintains the same aspect. "What color are you going to put on?" asked Seth Twiggs, as he looked over the gate, and mingled the smoke of his pipe with the steam of the boiling oil.

"It won't be blue, I'll warrant you," said Jotham Sparrowgrass, without waiting for me to give neighbor Twiggs a civil reply.

"Guess it'll be horse color," observed Jake Frink, who still remembers the cured horse-pond, and thinks every thing I do must have a shade of horse in it.

When I was a boy, it wasn't much of a question as to what color a man would paint his house. I don't think there were a dozen houses in Hookertown of any other color than white. It was claimed that white was the natural color of the lead, it was the least trouble to make, and looked best in the country, where it was so easy to surround the house with trees and shrubs. I have always noticed in journeying, that the more green you have around a white house the better it looks. In the last twenty years a great change has come over the taste of the people, and somehow they seem to paint other colors a good deal more than white—yellow, drab, light brown, lilac, and gray. This may be owing somewhat to an improvement in taste, but I guess fashion has got quite as much to do with it. A man paints his house to please his neighbors rather than himself, and if brown is the rage he paints brown. I am saved all trouble about the color, for Mrs. Bunker likes white and nothing else, so white it shall be. Our trees and shrubs have got so well grown, that white makes an agreeable contrast, and then it has always been white, and some of my friends might not know the house if it was any other color. The artists and architects make a good deal of fuss about blinds upon the outside, and the green color. But there is no substitute for a green Venetian blind upon the outside. It bars the heat, and lets in the breeze in summer, and is always agreeable to the eye. Houses are built for comfort rather than for show, and I think comfort should be studied more than anything else. If we can make taste go along with it, that is so much clear gain.

It makes a good deal of difference about the season of painting. In the heat of summer, the oil seems to strike all into the wood, and the lead washes off sooner. If I could have my choice of weather, I would select the clear days of spring or fall, with a north-west breeze, if any. Then, with good materials, the paint dries gradually, makes a good body, and will be a good deal more durable.

There is one thing I have just learned about painting, and it must be as true as preaching. Paint upon a building well sheltered by trees will last twice as long as paint in an exposed position. The gable end of the house, to which Mrs. Bunker called my attention, is almost bare, while the lower part has still a fair coat of paint. The reason is, that the upper part of the house is fully exposed to the raking winds, while the lower part is partially protected by the barn and the shrubbery. On the west side of the house is a covered piazza. The paint sheltered by this is almost as good as when it was first put on, five years ago. In violent storms the wind moves from forty to sixty miles an hour, and the rain is driven with this velocity against the sides of the house. Of course, there must be a good deal of mechanical violence done by this continual battering of the rain drops. A friend, who has three sides of his house sheltered by trees, is of the opinion that a coat of paint will last twice as long as upon the fourth side, which is without any protection. Trees break off the winds, and are of as great advantage in preserving a house as they are in warming it in winter. They should not stand too near a dwelling, so as to make it damp and unhealthy, but at a distance of thirty feet or more, they are a great comfort and ornament. In saving both paint and firewood, the evergreens have a great advantage over the deciduous trees. Their foliage is so thick and fine that they break the force of the wind more completely, and sift out the cold.

This will be a new argument for planting trees around farm buildings, and one of the strongest that can be brought forward. A man will save enough in paint in five years to pay for his trees and the cost of planting them.

Yours to command,

TIMOTHY BUNKER, ESQ.

Hookertown, Oct. 10th, 1861.

NO. 54.—TIM BUNKER ON THE VALUE OF MUCK.

"Hain't you got most tired on't, Squire?" asked Ben Jones, as I carted along my twentieth load of muck last night.

"Guess not. Why?" I replied.

"It's a mighty deal of hard work for nothing. I'd just as leeves have so many loads of snow banks in a barnyard."

"It's all moonshine about there's bein' any vartu in muck. I'd jest as soon dung a field with icicles," chimed in George Washington Tucker, who gets his ideas and his drinks from Jones.

"Them's my sentiments exactly," said Jake Frink, as

he met us in the road with a load of oats in bags, going down to Shadtown to market. "You see I was over-persuaded one year, when the Squire bo't the hoss-pond lot, to try some of the mud that come out of the side of the road, where the pond used to be. I guess I carted a dozen load, and thought I was going to see corn stalks as big as your wrist, and ears as long as a hoe-handle. And I du declare I never could see a bit a difference where I used it."

"How much manure did you put on to the acre?" inquired Seth Twiggs, as he drew a lucifer across the tap of his boot, and lighted his inevitable pipe.

"Wall, I made a whoppin sight that year, and slapped her on ten loads to the acre."

"Corn must 'av been skeer'd at such duin's, I guess," said Seth, with a twinkle in his eye that the smoke could not hide.

"Corn didn't come up well, did it?" asked Seth, pursuing his catechising.

"Wall, yes, it came up, but looked mighty yaller, and didn't begin to grow much till into June, and then it was spindlin, and a great many stalks didn't have any years on 'em. It was that cold frog mud that pizened the sile."

"How much corn du you git to the acre, take it by and large, Mr. Frink?" asked Seth civilly.

"I guess about twenty bushels, on an average, sometimes a leetle more—and sometimes less."

"And how much manure do you put on to the acre?" continued Seth, determined to get to the bottom of the matter.

"Wall, that is jest as it happens. I allers put on all I make, be it more or less, p'raps fifty or sixty loads on to eight or nine acres of plantin. It's real dung, though, and none of your bog moss and stuff."

"And how do you suppose Squire Bunker gits eighty bushels of corn to the acre?"

"Wall, his land allers was better than mine; and then he has more cattle to make more manure, and he buys lots of guanner and bone dust, and all the ashes folks makes in the village, and sets every boy that's big enough to run on tew legs to pickin up bones, and buys every ded hoss and rotten sheep, and murdered cat, shoemaker's parin's, old boots, ded hens, old rags, and feathers, sticks 'em into this muck, and makes manure. If a man has money 'nuff to buy carrion, he can make manure and make crops, but ye see it costs more than it comes to. And then, who wants to be runnin an opposition line to the crows! The Squire is great on ded hosses, depend on't. The crows haven't had a decent meal of vittles the last five years, the Squire's been so spry after every ded critter."

Jake Frink touched up his nag and disappeared rather suddenly after this display of his philosophy of big crops. There was, of course, some foundation in truth for his reflection upon *my* methods of making manure. But neighbor Frink displayed his own pride, as well as my humiliation, in his remarks. One would hardly think it, but Jake Frink is really above his business, and is ashamed to do what ought to be done, to make the most of the materials within his reach to enrich his stores of manure. You see, this digging mud is nasty business. You must soil your boots, and your shirt sleeves, and a splash of mud upon your shirt bosom is not uncommon. And the handling of dead horses and other diseased animals is not particularly savory. But then if a man is going to be a farmer, he musn't faint at the sight of such things, or carry a smelling bottle to keep down the stenches. Muck makes *clean* corn, yellow as gold, and the sweetest of meal, and all offal and putrid flesh in the laboratory of the soil is turned into luxuriant grass, which makes nice milk, cheese, and butter, and a plenty of it. Being a farmer, and "nothing else," as the boys say, I go in for muck and more of it every year.

You gentlemen that edit agricultural papers, attend the fairs, and see almost nobody but the best farmers, who carry out your teachings, think the world is almost converted to your faith. You have been preaching about muck for a dozen years or more, and you may think that every body understands it, and every body uses it as much as they ought to. You never made a greater mistake in the world. I tell you the millenium hasn't come yet, by a long shot. I guess one-half the farmers in these parts to-day have got Jake Frink's notion about muck, and it rests upon just his sort of trial—a single experiment based on an application of ten loads of half-made compost to the acre. No wonder that muck is considered poor stuff.

Now I am ready to give a reason for the faith that is in me. On my old land I can not make any money at farming without manure, and carting muck is the cheapest way I can make it. Indeed, I should not know what to do without swamp muck. Manure, as it is sold in towns and villages in the Northern States, brings from two to three dollars a *cord* of 103 bushels. As it *brings* this price it is to be presumed that it is worth this to the cultivators who buy it. These are generally market gardeners and farmers, who live within four or five miles of market. If manure is worth this to the farmer who has to cart it several miles, it is certainly worth as much, or more, to the farmer who makes it and uses it upon his own farm.

Now I claim for the muck and peat that I use, that I make a dollar upon every cord that passes through my yard and stables on its way to the plowed fields where it is turned under—reckoning its value at the lowest market price, two dollars a cord. The peat as it lies in the bed, yielding no income, is entirely worthless. It can be dug and thrown upon the bank of the ditch for twenty-five cents a cord. If it can lie a year, all the better, but this is not essential, as fresh stable manure will cure it without frost. It can be delivered in my yard for fifty cents a cord, but it would cost those who have to cart it half a mile or more, perhaps seventy-five cents a cord, making a dollar. Dry muck, in the process of mixing and curing during the winter, would be certain to lose neither in weight nor volume. In the spring it is worth two dollars a cord as it lies in the yard. In making compost I calculate to use about three loads of muck to one of stable manure. If I have animals enough to make a hundred cords with nothing but straw, I can make four hundred with muck.

On the muck that I am able to cure in the fields where I use it, I make a still larger profit, as I save one carting. This I cure with stable manure that I buy from the village, and with fish, dead animals, guano, or with lime and ashes, taking care not to use these latter articles with the animal manures. If any body doubts about my estimate of muck let him come to Hookertown and see my corn bin and porkers, my root cellar and cows, and my hay mows and horse stables. Jake Frink despises a dead horse and invokes crows. I think the carcass worth a "V," and save it. There is as much difference in folks as in any thing.

Yours to command,

TIMOTHY BUNKER, ESQ.

Hookertown, Jan. 11*th*, 1862.

NO. 55.—TIM BUNKER ON FAMILY HORSES.

"In faith, she's dead as a herring, sir," said Patrick, as he came from milking, yesterday.

"Poor old crature, is she gone indade?" asked Bridget, the maid, as she lifted the corner of her apron, and wiped genuine tears from her eyes.

This was sad news, though I had been expecting it for several mornings, and not a very good preparation for breakfast, which was already upon the table. I saw it was all over with the old mare, the mother of John's Black Hawk colts, and the faithful family beast of twenty-five years standing. She had been ailing for a fortnight, a little stiff in the joints at first, but nothing alarming considering her years. She had been serviceable up to that time, and though neither so strong nor so swift as in her younger years, was just as good for my purposes as a dozen years ago. When she began to refuse food, I resorted to the usual remedies, but soon saw that it was of no use. She died in her stall, on the fourth day after refusing food, full of years and full of honors. I own that I set more store by her than anything else that goes upon four legs. I had raised her, and ridden behind her to mill and to meeting for over twenty years. Her disposition was a great deal more human than that of the common run of mankind. She knew her place and her business better. She was so completely under the control of my voice that I never had occasion to strike her a blow. John lived upon her back almost, when he was a boy, and the women could drive her anywhere. She was the first horse John and Sally ever learned to drive, and she was associated in my mind with their childhood. It will go hard with John when he hears the news, down on the Potomac, for old Rose was the companion of all his boyish pleasures, until he was big enough to break colts. There is not a fish pond, or a trout stream, within a dozen miles of home, whither she has not carried him. He can hardly think of a pleasant spot, or a happy day in his childhood, a 'berrying with his schoolmates, or a 'visiting with his cousins, without recalling the nimble feet of old Rose.

It so happened that Sally and her husband were at home on a little visit yesterday, and it seemed to lighten the load a little, that we had children and children's children in the house, when there was so dark a shadow upon the barn. But it was rather a sad breakfast, even with these alleviations.

"She was just Sally's age, and—" remarked Mrs. Bunker, as she passed my cup of coffee, without being able to finish the sentence.

"What's the matter, grandma," asked little Timothy, who did not exactly understand the trembling lip, and the tears that the spectacles did not hide.

"One of the earliest things I can remember," said Sally, "was a ride to mill, after old Rose, with you, father, and John. I couldn't have been more than four years old. I know John got to sleep before we got home, and you left him under the shed to take his nap out. You must not laugh at us, Josiah," directing her remarks, by way of apology, to her husband, "for our tears for old Rose. She was the mother of our Charley, you know."

"A very remarkable beast, I have no doubt, from the impression she seems to have made upon those who knew her best," said Mr. Slocum, trying to enter into his wife's sympathies. "I have always thought horses approached nearer to man than any other domestic animal. The name of the horse recalls little Rose, in the Shady Side, who seems to have been as much afflicted at the sale of her father's horse, Pompey, as *you* are at the death of the family mare."

"Oh, yes," said Sally, "I remember the passage, and it is one of the best in the book, where Mr. Vernon, the clergymen, had to sell his favorite horse out of sheer poverty.—'The children got bravely through the dinner; but afterwards, seeing her father look sadly out toward the empty stable, little Rose climbed his knee, and whispered, 'Never mind, dear papa, we shall see Pompey again—in heaven,' she was about to say,—but suddenly recollecting, she added, 'Oh, no! he has no soul, has he? poor dear

Pompey!' and the tears rained fast through her chubby fingers, with which she tried to hide them from papa.'"

"I do not altogether sympathize with the theology that takes it for granted that there is no hereafter for brutes," said Mr. Slocum.

"I should like to think so," said Sally, "now that old Rose is dead, but I can not see what place there is for animals in a spiritual world."

"I believe the Bible has not much to say on that point," said Mrs. Bunker hopefully.

"Very true," said Mr. Slocum; "and it is worthy of notice, that the most pointed thing it does say against their immortality, Solomon puts into the mouth of an infidel arguing that 'man hath no preëminence above a beast, for all is vanity.' They fill their places so much better than multitudes of men, and seem to answer the Divine purpose in their creation so much better, that it seems very sad to think there is no hereafter for them."

"It is almost as sad to think that some men can never die," Sally replied very soberly. "Still I think we shall have to give up old Rose and all our dumb pets, when we become like the angels. You remember, Josiah, that passage in one of the 'Essays of a Country Parson' where the writer represents himself to be seated upon a manger, writing upon the flat place between his horse's eyes, while the docile animal's nose is between his knees. The book is here upon mother's table, I will read it:

'For you, my poor fellow creature, I think with sorrow as I write here upon your head, there remains no such immortality, as remains for me. What a difference between us! You to your sixteen and eighteen years here, and then oblivion! I to my three score and ten, and then eternity! Yes, the difference is immense; and it touches me to think of your life and mine, of your doom and mine. I know a house where at morning and evening prayer, when the household assembles, among the servants there always walks in a shaggy little dog, who listens with the deepest attention, and the most solemn gravity, to all that is said, and then when prayers are over, goes out again with his friends. I can not witness that silent procedure, without being much moved by the sight. Ah! my fellow creature, this is something in which you have no part! Made by the same hand, breathing the same air, and sustained like us by food and drink, you are witnessing an act of ours which relates to interests that do not concern you, and of which you have no idea. And so here we are, you standing at the manger, old boy, and I sitting upon it; the mortal and the immortal close together; your nose on my knee, my paper on your head; yet with something between us, broader than the broad Atlantic.'"

"That is charmingly expressed, my dear," said Josiah, "and it satisfies the reason very well, but still the heart pleads for its accustomed companionship in a better life. It is a point not definitely settled by revelation, and as the belief tends to make men humane in their treatment of animals, I am inclined to think that there may be another life for them."

Sally and Josiah had a good deal of discussion in this vein, all very well in its place, but I could not take any part in it. Sally, I guess, had the best of the argument, but that did not make me feel the loss of old Rose any the less. The tears from under the old spectacles at the other end of the table were a little too much for me, and I had to keep silence, or join the company of mourners outside. Twenty-five years, you know, make a great hole in the life of man, and when we are touchingly reminded that they have gone, even though it be by the death of a brute, it is very natural to think of the end. These domestic animals, especially the most intelligent of them all, the horse, have much to do with our moral training. The affection for them, which seems almost as natural and as strong as for our own species, tends to repress cruelty, and the abuse of the power we have over them. The civil law properly recognizes cruelty to brutes as a moral offence. Their kindly treatment is a virtue that makes better citizens, and honors the State.—As old Rose was so near to the family, we honored her with a decent burial. She lies under an old oak in the pasture where she used to graze. Peace to her ashes.

Yours to command,

TIMOTHY BUNKER, ESQ.

Hookertown, Mar. 15, 1862.

NO. 56.—TIM BUNKER ON THE "HORN-AIL."

"What is the matter with your cow, Mr. Frink?" said Seth Twiggs, as he leaned his elbow on the barn-yard bars, and looked benevolently at a very spare and hirsute animal, that Jake was milking.

"Can't tell exactly," said Jake. "Guess she's got the horn-ail, or some sich thing."

"I thought the trouble seemed to be in her legs, when she come by my house last night. She walked kind o' totlish," said Seth, knocking the ashes out of his pipe.

"Wall, that might be. Horn distemper generally affects 'em all over. Had Tucker up here to doctor her last night; he said it was horn-ail."

"What did he give her?"

"He gin her a slice of salt-pork, split her tail, put in salt and pepper, and bored her horns."

"Rather guess there was some squirming."

"Yes, it took three men and all the ropes in the barn to hold the old keow."

"Don't you think horn-ail hurts the milk?" inquired Seth hesitatingly, as he relighted his pipe.

"Wall, as to that, I can't say. It's all the keow we've got, as gives milk, and I shouldn't think any trouble in the horns would strike clean threw the beast. Milk is milk, I take it, no matter where it comes from. I never could see any difference in the taste."

"I rather guess milk wont be milk out of that animal much longer," said Seth ominously, and blowing a puff of smoke as blue as his prophecy.

"You don't think she's going to die, do you?" asked Jake solemnly.

"The crows have already held a counsel on that animal. Tucker told me so last night."

"The scoundrel! He told me he would warrant her to get well, if I'd give him a dollar for his doctoring."

Two days after the above conversation I was called in to administer upon the carcass of said animal. Jake said he had human feelings, and he could not skin a cow he had milked, and he did not even want to put her in a muck heap. I gave my neighbor due credit for the feelings of tenderness which the death of his cow seemed to call forth. But I could not help thinking that a little more of that tenderness manifested to the animal while living would have been much more wisely bestowed.

To tell the plain truth, the animal died of starvation, just as many cows die every year in this land of steady habits and Christian civilization. I noticed the cow last summer, and told Jake he would certainly lose her if he did not give her a better pasture. But he would keep her with his young cattle in the old cow-pasture that has been grazed to my certain knowledge for fifty years, and probably for a hundred, without plowing or manuring except the droppings of the pastured animals, and these were yarded at night. He kept six animals where there was not grass enough for three. They came out of the winter poor and thin, and this cow having the drain of milk upon her system grew thinner through the summer. The winter diet of corn buts, bog meadow grass, and salt marsh hay, cut short the work of starvation, and fulfilled Tucker's prophecy.

They have a great variety of names for this process of torture in Connecticut, and I suppose in other parts of the country. Sometimes it is horn-ail, or worm in the tail; again it is slink fever, or murrain, black leg, or black tongue, cattle disease, or pleuro pneumonia. It would not do for an intelligent, civilized man to see and believe that he starved his cattle to death. Conscience might trouble him, and possibly some of his neighbors might have him before the courts under the statute which prohibits cruelty to brutes. If I were called to judge in such a case it would certainly go hard with the offender. It certainly inflicts more pain upon a brute to starve, than to beat it. The whip upon ribs well lined with fat is a sharp torture soon over. But to keep a cow at the stack-yard through the cold, stormy nights of winter, to give her poor food, and not half enough of that, is a lingering torment, more cruel than that which the savage inflicts upon his victim bound to the stake. The poor beast can only speak through the hollow ribs and the bristling hair, and these signs of woe are usually attributed to disease rather than to a lean manger.

This is an evil that legislation will not reach, and I suppose nothing but public opinion will set it right, and that probably not in our day. It would seem that there was no need of losing neat stock under ordinary circumstances. I have kept cows for over forty years, and they have all died by the knife, proving as useful and ornamental in their deaths as in their lives. The starving of animals is so unprofitable that there is no apology for it. A half-starved cow hardly pays for her keeping. A well-fed one pays a handsome profit.

My recipe for the horn-ail is, one good warm stable well ventilated and well littered, one bushel of carrots or sugar beets daily, hay and water ad libitum, one card or curry-comb, and gentle treatment. I have never known this dose to fail of preventing the disease.

Yours to command,

TIMOTHY BUNKER, ESQ.,

Hookertown, April 10th, 1862.

NO. 57.—TIM BUNKER ON A "COMMENTARY" ON ROOTS.

"I should like to know what upon airth you dew to your cattle to make 'em look so slick?" said Jake Frink as he looked into my yard on a bright April morning.

"Dew to 'em, you fool," exclaimed Tucker, "he stuffs 'em with ile meal and corn, just as you would a sassage."

"I'm mighty glad I don't have the bills to pay," said Jones. "That animal has cost fifty dollars this winter, I'll bet a shad; and 'twouldn't sell for that neow." "Don't be so sure of that," said Seth Twiggs, as he joined the company at the gate, and looked admiringly at Cherry, who had dropped her third calf a few days before. "I am in want of a new milch cow, and will take her at that price without the calf."

"You will have to add ten more to get her, I guess, even if I want to sell," I remarked very quietly, as I showed a pail half full of milk after the calf had taken all he wanted to suck. "But you see I never sell a new milch cow. Making butter and cheese is my business, and milk is my stock in trade. A shoemaker might as well sell his leather, or a tanner his hides, as a farmer sell a new milch cow. The dairy farmer, who has his eye teeth cut, will sell cows only when they are well fattened, or at the close of the milking season."

"But s'pose he has mor'n he wants," said Seth inquiringly as he loaded his pipe.

"He has no business to be in that fix," I replied. He raises a given quantity of hay, and rough fodder, corn stalks, straw, pumpkins, roots, etc., and he ought to know just how much it will take to bring them out in good condition in the spring. If he has only fodder enough for twenty head of cattle, he makes a great mistake if he keeps twenty-one, and is foolish if he attempts to keep five and twenty. With food enough, he will make a profit on each; with too little, he will lose on every one."

"'Lose *every one*,' you ought to have said," interposed Seth, with a knowing wink at Jake Frink for his recent experience with the horn-ail.

"Cherry," I continued, "is what I call a living *commentary on roots*. Mr. Spooner has a good deal to say about the opinions of different commentators on this and that text from which he preaches. I always thought that the best commentary on a man's faith, was his *practice*. His life shows well enough what sort of food his mind lives on, and it is pretty much so with fodder. There's a good deal of truth in the old adage 'The proof of the pudding is in the eating.' The kind of pudding my Cherry has lived on all winter is turnips, sugar beets, and good hay. Not an ounce of meal, upon the honor of a gentleman, and she gave milk until within two months of her calving. You see, now, she is as sleek as a mole, with a bag as big as a milk pail, and a fine calf."

I put the case to my neighbors, Mr. Editor, in that way, and made them see it. I know a good many farmers say roots don't pay for raising, that they are all water when not frozen; and if they are frozen, you might as well feed your cattle on snow banks. I know that the chemists say that they are more than three-fourths water, and not worth half as much as hay, which may be true enough. But what do I care for these opinions, so long as roots make flesh and milk cheaper than any thing else I can raise? I am after milk and flesh by the cheapest method, and if giving water to the stock will bring them, I shall give them water, Jake Frink and Mr. Retort to the contrary notwithstanding.

White turnips stand particularly low in the scale of nourishment, and yet Cherry had white turnips, a half bushel a day, until they were all gone, and gained flesh upon them. She did better on sugar beets; and for that reason, I think they are worth more, and if they could be raised as cheaply as turnips, I should prefer to raise them. But I do not see how they can be. I can raise turnips among corn, as a stolen crop, for four cents a bushel, and I think all roots that require a whole season—beets, carrots, and parsnips—will cost not far from ten cts. a bushel.

My rule is to raise all the roots I can, of the several varieties, so that every animal may have a daily food of them from November until May. They like a variety of food, and with hay as a staple, I think the greater variety the better, feeding say two weeks upon one kind, then taking another two weeks. Many think they can get more fodder from an acre of land in grass or in corn than in roots. Not so:—An acre of land has to be highly manured to produce seventy bushels of shelled corn, and four tuns of dry stalks, worth at the market price not far from a hundred dollars, which is perhaps a fair expression of their value for feeding. The same acre, with rather more labor, will produce 1,000 bushels of carrots, worth from two to three hundred dollars in different markets, just as their value is known and appreciated. I have raised all the roots usually cultivated for feeding, and I come to the bottom of the root bins every spring with a stronger conviction of their value. *The living commentaries* tell the story a great deal better than I can, and some of my neighbors have got the lesson. Deacon Smith learned it before I did. Mr. Spooner got hold of it early, and he always drives a fat horse, that goes round the parish preaching carrots, wherever he calls, just as plainly as Mr. Spooner preaches election in the pulpit. Now I have nothing agin Mr. Spooner in the world, and I don't mean any reflection on him when I say that the old horse has more "unction" in his preaching than any thing we have in the Hookertown meeting-house on Sundays. There hasn't been a rib in sight since he has owned him, and when he drives up to the door on Sunday morning the horse comes up with a prancing gait, and a coltish air, that says "carrots," as plain as if Mr. Spooner had a bag of them under his carriage seat. I don't talk such things Sundays, but you know a man can't help thinking.

And there is Seth Twiggs, whose brains one might think were all smoked out, has got ideas straight as a ramrod on roots, and raises heaps of them every year, though he has but a few acres of land. Even Jake Frink is waked up by the preaching of Mr. Spooner's horse, though he never hears the man—except at funerals. He goes in for a crop of sugar beets this season, for the first time. Tucker and Jones are not yet converted, but I am expecting even they will be brought in before long.

One of the advantages of the root crop is, that it may be put in late. Ruta-bagas and carrots may be sown without any detriment any time in the month of June, white turnips a month later, and the first week of June will do very well for sugar beets and mangel wurzels. This last is the most productive of all the roots, and but little inferior to the sugar beet in quality. The "commentaries" on roots are multiplying here.

Yours to command,

TIMOTHY BUNKER, ESQ.

Hookertown, May 15, 1862.

NO. 58.—TIM BUNKER ON STEALING FRUIT AND FLOWERS.

"Where did you get them lalock blossoms and roses?" asked Seth Twiggs, as he saw Kier Frink driving home his empty coal cart, with his horse profusely decorated. There was a large branch between his ears tucked under the bridle, and a dozen or more of Dea. Smith's large damask roses nodding from the hames.

"Shouldn't 'zactly like to tell. I'm 'fraid you'd all be arter 'em, they're so handsome."

"Well, I can tell, you scoundrel," said Seth, as he tucked his stub of a pipe into his pocket. "The roses came from Dea. Smith's, and the lalocks from my yard, and they haven't been picked more than five minutes. You miserable White-oaker and thief, don't you know any better than to steal such things? I'll have you sent to Har'ford, for theft, sure as I am a live man."

"I should like to see you do it. They are nothing but posies, and haven't any more vally than the smoke of yer pipe, Mister Twiggs. They hung over the road tu, and I should like to know if anybody haint a right to what grows in the road. I wanted to make the ole hoss look kinder gay, and bring home something nice to the old 'oman and the young ones. I didn't mean any harm."

"Harm? you miserable scapegrace!" exclaimed Seth, shaking his first; "I would rather you'd taken the calf out of my stable, or the pig out of my pen. Didn't wife plant that bush, and hasn't it been growing these four years, and now it is all broken and ruined, and the flowers hang on that wretched carcass of a coal horse. It's enuff to make a Christian swear to see lalocks and roses put to such a use. If there is any justice, you shall go to Har'ford jail."

There, you see, was the rub. Seth Twiggs got angry to very little purpose. There is no law that touches these vexatious trespasses upon flowers and fruit;—or if there is, we have no public sentiment to enforce it. The majority of the public, even in this Commonwealth, which I am bound to believe is head and shoulders above any other in this respect, have no taste for flowers and the finer kinds of fruit, and they look upon the people who cultivate these things as lawful prey. Their own flower gardens are limited to a patch of bouncing bet and tansy in the back yard, with may-weed and catnip in front; and as they do not attach any particular value to these things, they think their amiable neighbors who cultivate roses and flowering shrubs prize these just as little. They would as soon break down a moss rose in a neighbor's yard, as a sweetbrier growing by the road-side. They admire gay colors and sweet odors, as most savages do, and that is the extent of their taste for flowers. They have no other measure of value than money, and as flowers in the country do not sell in market, they have no value. A pound of butter brings twenty cents, and is worth the money. A rose, though it affords pleasure to the eye and to the smell, and gratifies our love of the beautiful, brings no price, and is therefore worth nothing.

It is pretty much so with fruits, though there is a little more conscience about stealing them, for fruit has a money value, though it be small. Apples are common, even among these rude people; but they are of the ungrafted sorts, and hardly pay to carry to market where the better sorts are known. But they think their neighbors prize fine pears, grapes, and the smaller fruits, as little as they do their seedling apples. It was only yesterday that I found a woman and her two children in my strawberry beds, helping themselves as leisurely as if they had been picking in a cow pasture. They had brought their baskets with them, and had got them nearly filled, when I had to lay down the law to them. They had at least a dollar's worth of my property, and were about to walk off with it.

Now I don't want to say a word agin' Hookertown, or damage the reputation of the place. I suppose it is a full average of Connecticut towns, and in some respects a good deal better. But to speak the plain truth, there is a good deal of stealing among us in this small way. And it can't be laid to the door of the pulpit neither. Mr. Spooner is faithful—preaches total depravity just as hard as if people did not illustrate that doctrine themselves—warns, entreats, and expostulates with all long-suffering and patience. But, you see, the most of these people don't come to meeting, and the preaching that is going to reach them, I guess, will have to be in men's lives rather than in meeting-houses.

The notion that nothing is of any value unless it will sell, seems to lie at the bottom of a good deal of this wickedness, and I think a word or two ought to be said upon it. Now this may be true with a great many people. They are so mean that they would skin flints to make money. But among decent Christian people this can't be so. A man prizes a good many things that have no money value, far more than if he could turn them into gold. There is an old lapstone, such as shoemakers use, in my garret, that belonged to Sally's grandfather. He used to use it, and when she was a little child she remembers seeing the old man pound leather on it. Now I don't suppose the stone would sell for a red cent, but Sally says she would not part with it for the Kohinoor diamond, and all the crown jewels of Victoria. She is an honest woman, and I am bound to believe her. Anything that our affections enter into has a value that can not be measured by dollars and cents; and to rob us of these things is to do us a greater injury than to steal sheep and horses. I can't blame Seth Twiggs for raving about his lilac bush. His wife planted it and had a right to rejoice in it. It was rather hard to see the growth of years destroyed in a moment by an ignorant boor.

We cultivate flowers and learn to love them for their beauty, and for the pleasure they give our wives and children. They cost considerable time and money, and really give more pleasure than many things that cost ten times as much. They are associated with our leisure hours and our domestic enjoyments. They seem to belong to the better side of our natures. We have a moss rose under our bed-room window that little Sally planted when she was a school girl. It hangs full of blossoms every year—not worth a cent. But I declare I had rather lose a half dozen of the best apple trees in my orchard than that worthless shrub.

It is very much so with our nice garden fruits. We raise them because we can't buy them in the country, and don't want to beg or steal them. I cultivate grapes and pears, and get a good deal interested in the vines and trees. I spend days in training them, and enjoy my power over them. They have a value to me above the market price, because they are the product of my skill. I have watched that bunch of grapes from its blossom to the purple bloom upon its ripened berries. I have watched those ruddy cheeked pears quite as anxiously, and anticipated the delight of setting them before my friends, when they pay me a visit. When the friends are gathered for the feast, it is a sore vexation and disappointment to find the fruit missing. We need more efficient laws to protect us against fruit and flower thieves, and above all a wider diffusion of a taste for these things, which will prove the best safeguard against their loss.

Yours to command,

TIMOTHY BUNKER, ESQ.

Hookertown, June 14, 1862.

NO. 59.—TIM BUNKER ON THE COST OF PRIDE.

"Father, have you seen the *Agriculturist?*" asked Sally, as she handed her second baby to her mother and the paper to me. I had been to the post-office that afternoon, and had not had a chance to look at it, even if I had been in the house long enough to do it. This is generally the way; the women have the first cut. I have known Mrs. Bunker to leave a batch of dough she was mixing to read the paper, and that, I guess, is about the last thing a house-keeper ought to leave, especially if the yeast is good.

You see it so happened that Sally and her children came over from Shadtown that afternoon, to make us a little visit. She has always been good about coming home, and since John has been gone to the war we have seen more of her than usual, which is very thoughtful in her.

"Well no, I haven't. What is in the wind now?"

"Just read what a Western Farmer says about your taking lessons in spelling. You see you get great credit for my correcting your letters."

"Credit, girl! The man is poking fun at me for writing out of character. I knew it would come to this, if you and the printers didn't let my spelling alone."

I have never told the public what lots of trouble I have about these letters, being a modest man, and not caring to push my private matters into notice. Folks are so awful proud nowadays that everything has to be fixed up before it can show itself, from a baby's dress to a President's proclamation. They even find fault with Lincoln's State papers, because the rhetoric isn't quite tall enough, and the grammar don't always break joints. I'm expecting nothing else but they'll get out a new edition of the catechism, and our children will be taught "The chief end of man is to fix up."

You see in the first place I didn't want to write at all, considering that I understood the use of a plow enuff sight better than the use of the pen, and remembering that old saw "Let the cobbler stick to his last." I still think there is wisdom in that saying. But, you see, the editor thought I had better write, that I ought not to hide my light under a bushel, and all that sort of thing. He was very civil in his compliments, and what was I that I should set up for knowing more than an editor, and the editor of the *Agriculturist*, too? I thought he ought to know what sort of talk would edify farmers, and I didn't pretend to be anything else. So I promised him that I would write for one year, and have kept on ever since.

Then Mrs. Bunker didn't want me to write; 'twould make a public man of me, and folks would come to stare round the house, as if they expected to see a lion in his cage; lionizing, I believe she called it, and I suppose that was about what she meant.

Then Sally put in agin' my writing; said she should be ashamed to have my letters to her printed, because the spelling was awful. She admitted the sense was good enuff, about equal to any thing they had in boarding school, but the grammar and the spelling wanted fixing. So I had to tell her if the spelling didn't suit her, she might fix it to suit herself. For my part I couldn't see why it wasn't just as well to spell words as they sounded, as to follow the dictionary. I thought plow was about the same tool, whether they spelt it with a *w* or *ugh* at the end; one was considerable shorter than the other, and would save ink; besides, every body would know what I meant, and that was the end of talking or writing, to be understood. But I couldn't convince her by any common-sense arguments, that my spelling was good enuff.

So "Western Farmer" and the public will see that my

ideas have to go through about as much grinding and fixing before they come to light, as a bag of wheat does before it comes on to the table in the shape of bread. Sally must have her say, and the editor his, and the printer puts in the stops and pauses; so that by the time my ideas get back to me in the paper, I don't hardly know them. Some of them look as if they had been to college, and some to boarding school, and some brought up on a farm. But I take it the sense is understood, which is the chief thing.

There is one thing I don't exactly understand, why they should put in what Jake Frink says, and Uncle Jotham, and the rest of them, just as I write it, and practice their fixing up on me. I talk for all the world just like Seth Twiggs, but Sally says that is the vernacular, and don't look well in print. Perhaps it don't. Tastes differ. I don't think it pays for altering. In my opinion Sally had better mind her babies than to be tinkering with my spelling, and I guess the public would understand my writings quite as well if the printer didn't spend so much time on the commas and exclamation points. Why, any fool would know when a question was asked, without the sign. They say they keep a fellow in the printing office at about $3 a day, just to tend to this kind of tinkering. I don't think it pays; but that is none of my business.

This pride shows itself everywhere, and is about as troublesome on the farm as in the city. I am afraid it will be the ruin of the nation yet. It seems to grow worse the longer I live. It costs me a great deal more to live than it did my father, and if John ever gets back alive from war, he will never be able to live in the simple way I have done. Pride costs more than all other necessary family expenses. It has made many a man a bankrupt, and it keeps a good many of my neighbors poor. Every thing they earn is spent upon their backs, or upon ornamenting and fixing up their houses and farms. Farming is a good business, and pays all decent demands upon it, but it will not support much pride. A fence that costs a dollar a rod will turn cattle just as well as a faced wall of hewn stone, costing twenty times as much. The nineteen dollars extra goes to the support of pride, and farming ought not to be expected to foot the bills. A barn that will shelter hay and cattle is just as good as one costing four times as much, finished as elegantly as a dwelling. Farming will not pay for the clapboards, the lath and plastering, the ceiling and varnish. If a man has made a fortune in trade, there is no objection to his building a country seat, and living like a prince. His profits will support his pride. But the profits of ordinary farming will not justify a like expenditure. He may keep, if he will, a servant to each member of his family, but a farmer must serve himself. When he gets above his business he had better leave it. It strikes me that a farmer's pride ought to run to his business, rather than to his walls and buildings. Other folks have to have dwellings, barns, and fences, and it is no great shakes to own good lumber and paint. But farmers only have a deep, rich soil, fine wheat and corn fields, and luxuriant meadows. It will pay for a farmer to cure a horse-pond, to drain a swale, or to turn a barren pasture into a meadow that will cut three tuns of hay to the acre. It will pay for him to raise fine horses and cattle, pigs and sheep. He ought to gratify his pride in the line of his calling, and not undertake to rival merchants and nabobs. If he fixes up his fields and breeds good points in his stock, people will not trouble themselves very much whether he says *cow* or *keow*, or attends spelling school late in life.

Yours to command,

TIMOTHY BUNKER, ESQ.

Hookertown, July 15, 1862.

[Squire Bunker's, like the rest of our correspondence, has to go through the mill.—ED.]

NO. 60.—TIM BUNKER ON SWAMPS TURNING INDIAN.

"So you see it's turnin' Injun agin," said Deacon Little, as he looked into the horse-pond lot where I was mowing with the machine.

"I guess you didn't make so much eout of me in that bargain as you tho't for, Squire Bunker," said Jake Frink, as he joined the Deacon at the fence a few days ago.

"What evidence of Indian do you see in this grass?" I inquired.

"Plenty on't," answered the Deacon. "There's dock, and rushes, and brakes—I told you so. I never knew it to fail. A reclaimed swamp allers turns Injun arter a year or two."

"And you hain't got more'n half the grass you had last year," chimed in Jake Frink. "Neow Squire, I du say, if you're sick of your bargain, I'll take that lot back agin at jest half the price you gin me—and that is mighty fair."

"How much hay will I get here to the acre, think you?" I inquired of Jake.

"Wall neow, naber, it'll be tight squeezin' to git a ton and a half, and the first crop was three tun three year ago."

"And that tun and a half," I replied, "will be worth $25. Taking out $3 for cost of harvesting, and $4 more for interest of land and cost of manure, it leaves $18, or the interest on $300 an acre. Should I be a wise one to sell it for $10 an acre?"

"But see them rushes and brakes, Squire Bunker!" exclaimed the Deacon." You see the Almighty made that a swamp, and I guess you won't make any thing else eout on't if you keep tryin' from neow till doomsday."

"Well, Deacon, you see nothing else grew here but such things, and sour grasses, four years ago, and since I put in the drains, and stocked it down, we have had less of them every year. There is a hundred pounds of good hay where there is one pound of such stuff. You can not expect sile that is full of old brake roots, and rushes, to say nothing of foul seed, never to show a sign of the old vegetation."

"Nothin' will come of it. You never can make upland where the Almighty has made a swamp."

"That's so," responded Jake. "Better take $10 an acre, and trade back. It will be all moss another year—see if it ain't."

This talk of a July morning shows pretty well the prejudices of some of my neighbors against draining. They want to find an excuse for doing nothing, and thus set up a standard for reclaimed land, that they would not think of applying to land that needs no draining. If it shows any remains of the old grasses and rushes, it is, of course, going back again to swamp. If it don't continue to bear three tuns of hay to the acre, they hail you with, "I knew it would be so; the land is running out."

Now I hold that we ought not to expect any more of reclaimed land than we do of any good upland. If it performs as well as that, it is clear enough that draining pays. No upland that I have ever cultivated will keep up a yield of two or three tuns to the acre, without manure. It is very good land that yields a tun and a half three years after laying down. I never expected the horse-pond lot to do any better, but it has disappointed me in this respect, and has held out better without manure than any undrained land upon the farm. I should have given it a top-dressing last year, if I had not wanted to see how it would hold out. The yield was quite two tuns, though Jake Frink saw a quarter less. With manure I can get three tuns easier than I can get two upon upland.

The rushes and sour stuff that Deacon Little makes such a fuss about grow smaller every year, and will soon disappear entirely. There is, however, a need of one more drain in this lot, to make perfect work, and that I calculated on when I began the job. I did not care to be at the expense of putting it down unless it was necessary. It was just fifty feet between the last two drains I laid down, and I can see now that it needs another just half way between. It has always been too wet along this middle line, the grass has not been so heavy, and it is here that the brakes and rushes are found principally. It is as clean as ciphering can make it, that there ought to be another drain there. Indeed, I have lost considerable money by waiting so long, say half a tun of hay annually for three years. But what I have lost in money I have gained in knowledge. It is worth something to know just when and where to drain. For such land as this twenty-five feet is none too near, and three feet is none too deep. I would drain three inches deeper if I could get the fall. But three feet makes very good work, and land so drained I am sure will never turn Indian.

I never was fool enough to suppose that such land would keep up to three tuns to the acre without manure of some kind. But some men demand this, and because drained swales and swamps will not take care of themselves, they think draining a failure. This is unreasonable. Parson Spooner preached a few Sundays ago about "not muzzling the ox that treads out the corn," applying it, among other things, to giving a good bounty to the soldiers. You see, Hookertown took the hint next town-meeting day, and voted $100 to every man that would enlist. I thought the truth would apply to the sile, as well as to soldiers and oxen. It is about the best worker man has got, and we have no business to starve it. I suppose I ought to have been thinking of something else on Sunday, but the application hit my case so exactly, that I made up my mind right off that I wouldn't muzzle the horse-pond lot any longer. It got a dose of manure right away after mowing, without fail. The grass looks as green as a leek now, as much as to say, "Thank you, Squire Bunker, for your kind attentions."

But Mrs. Bunker's mind took another tack, thinking, I suppose, how the bounty was going to help enlistments, and that the new soldiers would help John down on the James River; she thought it wa'n't worth while to have Parson Spooner muzzled after such a sermon, and hinted that I had better leave a barrel of potatoes and a hind quarter of lamb at the parsonage next day. Well, you see, that was a scriptural application of the doctrine, and as I believe in facing the music, I left them, and added a bag of corn on my account, and a beef ham, that he might know that the oxen and corn part of his text at least was remembered.

But to return to the subject, as Mr. Spooner sometimes says in the pulpit, I think we make a great mistake in not top-dressing our meadows oftener, say as often as once in two years. In a small lot of an acre and a quarter, where I cut four tuns last year, I only cut three this, and the only difference was in manure. Five dollars' worth of compost would have made a difference of at least one tun of hay.

Deacon Little and Jake Frink are mighty afraid of having too large grass. Jake often says that he had rather have "two tun than three to the acre." Now I don't believe this notion, that heavy grass makes less nutritious fodder than light. A beef steak out of a corn-fed ox is enough sight better than one out of a thin, grass-fed animal. Why should not grass from a well-fed soil be more nourishing? I have watched this thing at the manger pretty close, and have grown three tuns and a half to an acre, and I have never yet got hay so big that the cattle would not eat it up clean. Cut your heavy grass a little earlier, and cure it well, and there is no trouble about making good fodder. A well-drained, corn-fed sile never turns Indian, Jake Frink to the contrary notwithstanding.

Yours to command,

TIMOTHY BUNKER, ESQ.

Hookertown, Aug. 15, 1862.

NO. 61.—TIM BUNKER IN HIS GARDEN.

"What kind of pears do you call them, naber?" asked Jake Frink as he stood admiring a dwarf Flemish Beauty, loaded with ruddy, russet fruit.

"That is a dwarf pear tree," said I.

"It looks like a giant," said Jake, confounding the tree with the fruit. "I never see such pears in all my life. Nothing but perries 'll grow on my place. I've heern of them dwarfs, but never tried 'em. Do all come as big as that?"

"Well, you see, they graft almost any kind of pear on quince, and that makes the tree grow small. But the fruit is generally bigger than it is on the pear stock. Dwarfing does not alter the fruit. It only makes the tree small."

"Dew tell! You see, I thought dwarfs was all of one kind. I shall have to own up on these pears, naber. I tell'd you at the time you were settin 'em eout, five years ago, that they never would come to nothin'. Uncle Jotham sot eout a lot, and his'n didn't dew nothin'. They grew miserable scrubs, got lousy and worm-eaten, and I guess there wa'n't one left arter three years. But now I see Jotham Sparrowgrass and Timothy Bunker are tew individuals, if not more."

Jake Frink's eyes hung out as he went round the garden, spying the pears, about as much as when he saw that first crop of hay in the horse-pond lot. I have kept back my pears from bearing more than most cultivators do, and think I find my account in it. Gentlemen who own small lots in the city or country village are apt to be in a hurry to realize; they let every fruit that sets hang on, even the first year. This is particularly bad for the bottom limbs of dwarfs, which are the most difficult to coax into a generous growth. If they bear much fruit they will not make wood, and the bottom of your pyramid is spoiled. I have seen a good many dwarfs killed outright by overbearing. With the standards there is not so much danger —indeed, none at all, if we except the Bartlett, and a few other early-bearing varieties.

I picked off all the fruit for three years, and threw all the force of the trees into wood. If I can get good, stout wood, well ripened in the fall, I consider this the best crop a tree can bear for four years at least. If a tree is a bad grower, I keep it back still longer. I have some standards out nine years, and dwarfs six, that have never borne a fruit, and I guess I know what I am about. They have blossomed profusely, and some of them set fruit—but I have pulled them off, though it went very much against the grain.

When they come into bearing, after such delay, there is great satisfaction in looking at the fruit, some in eating it, and more still in giving it away. You see, in growing a handsome fruit, perfect after its kind, a man enters into co-partnership with nature. He helps nature to do something which would be impossible without him, and nature helps him. The joint product is as much an honor to man as it is to nature. A basket of fine pears glorifies a gardener as much as a great speech does an orator. The giving away of the fruit or putting it upon exhibition is the publication of his speech. It sets the gardener to talking in a very mute kind of way that all sensible people comprehend. I should call an orator rather stupid who spouted his speech to the winds. He wants an audience. That gardener lacks both wit and manhood, who is content with eating his own pears. They should have a chance to speak for him.

And this reminds me of a circumstance that has just happened in Hookertown. You see, a week ago Sunday, Mr. Spooner preached a sermon on the text "By their fruits ye shall know them," applying the doctrine, among other things, to Slavery, and showing up this wicked war as one of its fruits. He pictured out a big tree, and the branches hung with treason, rebellion, oppression, theft, murder, and about all the vices that disgrace mankind. Now, you see, human nature is weak, and my mind, instead of following the thread of discourse, was running on the fruits in my garden. My Bartletts were just in their glory, and a man couldn't have said fruits on any occasion, without my thinking of them. So when we got home from meeting, I said to Mrs. Bunker: "Sally, we needn't be ashamed to be known by our fruits; suppose we send Mr. Spooner a basket of Bartletts."

"Very well," she said. "Send the basket heaping full and send it the first thing in the morning so that he will know what it means."

Sally, you see, is one of Mr. Spooner's right hand men, or rather women, a modern Dorcas, to whom it seems to come natural to help the poor, and make other folks happy. So I thought it fair to credit her while I credited the minister, and put on top of the basket a card: "With the compliments of Mrs. Bunker, Matt. 7 : 20."

I am getting to be pretty well along in life, and my enjoyment of gardening increases with my years. I am only sorry that I had not begun to plant fruit trees earlier. I hope your young readers will learn wisdom and improve the present season.

Yours to command,
TIMOTHY BUNKER, ESQ.

Hookertown, Sept. 15, 1862.

NO. 62.—TIM BUNKER ON RUNNING ASTERN.

"A great crop of corn this," said Patrick, as he threw the tenth red ear over the heap of stalks from which he was husking.

"'Taint nothing to what I've seen over on the Island when I used to live there," said Uncle Jotham Sparrowgrass, with a look that would have annihilated anybody but an Irishman.

"An how much d'ye think ye've seen over there, old fellow?" asked Pat, determined to sift matters to the bottom.

"Eighty bushels to the acre of clean shell corn, and nothing used but fish manure neither."

"An sure that was some corn, but the Squire will have a hundred as sure as ye're born. That is the tenth red ear, and we have not been husking an hour yet, and every red ear marks ten bushels, they say."

"Red ears! you fool!" exclaimed Uncle Jotham, "the corn is more than quarter red ears. There won't be seventy bushels to the acre on any part of the Squire's farm, I know."

"You must go over to neighbor Frink's to see corn," remarked Seth Twiggs, drily, as he sat on his milking stool at the end of the heap, puffing away with his pipe, while his hands were busy with the ears.

"Now, Jake, own up," said Tucker, "and tell us whether the crop on that lot was ten bushels and three pecks, or three bushels and ten pecks."

"It was plump twenty bushels, and no thanks to you either," said Jake indignantly. "It is enuff to make any man go astarn to have such a hand to work for him as you are. The weeds grew faster than the corn, a mighty sight."

These remarks were made at a husking bee on my barn floor a few evenings back. I approve of huskings if they are rightly managed, though they probably do more to promote good neighborhood than they do to help on the farmer's work. They make a pleasant gathering of old friends and neighbors, and sometimes relieve a man in a pinch. The scene was a good deal like that in Whittier's song of the huskers:

"Swung o'er the heaped-up harvest
From pitchforks in the mow,
Shone dimly down the lanterns
On the pleasant scene below;
The growing pile of husks behind,
The golden ears before,
And laughing eyes and busy hands,
And brown cheeks glimmering o'er.

Half hidden in a quiet nook,
Serene of look and heart,
Talking their old times over,
The old men sat apart;
While up and down the unhusked pile,
Or nestling in its shade,
At hide-and-seek with laugh and shout,
The happy children played."

You see, Whittier is an old fellow down in Massachusetts, that writes songs, and once in a while he touches up the farmers as well as the negroes. I suppose it is because he thinks they are both rather sad cases, and need sympathy. Mrs. Bunker says he is the best ballad maker in America, and I believe our Sally is pretty much the same way of thinking. At any rate, I guess he has been to a husking, and knows pretty near how they go on. The old folks that evening had the barn floor pretty much to themselves, the young ones preferring out-of-doors, where they had a plenty of moonshine in the heavens, and I guess some below.

Jake Frink's corn field of course came up for discussion; for I never saw men at a husking but they wanted one more *butt* than they found in the corn heap. It was certainly the poorest piece of corn in the neighborhood, and if there is any poorer in town, I have not seen it. It wasn't so much because the land was poor naturally, for his farm joins mine, and there can't be a great deal of original difference in the soil. His corn field and mine were not a quarter of a mile apart, but there was a good deal more than that difference in the yield. Tucker probably made an under-statement in putting it at ten bushels and a fraction, but there could not have been over twenty bushels, and one-third of that was soft corn. It was hoed only once, and the crop of wild mustard and wormwood was very generous. Grass was so plenty that Jake's cows found the best pasture upon the corn field.

"What is gwine to be the price of mustard this fall, naber Frink?" inquired Seth Twiggs.

"I don't care," said Jake, "I sha'n't have any to sell. It makes tol'able fodder."

"You'll make beef on't, I suppose," remarked Tucker, very gravely.

"How much profit d'ye spose ye've made on that crop?" inquired Uncle Jotham.

"Profit!" exclaimed Jake. "I don't farm for profit. I'm thankful enuff if I can get a livin'. I've allers had a hard time on't, and this year have run astarn a little more than common."

"And where do you 'spose the leak is, in your pocket?"

I inquired. "Wall, neow I can't tell," said Jake, scratching his head. It seems as if the trouble was at the top of the pocket instead of the bottom, and I've been allers siferin' to find out why money didn't git into my pocket. Mine allers gits eout afore it gits in, so that the most of the time I don't have nothin'. I've allers ben runnin' astarn since I begun to farm it, and I don't know what the matter is."

Jake's puzzle is that of a good many others, though few, it is to be hoped, are quite so bad off as he is. They do not make any headway, but are rather getting in debt every year. Many have to sell out and change their business, or emigrate to the West, where the land has not been so long abused as it has in the older States. There is something in Jake's insinuation that bad help is the cause of bad crops. This is apt to be the case where the employer is not in the field himself with his hands for a large part of the time. I have never yet seen a farm that would thrive without the constant oversight of the owner. Farming necessarily confines a man at home as closely as any other business. There are occasions of loss every day in seed time and harvest, if he is away from home. But Jake's trouble is not here, for he does not hire much help of any kind, and what he does hire is a fair average of farm help.

One thing that makes him run astern is the want of all system in making manure. He does not feel that this is an essential part of a farmer's business. He does not make one load where he has the material to make ten. An empty barn-yard makes a barren corn-field. This makes a man discouraged, and he does nothing promptly and with a will. He runs astern in every crop through the season, and in his pecuniary affairs at the end of the year.

But this is not all the trouble with my neighbor. Jake is not what he ought to be morally, and this, perhaps, lies at the bottom of his poor farming, as is the case with a multitude of others. It takes something more than a strong body and a sound mind to make a successful tiller of the soil. Manhood is as much an element of prosperity in this as in any other calling. If a man goes to the village and haunts taverns, nothing will save his business from disaster. He will make foolish bargains, sell what he ought to keep, and buy what he does not want. If he is tricky in his business dealings, he will soon lose the confidence of his fellow men, and the market for his produce. Temperance and integrity are about the best stock a man can keep on the farm, and with these, I have rarely known a farmer to run astern.

Yours to command,

Timothy Bunker, Esq.

Hookertown, Nov. 15, 1862.

No. 63.—TIM BUNKER ON EXTRAVAGANCE.

"Forty-five thousand dollars for jewelry, at one store, in one morning!" said Mrs. Bunker as she took off her specs, and laid down the Times, in which she had just read that account.

"And how many stores do you 'spose they've got in New York, where they sell them 'ere fixins?" inquired Mrs. Seth Twiggs, who had dropped in with her knitting, and sat in a meditative mood, while Mrs. Bunker read the war news. (Seth used to take the daily paper himself, but since the rise in price, he says he can't afford it. Twelve dollars a year for a daily paper, he says, is a leetle too mighty for a poor man who works for his living. That would more than buy a barrel of flour, and it only takes two barrels to carry his family through the year. I have noticed, however, that he and his wife are more neighborly than common, since they stopped the daily paper. I am not particularly sorry, for Seth is good company, if it wasn't for his everlasting pipe, which I abominate, as all sensible people should. What upon earth a man should want to make a chimney of his nose for, I never could see. We are kind o' lonesome since Sally got married and John went off to the war, and neighbors don't come amiss. Seth also has a son in the war, and we have a considerable fellow feeling.)

"There's a hundred of them stores at least," replied Mrs. Bunker.

"You don't mean a *hundred* on 'em ?" exclaimed Mrs. Jacob Frink, whom the neighbors all call "Polly," for short—except a few of us older people, who say "Aunt Polly."

"What a sight of silver spoons and forks, tea-pots and tureens, fruit knives and porringers, they must have down there, if all the stores sold as much as that 'ere one you read about!"

"It would make four millions and a half of dollars, spent in gewgaws in one morning," said I, willing to increase Aunt Polly's astonishment.

"You don't say so, Squire Bunker!" said she. "That is more than Jacob could carry in his cart."

"Well, I guess it is. It would line Broadway with silver, from the Battery to Central Park," said I.

"Provided you did'nt lay it on too thick," added Mrs. Bunker, squirming in her chair, at the extravagant expression.

"I said *line* it, Sally, not cover it." I responded.

"Wall, it is an awful sight of money any way!" said Aunt Polly. "I fear I should covet, if I see it."

"And where do you suppose it all comes *from?*" asked Mrs. Twiggs.

"I can tell you where some of it comes *to*," answered Aunt Polly. "You see, Kier has just got home from the war, wounded in his left arm. And he stopped in New York jest to see the sights, and to get something to bring home to the old folks, and to his family up at the White Oaks. And don't you think he brought me home a pair of gold specs and a gold thimble for his wife, and a silver trumpet for his boy, Jacob Frink, jr., who aint more than six months old. Now we didn't need these things any more than a cat needs tew tails. I had a pair of steel bows that Jacob got me five years ago, and they are jest as good as new, and I can see in 'em just as well as in the new ones, and a trifle better. And then his wife had thimbles enough, rather more than she used, any way, judging by the looks of Kier, when he used to drive the coal cart. She never kept him tidy, and I don't believe gold thimbles will help her case, if she had a cart load of 'em. And then as to that boy, he won't be big enough under a year to blow a squash leaf squawker, to say nothing of trumpets. A silver trumpet! It is the only article of silver in the whole neighborhood of the White Oaks, barring the small change they've got stowed away in their stockings, agin it comes into fashion agin. Now Kier paid ten dollars for that 'ere trumpet, and he had no more use for it than his wife has for a pianny. You see, he had just got paid off, and he had never seen so much money before in one pile, in all his life. He wanted to make a sensashun in the White Oaks, and I guess he did it, when he bought that article. Not less than twenty-five dollars, the price of blood, as it were, all spent for nothin! Ah, if he had only got a raw hide for that youngster there would have been some sense in it."

Aunt Polly paused for breath, and looked red in the face as she doubtless remembered the wallopings she had bestowed upon Kier in his juvenile days. But there is a deal of sense in what the old lady says. You see, this war has made money awful plenty, such as it is, among a certain class of people. It has got into new hands, and they are itching to let the world know that they have got it. I know of some fellows that have gone to the war that are earning more money for their families than they ever did before. There are Tucker's two boys that never did anything but hunt, fish, and loaf, but they are now earning their rations and thirteen dollars extra, a thing they never did before, without the extra. There are hosts of contractors for steamboats, for iron-clads, for army clothing, for horses, for mules, for forage, for flour, for rations of all kinds, that are getting a big slice, and piling up money by the hat full. This money is distributed all through the country, and farmers come in for their share. Well, now, it is mighty natural for folks that have been stinted for a good while, when they get hold of the cash, to make it fly. So it goes for jewelry, for bonnets, and silver trumpets, and all sorts of jimcracks that tickle the women and children, and don't do any body much good.

You see, George Washington Tucker, jr., that enlisted in the beginning of the war, sent home fifty dollars to his intended, Miss Almeda Georgiana Bottom, and told her she might *swell* for once, as she had never had a fair chance in life. The next Sunday I rather guess there was a sensation in the Hookertown Meeting-house that kept sleepy folks awake, if the sermon didn't. She had on a pair of ear-rings, a big, gold-washed watch-chain, and bracelets like Col. Smith's daughter, a monstrous swell of hoop skirts, one of those two story bonnets with pink flowers in the second story and a top knot of feathers, and to top all, or rather to bottom all, a pair of new calf-skin shoes that squeaked like a cider mill. She came sailing into meeting just after the first hymn, when Mr. Spooner was reading scripture where it says "Behold the lilies of the field," etc. The shoes made such a squeaking that he had to stop until the young woman got seated. Some of the young folks in the pew behind me tittered, and an old lady in my own pew put her handkerchief to her mouth. I suppose she wanted to cough just then, and didn't like to disturb the meeting. Mr. Spooner looked astonished, as if he had seen a vision.

Now, you see, this sort of thing is going on all over the country, and there is a good deal of extravagance in folks buying jewelry and knick-knacks that they do not have any use for. I suppose it is rather worse than common just now, but there has always been a good deal of it. If a man buys what he don't need, I call him extravagant, whether it is an extra acre of land, a two story bonnet, or a bogus gold watch chain, without any watch. If a man can do his business with a wheelbarrow, he should not invest in a horse and cart. If his farm only affords occupation for one horse and cart, he should not buy a yoke of oxen and cart. If he has only capital to work twenty acres to advantage, he is very extravagant to purchase fifty. If he has only feed for six cows, he should not keep eight. This is one of our greatest faults as a people, and I am afraid this war, if it ends in the triumph of the government, as we hope it will, will not remedy the evil. We buy cargoes of silks, and jewelry, wines, and brandies, that we have no need of. Miss Almeda Georgiana Bottom is not the only sinner among us, not by many hundred, I tell you.

Yours to command,

TIMOTHY BUNKER, ESQ.

Hookertown, Jan. 1*st*, 1863.

NO. 64.—TIM BUNKER ON THE FARMER'S OLD AGE.

"*Sallie Bunker Slocum* is the baby's name," said Mrs. Bunker, as she took off her spectacles and laid down the letter from Shadtown, which I had just brought in from the Post-Office.

"I like the name well enough, except the spelling of it," she continued. "Sally was my mother's name, it is my name, and my daughter's, and if they wanted to keep up the name in the family, I don't see why they didn't spell it in the old way. If I set out to do a thing I would do it right."

"I suppose it is a little more genteel," I replied. "That is the way they spell it among the aristocratic families of the South."

"That is just what I don't like," said she. "It is a miserable affectation of women who read novels more than they do their Bibles. We have no aristocracy up here, and judging from what I saw when I was down South, I never want to see any. Isn't this wretched war carried on to bolster up an aristocracy, and that a few families may live in idleness at the expense of the poor? I don't want to see any aristocratic trumpery on my grandchildren. *Sallie* won't look well on a grave stone."

"What does Sally write about it?" I asked.

"Not a word about the spelling. She seems to think it is all the same. She writes: 'We carried the baby out to meeting for the first time last Sabbath, and it was baptized Sallie Bunker. We never thought of calling her any thing else, out of regard to you and grandmother, though we did not tell you at the time you were here, lest you should be too much puffed up with your honors. She is a nice child, and little Timothy thinks a world of her.' That is all she says about it. I shall write her immediately," said Mrs. Bunker, with emphasis, "that my name is not *Sallie.*"

Now we do not always agree on small points, but on the larger matter of having grandchildren, we see pretty much alike. It is one of the greatest comforts of old age to have children's children around us, to cheer us while we live, and to bear our names and to take our places when we are gone. We can hardly have too many of them, and I shall not be very particular whether their names have a letter more or less, if we only have the children.

This is a matter of considerable solicitude, not only here in Hookertown, but in a great many farming towns around us. The present generation is getting pretty well along in life, and we do not know who is going to take our places. You would be surprised to see how few young men there are at the meeting-house on Sunday. The men who sit at the head of the pews are almost all gray haired, and some of them are about as white as snow. It looks a great deal worse than it did a year ago, before so many went to the war. Uncle Jotham Sparrowgrass has no son to take his place, and Seth Twiggs, Jake Frink, and myself, have boys in the army, and a dozen more went from our parish. It is about an even chance whether we ever see many of them again. The war bids fair to be a long one, and what the bullets don't kill, the hospital will be likely to finish. But then we ain't sorry the boys have gone, and if they don't come back, *we are going ourselves,* if the rebellion is not crushed. It is pretty certain that our farms won't be worth much to ourselves, or to our grandchildren, if Jeff. Davis is going to rule. It is the old battle of despotism and liberty, and we are bound to see it through, whatever may be the cost.

We have got things fixed up pretty comfortable, and

it will be pretty hard to go off and leave them, but we might say that, I suppose, when we start on a longer journey. We can't expect to stay here forever, and a few years more or less won't make any particular difference with us, when we get into the promised land. Most of us here in Hookertown have kept old age in view for a good many years, and I guess we are about as comfortable and jolly a set of old people as you will find among your hundred thousand readers. We have most of us got good houses that keep us just as comfortable and entertain our friends as well as a house that rents in the city for a thousand dollars or more. We are as independent as wood-choppers, on fuel, for if coal runs up to ten dollars a ton, as it has this winter, we can say to the coal merchant, "No you don't, Mr." and turn to the wood-pile. We have been using coal for several years, because it was cheaper than it was to hire labor, and chop and cart the wood. But there isn't a man of us but has a good wood lot, and I guess there is more wood in this town than there was fifty years ago. It is a great consolation to know where your fuel *can* come from, in case of a pinch. And then in case the house or barn wants repairs it is mighty convenient to know that you have a living lumber yard close by, where every shingle, plank, and timber, you need is on hand. Twenty acres of woodland that you have watched the growth of for forty years or more is about as good as any bank stock I know of. I suppose I could sell the timber on any acre of mine for two hundred dollars, to say nothing of the fuel. That same land cost me only seventeen dollars an acre. Perhaps some folks who are in such a mighty hurry to cut off their forests might as well stop and cipher a little.

And while I am talking of trees as a shelter for old age, I want to say a good word for orchards, apples, and indeed fruits of all kinds. I waked up to planting apple trees when I was young, and I think I have now about as good an orchard as there is in town. With the low price of fruit this last year, it has brought me in over three hundred dollars, sold on the trees to the buyer. I only regret that I had not begun to plant pear trees sooner. They are quite as hardy as apples, yield as well, and sell for more than double. A man with a dozen acres in pears, of the right kinds, would have a comfortable income for old age, if he had nothing else. But aside from profit, a plenty of fruit in the family is a great comfort and luxury, and an important means of health. We have seen very little of the doctor in forty years, and we have had fruit in some shape every day in the year. Put these two things together: long-lived people eat much fruit.

Perhaps we don't live quite so well out here on the farm as some of the nabobs in the city, though about that there is room for a difference of opinion. All the raw materials of their extra fixings come from the farm—poultry, eggs, milk, cream, butter and cheese, and the fine fruits. They have better cooks, perhaps, though some of us out here have things about as nice, in that line, as it is safe for sinners to enjoy. I should be loth to swap my cook for the best you have got in your biggest hotel. When Mrs. Bunker gets on her checked apron and spectacles, and lays herself out on a soup or a roast, you see, common cooks might as well retire.

In the matter of dress, we in the country are not quite so independent as we used to be, when there was a spinning wheel and a loom in every house, and men wore the linen and woolen made at home, because they had nothing else. But we clothe ourselves easier now, for we can buy cloth a great deal cheaper than we can make it. But if the war continues, and prices keep going up, we may have to go back to homespun again, and then I guess the old folks will be about as independent as any body, for we know how to use the spinning wheel and loom. But that day is some ways off, I guess, judging from the finery we see in the Hookertown meeting-house on Sunday. That two-story bonnet of Miss Almeda Georgiana Bottom has done the work for our young women. They tittered at it at first, but it was no use laughing at the fashions. They had to cave in, and the meeting-house on Sunday now looks like a big flower garden. The old ladies who were freest in their remarks, I notice have bonnets as high as the highest. I suppose I should not have said so, but I couldn't help asking Mrs. Bunker, as we started for meeting, if she would have the carriage top let down.

Yours to command,

TIMOTHY BUNKER, ESQ.

Hookertown, Feb. 20th, 1863.

No. 65.—TIM BUNKER ON SHEEP TRAPS.

"What upon airth d'ye call that?" asked Uncle Jotham Sparrowgrass, as he hailed Seth Twiggs in the street, this morning. Seth had a gun over his shoulder, and held in his hand what might have been mistaken for game, at a short distance. On closer examination, the object revealed a pair of short ears, a prominent nose, a long, clean pair of jaws, well armed with sharp, bloody teeth. It was what is left of a dog after his tail has been cut off just behind his ears.

"That is what I call a sheep trap," said Seth, as he flung the head upon the grass, pulled his pipe out of one pocket, and a match out of the other, and lighted.

"Why, that is Jake Frink's dog!" exclaimed Uncle Jotham.

"Taint Jake's any longer," replied Seth. "Ye see, I

caught him in the act, this morning airly. He was gnawing away at a sheep he had run down, and that is sheep's blood you see on his teeth now. I put that bullet between his eyes, and he hadn't time to clean his teeth before he emigrated to t'other country. That trap has caught three sheep of mine this spring, besides lots of my neighbors', to say nothing of the lambs; and I was so afraid the trap might be set again that I jest cut his head off after I shot him, to make sure work of it. That critter has destroyed a hundred dollars' worth of property this spring, I haven't a doubt. Sheep have been found dead, and badly maimed, and he has been seen chasing them. When complaint has been made to Jake, he could not believe he was guilty of even chasing sheep. He did not allow him in such tricks. His dog was as innocent as a lamb. Children could play with him, and he wouldn't even growl. To hear Jake talk, you would think the dog's mother must have been a sheep. Waal, now, ye see, that talk didn't go down with me. I can tell a sheep stealin dog as soon as I lay my eye on him. There is a kind of guilty look about the critter, that says mutton, as if it stuck in his jaws. Jake has never been able to raise sheep. If he tried, his lambs disappeared mysteriously when that dog was a puppy. He always laid it to other folks' dogs. But Rover was the guilty wretch that drunk lambs' blood. I have been watching him for about a week, and ye see this morning I got him jest where I wanted him. There was a piece of mutton in his mouth when I fired. It will take a smarter man than Jake Frink to get away from that fact."

"I guess you'll catch it when Jake hears of it."

"He won't have to wait long, for I am going to take home Jake's sheep trap this morning. I wouldn't have you think that I'd shoot a man's dog, and then not own it. That would be too much like a sheep stealing dog. I calculate to take the responsibility."

This conversation of my neighbors shows the way the current is setting on the dog question, and the progress the reform is making, under the new laws, and especially under the high prices of wool and mutton. This last, I think, has more to do with dog killing, than all the laws that have been enacted. With wool at a dollar a pound or in that neighborhood, every body that owns land wants a few sheep. Even Jake Frink rubs his eyes and wakes up to the fact that sheep raising will be a profitable business. Sheep will live and do well on his poor pastures where his cows grow poor. He will bluster, of course, when he learns that his dog is killed, but he will be resigned and conclude that his sheep as well as his neighbors' will be safer with that sheep trap out of the way. A large number of poor farmers, and rather poor citizens, who have the dog mania, will invest in sheep, and that will make *them* the natural enemies of dogs. I have noticed that it makes a mighty deal of difference whether it is your sheep or your neighbors' that are bitten or killed. Resignation is a virtue easily practised when a pack of dogs get into your neighbor's flock, and worry and slay. But when you go out some fine morning and find your fattest wether half eaten up, or your full blood merinos made into mutton prematurely, it stirs the blood at once against dogs. You owe the whole race a grudge. You think of steel traps, bullets, and small stout cords in close proximity to dogs' necks. You talk fiercely and threaten vengeance. Men in such a humor are prepared to legislate rationally upon the dog question. They see very clearly that one vile cur, not worth a copper to any body, may easily destroy a hundred dollars' worth of their property in a single night. With sheep at two or three times the old prices we shall not only have good dog laws, but we shall have men that will execute the laws, and the dogs at the same time. The old arguments on this question are just as good as any new ones that can be brought forward, but men see them a great deal better. A sheep is a creature of consequence, just about three times bigger than it was two years ago. The dogs have grown small, and a multitude of them have grown out of sight entirely.

There used to be a dog on about every corner of the streets in Hookertown. Some families kept a half dozen, and they had a tight match to get enough for their children to eat, too. Now they are getting scarce, and I am in hopes that the time is not distant when they will be confined to cages, and shown up as curiosities at Barnum's. It does my eyes good to see children and lambs fat and happy, and dogs lean and miserable. Fat dogs indicate a low civilization like the Chinese, or a low state of morals like the White Oaks, where the dogs are more numerous than the people.

I have hated dogs ever since I was a boy. My father kept sheep and was a lover of choice mutton, and chose to do his own butchering, in a humane and decent manner. I remember an old ewe with twin lambs, a cosset who came home with the cows to be petted and cared for as if she were a member of the family. One morning she was found dreadfully torn by the dogs, just alive, but unable to move and her lambs missing. I have hated the sight of a dog ever since, and never pass one in the street without an apprehension of a bite, and a great longing to brain him on the spot. Seth Twiggs has given them the right name, "Sheep Traps."

And the morality of keeping a sheep-killing dog is on a par with that of a malicious neighbor who should set steel traps in the sheep walks of your pasture. I would much rather have steel traps than the dogs. The trap would be certain to dispose of only one sheep in a night, while the dog might kill or maim a dozen. The trap and the victim would be found together in the morning, and the mystery of the broken leg would be cleared up. But your cowardly, sneaking dog does his work by night and is miles away in the morning, with his chops all licked, and lying by his master's door, as meek looking as if he never dreamed of mutton. The owner of a steel trap is a responsible being, but the owner of a dog seems to think that his brute is what Mr. Spooner would call a free moral agent, fit to do business on his own hook. He is not accountable for the deeds of his dog. I go in for trapping rats, skunks, foxes, weasels, and other vermin. If we must trap sheep and lambs, I prefer an article with steel springs and chain, to a pair of living jaws on four legs. The latter catches too much game.

Yours to command,

TIMOTHY BUNKER, ESQ.

Hookertown, May 10th, 1863.

NO. 66.—TIM BUNKER ON OLD STYLE HOUSE-KEEPING.

It was a rainy morning in August; I had five tons of hay down, and it was "morally certain," as Mr. Spooner says, when he is putting a thing strong, that I shouldn't have any hay weather, so there was nothing to do but set in the house, and see things grow. There is a great satisfaction in that, and blessed is that man who has his fields and meadows where he can see them from his window. I have seen some rather handsome pictures down in your city in the Academy, and other places, but there are none to compare with the view from my dining-room window. There lies spread out before me, the horse-pond lot, all nicely mowed, and looking as smooth as Mr. Olmstead's lawns in your Central Park that you think so much of; and just beyond, a four-acre field of corn, in full tassel and spindle; and beyond that, a side hill covered with wood and rocks, and a little to the right hand, a glimpse of the sea covered with sails. There is a pasture dotted with cattle and sheep, that beat anything I ever saw on canvass. It don't cost half so much to build a house with the picture gallery outside as it does to have it within, and then you are never pinched for room, and it costs nothing to have your pictures retouched, and the frames regilded. It is a source of endless entertainment and instruction to study this out-door picture gallery, and rainy days give us the leisure, and a new light to see them in.

Mrs. Bunker had got her cheese in the press, and the milk things washed up, and things put to rights generally, when I saw her overhauling a bundle of old yellow papers that looked as if they were a hundred years old. One of them was an old account book of her grandfather's, made by doubling a sheet of foolscap twice, and sewing it together. The thread is stout linen, such as her grandmother used to spin on the linen wheel.

"Now," says she, "Timothy, I like to look over these things and see how differently folks live now, from what they used to when my mother was a girl. Here is the account of my mother's 'setting out in life' when she was married, in the handwriting of my grandfather, Amos Dogett."

"When was that?" I asked.

She read from the manuscript: "Our oldest daughter Sally was married to John Walton Jan. ye 29th, 1784."

"That was just after the war of Independence."

She continued "Things that I let my daughter have was one horse, 10 pound, one new side-saddle and bridle, 5 pound." "Horse-flesh was pretty cheap then," I remarked. "Reckoning the pound at three dollars and a third, which was its value in the New England States, it would make the horse worth only thirty-three dollars and a third, and the saddle and bridle half as much—which is only about one-quarter of the price of good sound horses in Hookertown to-day. Side-saddles have not fallen off much. They were a good deal in demand then, and not much now. You see Mrs. John Walton, bride, had no other way to get to her new home but on horseback, and all other brides, and damsels in general, had either to try the saddle or go on foot. Happy was that damsel who could boast of a horse on her wedding day."

Immediately following the saddle was the entry of "one pot, 8 shillings, one small iron kettle, 6 shillings, one iron spider, 4 shillings, one pair of flats." It would seem from this that Mrs. Walton was expected to cook her husband's dinner, and to iron the clothes. Mrs. Bunker says she was a capital cook and laundress. I think it must run in the blood. I have no doubt I am indebted to that pot and spider for all the good dinners I have eaten under my own roof.

Then follows, in the bridal outfit, "two candle sticks, two shillings." These must have been iron, such as went out of date about the time I was a boy. The bottoms of the dilapitated sticks used to figure on butchering day, in scraping off the hair from hogs, and nothing better has been invented since. Then follows "one case of knives, one fire shovel, one large iron kettle, one teapot, one teakettle, one trammel." Then for personal adornment the bride had "one gauze handkerchief, 3 shillings sixpence, one pair of gloves, same price, one pair of English shoes, 6 shillings, one pound of whalebone, and four and a half yard moreen for a skirt," which shows what the whalebone was intended for. Our grandmothers probably split their own whale-bone, and never dreamed of steel. hoop skirts.

The fitting out of the bridal chamber was "one feather bed, 4 pound 10 shillings, two under beds, 1 pound 1 shilling, four pairs of sheets, two coverlids, two fulled blankets, one chest and lock, and one looking-glass, and one paper of pins." There was no wash-stand with bowl and pitcher, soap-dish, and mugs, towel-rack, and other indispensable articles in a modern bed-chamber. The morning ablutions were probably made in the kitchen, or at the back door from a stone hollowed out for the purpose. Possibly they kept as clean as those who have better facilities for washing.

The table furniture was rather meager,—one set of teacups, nine plates, four platters, half a dozen spoons, half a dozen teaspoons, two basins, two porringers. There is nothing said of table linen, and probably Mrs. John Walton was in the hight of fashion, not only at tea, but at every meal, eating from a *bare board.* This, I mistrust, was not mahogany or black walnut oiled, but plain pine or maple, which was scrubbed daily for the whole term of her natural life.

A significant entry was " one little wheel, one pound." This was the linen wheel on which all the sewing thread was spun, and the fine linen for shirts and sheets, and other articles for the bed, and for the person. There was also " one set of loom irons, 3 shillings." John was expected to make the loom himself. Fortunately it consisted mainly of wood, and the framing was not difficult. This brings back the good old days of homespun. In that loom was woven all the clothing, woolen and linen, of herself, husband and children, for a whole generation. What visions of solid work and happiness the loom and wheel open to us!

We find also among the bridal items "hard money for to buy a cow with, 5 pounds 8 shillings." The *hard* money indicates the abundance of paper currency at the close of the war. The price of cows was relatively much higher than the price of horses. Twice the sum would now buy a very good cow. That cow laid the foundation of John Walton's fortune. His wife understood the mysteries of the dairy, and the one cow grew in a few years into a herd of thirty, and the Walton butter and cheese became famous.

The whole outfit foots up forty-four pounds nineteen shillings sixpence, or less than one hundred and fifty dollars. That stocked a housekeeper in 1784, and probably she was better off than most of her neighbors. The whole would not equal the cost of the piano now in many a farmer's parlor.

"The tea set that Dea. Smith gave Eliza at her wedding cost $200," added Mrs. Bunker.

"I know it; and the rest of the presents were worth a thousand dollars, to say nothing of the furnished house into which she entered when she got back from the bridal trip."

"A single looking-glass costing eight shillings, and a mirror covering half the side of a parlor, and costing three hundred dollars, is another contrast worth looking at," said Sally.

"And the young brides that prink before them are no handsomer or smarter than Sally Walton's daughter forty years ago." "It is time you forgot that, Timothy. It is a long while ago."

Here the dinner bell rung and the dingy account book was returned to its place in the bundle.

Yours to command,

TIMOTHY BUNKER, ESQ.

Hookertown, Aug. 10th, 1863.

NO. 67.—TIM BUNKER ON KEEPING A WIFE COMFORTABLE.

"How long have we got to wait for dinner, I should like to know?" said Jake Frink to his wife Polly, one day in hoeing time. "Its tu bad to keep three men waitin' an hour for their grub."

"You've got to wait till the brush is cooked, with which to cook your dinner," said Aunt Polly snappishly. "None but a greenhorn would furnish green wood for his wife to cook with—and green brush at that. You know, Jake Frink, that you have never had a second cord of wood at your door any time since I have lived with you, and that is going on seven and thirty years. All that time green brush has been the chief article of kindling. One might think that your whole farm was a brush pasture teetotally. I should like to have you try cooking with green wood a little while, and see how you would like it."

"Wall, Polly, hurry up any way," said Jake, "for we are all mighty hungry, and the corn wants hoeing badly. You see, brush is economical, and what I can't sell at the store, I can use at home. It would kind o' rot on the ground ef I dident burn it up."

"Pretty economy it is, to keep your wife in a stew all the while, and hired men a waiting hours every day because green wood wont burn! It is smoke, siss, and fizzle, from morning to night, and I no sooner get a blaze agoing, than I have to put on more green wood, and then there is another sputter. I never see such a house as this is," said Aunt Polly, with great emphasis, and with a face as red as a beet.

Jake is a great sinner, although he thinks he is so good

that he does not need to go to meeting and hear Mr. Spooner preach. He would try the temper of a much more saintly woman than Aunt Polly, and keep her on the rack. He might just as well put red pepper in her eyes, as to keep her kitchen always smoked up with green brush. Her eyes always look red, and it is nothing under the sun but that smoky kitchen. The draft of the chimney is none of the best, but that would be remedied with well-seasoned wood. Now, you see, that man had Christian marriage, but he don't care no more for his wife than for a dumb animal. I guess he would lift a sheep out of the ditch, especially in these times, when wool is a dollar a pound. But he keeps his wife in the ditch about all the while, and never suspects that she is a bit uncomfortable. He thinks he saves something by burning brush, but it don't pay unless you have a machine to chop it up fine, and keep it under cover until it gets dry. To work it up with the axe into fuel for a stove, it costs more than it is worth. If it lies on the ground in the woods, it rots and makes good manure without any expense. Then if you have it, or any other wood, green, there is a matter of uncertainty about meals, which throws the whole work of the farm into confusion, and puts every body out of humor.

But this is only one way in which a wife is kept uncomfortable. It does seem as if some men took less care of their wives than of the dumb cattle in their fields. If the rooms in their houses had been thrown together by chance, they could not have been more inconvenient. A good arrangement of the rooms saves one-half the labor. Some times the sleeping room is on the second floor, and there is many a journey up and down stairs during the day for a woman already overburdened with care. Sometimes the store room is in the garret, and other journeys have to be made daily, for supplies for the table. Every thing that she needs for her work should be upon the first floor, and close at hand. There is no unnecessary waste of strength then in filling her place as housekeeper, cook, dairy maid, laundress, wife and mother; for many a farmer's wife is expected to fill all these offices, and to be always cheerful and happy, waiting for the coming of her liege lord, as if she had nothing else to do but to be a wife.

The lot of a farmer's wife, as it generally runs, is rather a hard one, and is made hard very often from the want of attention to little things. If a man needs twenty cords of wood for the year, it costs no more to get it in the winter, in a time of leisure, and to have it chopped, split, and packed under cover, than to get it, a load at a time, and have the torment of a slow fire all the while. This not only makes more labor, but it frets and worries, which is a good deal worse than work. Dry wood is one of the secrets of a comfortable wife. That is what makes Mrs. Bunker so hale and handsome, past sixty. She says she wouldn't know how to keep house without dry wood. I guess she wouldn't, for she has never had any thing else.

Deacon Smith is a good man and means well, but he does not know how to use a wife. His well has hard water, that wont wash, and all the water on washing day has to be brought from the brook, more than forty rods from the house. To be sure he keeps a servant, but it makes a world of work for servant and housekeeper. He might have a cistern that wouldn't cost twenty dollars, and it would save more than that value of labor every year. He has roofing enough to keep it supplied with water all the while. And then the Deacon carries on a large farm and keeps a half dozen hired men, and boards and lodges them all in his own house. Now what a burden this brings upon a woman, when they might be much better accommodated in small farm-houses of their own. It is quite as easy to hire a part of the labor needed on the farm from those married, as from those who have no homes of their own. This leaves a farmer's wife with no family but her own to attend to, which is much more pleasant.

Then I guess a man has to do something to himself as well as to his house, to make every thing go smooth with his wife. She bargained for a man when she got married, and she has a right to be disappointed, if she finds she has nothing but a working animal always jaded and unfit for social life. I know of some farmers who rarely go anywhere but to meeting and to market. They feel that they can not afford the time to dress up and go and see their friends, and dine or take a cup of tea. They have so slid out of society that their friends rarely come to see them. They are so hurried with work that they do not make friends very welcome. They seem to have no appreciation of life, but as an opportunity to make money. They prize work for this end, and time that isn't turned into money is lost to them. Their muscles not only become hard, but their hearts grow hard and unsympathizing. They lose their taste for reading, if they ever had it, and very soon fall asleep if they attempt to read or hear reading. If they are active in the field, they are stupid and dull in the house, like tired animals in their stalls. There is no mental growth, no development of manhood in their lives. This discovery I think makes a woman more uncomfortable than green wood and smoky fires. She married a man—a creature of intelligence and affections—and she has the right to the companionship of a man while she remains a faithful wife. No man has a right to prostitute himself to mere money getting, no matter how honestly, or to turn all the energies of his being to muscular exertion. Manhood is the most precious product of his farm, and whatever else suffers, *that* ought to be kept strong and vigorous. That article has become mighty scarce on Jake Frink's premises, and it is this fact that makes the green wood so very green, and the smoke so trying to

Aunt Polly's eyes. Poor woman! I shouldn't wonder if there was something else in them besides smoke sometimes.

Yours to command,

TIMOTHY BUNKER, ESQ.

Hookertown, June 6th, 1863.

NO. 68.—TIM BUNKER ON STARTING A SUGAR MILL.

"Who'd have thought of ever seeing a sugar mill in Hookertown!" exclaimed Seth Twiggs, as he looked at that new institution just put up on the Shadtown road.

"And such lots of sorghum too!" said Deacon Smith. "Almost every farmer has a patch."

"The age of meracles ain't past yet," said Tucker in a meditative mood.

"I wonder if there 'll be any rum made of the leavings," inquired Jones expectantly, recalling his experience on a sugar plantation.

"Not a bit of it," said Seth, with a twinkle in his eye and an extra puff at his pipe. "Suckers will go dry in these parts."

Ten years ago, I should as soon have thought of seeing an elephant in my barn-yard, as of seeing a sugar mill in Hookertown. In the first place there was nothing to make sugar of, except a few maple trees, and they did not require a mill. And then there was not enterprise enough to start a new project of that magnitude. We most of us believe in foreordination, and had not put down sugar making as among the things that were destined for Hookertown. We expected always to get our sweetening by barter, just as our fathers and mothers did before us—a pound of cheese for a pound of sugar, and brown sugar at that. We expected, too, to eat a slave-grown article because we could not get any other. But they say they are getting off the notion of forced labor on the sugar plantations in Louisiana, and I suppose when the Fates got to making a change, they thought they might as well make a change all around, and have free sugar North and South. At any rate it is a settled fact that we have a sugar mill, where they are going to make molasses this fall, and where they may make sugar by and by. I suppose half the farmers in town won't pay a dollar for sweetening next year, and some will have a few barrels of syrup to sell. The world moves, notwithstanding the war, and I am not sure but the war has given a good many enterprises a new hoist. You see, it has made sugar and molasses dear, and that has set Yankee wit at work to get these things out of our own soil. In raising sugar at the North, it makes a great deal of difference whether that article is eight cents or sixteen cents a pound.

We have been getting ready for this business some years. The seed sent out from the *Agriculturist* office introduced the plant, and taught us that we could grow it as well as corn. Jake Frink could see that it looked like broom-corn, and was no humbug. It would pay to raise it for fodder for cattle, and hogs ate it greedily, and would thrive upon it wonderfully well. There was no chance to lose much. Some made syrup from it, the first year, and put it up in bottles, and exhibited it at the county fair. It looked like syrup, tasted like it, and went well on buckwheat cakes. But we had no mill to grind the cane, and no conveniences for boiling down the juice, and that was the great objection to going into the business.

Last winter we talked the matter up in the Farmers' Club. Men in whose judgment we had confidence said the thing would pay. Mr. Spooner, who is ready for every good word and work, said there was no good reason why we should not make our own sweetening at home; that the farmers in the town paid out twenty thousand dollars every year for this article, and they might just as well keep that amount in their own pockets. Deacon Smith read extracts from the agricultural papers, showing what they were doing out West, raising two and three hundred gallons of syrup to the acre, and clearing over a hundred dollars above working expenses. He said the crop last year was worth several millions of dollars, and that the business was increasing rapidly wherever they had learned to make the syrup.

Seth Twiggs said they had started a mill at Smithtown, and it worked well. He brought along several bottles of the syrup made at the mill, and to convince the skeptical, sent it around for trial. It was found that it made good gingerbread, it sweetened coffee, and filled the place of molasses completely. After a fair trial, and several weeks' talking, in which every man made sure that the syrup would not bite, we got the Club up to the question—"Shall Hookertown have a sugar mill?" This was the name the thing seemed to take of itself, though I suppose they will make nothing but syrup at present. It was agreed that the syrup was the thing we all wanted, and we were all ready to go into it if the thing could be made to pay. Two men agreed to build the mill, and put into it every thing necessary to grind the cane and boil the syrup, if they could have cane enough to make it an object. They wanted three hundred acres pledged. This, with what they raised themselves, they thought would make it a safe enterprise.

To get the cane pledged in a community of small farmers, many of them not having more than ten acres under the plow, was a good deal of an undertaking. It was agreed to appoint a committee for each school district, to see how much could be raised. There were fifteen districts in the town, and it would take about twenty acres to each district. Mr. Spooner took the matter in hand in his district, and worked as hard as any of us. Some subscribed two acres, and some a half acre. We raised about three quarters of the pledges here, and for the rest we had to go to Shadtown.

The results of the winter's work are, that we have a wonderful increase of sorghum in all this region. A patch may be found on all the best farms and on some of the poor ones, and even in the gardens of the mechanics. A quarter of an acre of sorghum will make a barrel of syrup, if it does only moderately well. We shall not have syrup enough to supply the town, perhaps, but we shall give the business a good start, and wake up the sleepers. I should not think it strange if we became exporters of syrup in a few years, and Connecticut syrup may yet stand as high in the market as Connecticut River shad. The mill is all up, and the machinery in, and they will be ready to grind as soon as the cane is fit. I do not see any reason why New England should not raise its own molasses. We have plenty of unoccupied land, and capital to invest in the crop and in mills to manufacture it. All that is needed is a few individuals in each town to talk the matter up, and show how it can be done. There must be concert of action, and then the whole business will go easy. The sorghum is coming into favor much more rapidly than the potato did, and it would not be strange if it wrought as great changes in our husbandry.

Yours to command,

TIMOTHY BUNKER, ESQ.

Hookertown, Sept. 10th, 1863.

NO. 69.—TIM BUNKER'S REASONS AGAINST TOBACCO

"Why don't you use tobacco, and raise it like other people, Squire Bunker?" asked Seth Twiggs one day of me, with a discharge of smoke from his pipe that would have done credit to a locomotive.

"Because *you* do!" I replied a little gruffly.

"Wal, neow, I don't see the peth of that, Squire."

"I do. You see, Seth, you and your farm are a standing argument agin tobacco. You are always smoking, smoking, smoking, and you have pretty much smoked your brains out."

"You weren't in any particular danger on that pint, Squire."

"Well, I admit I'm not so smart as some of my neighbors, and it becomes me to take care of what little brains I have got."

"Jest so," said Seth. "I see."

"Your eyesight is darkened half the time," I continued, "by that cloud of smoke, and you don't know exactly what you're about. You waste time and money as well as brains. It takes you about one-half the time to load your pipe, and the other half to smoke it. And it is a great deal worse since you have got them big Dutch pipes, with big bowls and crooked stem, than it used to be when you had that old stump of a clay pipe that lasted you five years. Then you only put in a pinch of tobacco, and you had to stop in about ten minutes, to take breath and charge anew. But with these big-bellied things, that hold half a paper of tobacco, you smoke and smoke, and it seems as if you never would stop. You make every place blue, where you go. You go out to feed the pigs in the morning, and it takes you twice as long to do that chore as it used to. You go into the garden to hoe, and you pay more attention to your pipe than you do to your hoe. You stop and squirt around every cabbage as if it was covered with lice, and you don't do an hour's work in the whole morning. The weeds get a start of the cabbage, and your garden looks—well, I can't compare it to anything else but Seth Twiggs in all the world—*weedy*. You go into the field to work on the tobacco, and the worms get the start of you, and what the worms don't kill, the weeds smother, so that your tobacco fields look worse than your garden. I wouldn't have a man on my farm that used to tobacco, at half wages. Now maybe you can see that I don't use tobacco, because you do."

"Yes, I see," said Seth, "and Parson Spooner couldn't have said it better. This has been a dreadful season for weeds."

"Season!" I continued, "don't lay it to the rainy season. This thing grows upon you, and laziness goes down into your bones, as smoke goes up into the heavens. You go about dreaming you're making a great stir, and when night comes you find next to nothing done. Tobacco, like wine, is a mocker, and if a man don't want to be befooled, he'd better not touch it. That is my opinion on tobacco as illustrated in the life and services of Seth Twiggs, the smoker."

Then, to come to the question in the abstract, it is nasty; there is no other word that just expresses it. Don't a man belong by nature to the clean beasts, and what right have I to make myself a nuisance among my kind? It is offensive to every sense. Look into the smoking room of a hotel, or a steamboat, and was there ever a stable fouler?—splashes of juice, ejected quids, cigar stumps, and a reek "that smells to heaven." Wont the world be foul enough without my joining the smokers and chewers?

And it is a very expensive habit. Your tobacco would cost you thirty dollars a year if you did not raise it, and if you take into account your losses of time under the influence of the weed, it costs you four times that sum. You stop to talk with a neighbor, and it makes you long-winded, for your brain is so befuddled that you never know when you have done. Many a man spends fifty dollars a year for cigars, and if one has a good deal of company, it is mighty easy to use up a hundred. Your friend who smokes never knows when he has enough. He always wants one more of the same sort, and the result is, that your box of Havanas is gone mighty quick, and you can't tell how or where. This makes quite a hole in the income of a man who lives by his hands, or by his brains. I have brains enough to see that I can't afford it.

It is very bad for the health. The doctors are all agreed on this, even those who use it. It don't help digestion. It don't save the teeth. There are better ways of reducing the flesh—eating less, for instance. And if the doctors were not all agreed, every man who has his eyes open can see that no man has sound health who uses it in any shape. They call themselves well, but have headaches, indigestion, don't sleep well, are nervous, have the fidgets, or some other complaints. Occasionally they break down under paralysis. Many make complete wrecks of their bodies. Always life is shortened. Now what right have I to make an invalid of myself, and go through life sighing and groaning, when I ought to be well? It is worse for a man's mind than it is for his body. It makes him forgetful. He loses the control of its powers, and can't think connectedly. He forgets the names of persons and places, his own plans, and in short about everything except to smoke. There was our minister, the one we had before Mr. Spooner, smoked himself out of his pulpit. His health failed and his sermons failed worse than his health. They were so foggy that even

Hookertown, that never dismissed a man before, could not stand it any longer.

Then it is a bad thing for morals. It begets a great craving for stimulating drinks, and very generally leads to their use, and when a man gets to drinking, he is in a fair way to do almost any thing else. What right have I to endanger the morals of my neighbor, even if I could smoke with entire safety?

Then I have got children and grandchildren, and I think the best inheritance I can leave them is a good example. John would smoke if I did, and I should have more fears of his pipe in the army, than from all the bullets of the enemy. If he dies now, I am certain he will die sober, and without one vicious habit. What right have I to pollute the faces of my grandchildren with the stench of tobacco? I want them to have pleasant memories of their grandfather's home in Hookertown, and I should not feel sure of it, if I scented myself and my house with tobacco.

Then I am the husband of Sally Bunker, and I think she has the right by marriage vows to a decent companion in life, with a clean mouth and shirt bosom. What right have I to make a nuisance of myself in her home, to scent her bed with this unsavory perfume, and to befoul her spit-boxes with quids and stumps? I am a little too proud to do that.

And lastly, and to conclude, as Mr. Spooner would say, I expect to give an account of myself hereafter, and if I were to be charged with the use of this weed, I should not know exactly what to say. That fifty dollars a year burnt up and wasted, I think would weigh against me. If I gave it for Sunday schools, or for any good cause, I should not be troubled about an answer.

Then as to raising this crop, it is a bad thing for the land, affecting other crops injuriously, so far as I have observed. But if this were not so, I could not tempt my neighbor to use what I would not use myself. When I look at Seth Twiggs' farm and my own, I like the contrast.

Yours to command,
TIMOTHY BUNKER, ESQ.
Hookertown, November 7th, 1863.

NO. 70.—TIM BUNKER'S TRIP TO WASHINGTON.

MR. EDITOR.—Being a modest man I was considerably surprised when I saw in the February *American Agriculturist*, that you had many inquiries after my health. Indeed I was never so much surprised afore, but once, and that was when the people of Hookertown made me a Justice of the Peace—an office that I still hold to the general satisfaction of my fellow citizens—that is, if they don't lie. I wasn't particularly flattered, however, that they should think that I had been sick, as if an honest man had nothing to do in the world but to be sick, or to write for the papers. You see, I hold that a man who comes into the world with a good constitution, (which, by the way, is the richest inheritance parents can leave to their children,) and lives temperately and virtuously, has no business to be sick. If he indulges in drink and tobacco, late hours, and fast living, he is very likely to have fevers, colds, headaches, and all "the ills that flesh is heir to." To hear inquiries about my health looked a leetle as if there was a suspicion that I had been doing something that I ought not to. I am happy to say to your numerous readers, that I have not been robbing hen roosts, and haven't been sick.

And to prevent any anxiety in their minds in the future, in case I don't write, I may as well say that I manage a farm in Hookertown, and *that* is my business, except when I hold a Justice's Court, or something of that kind. A man who is feeding cattle, getting up his winter stock of wood, drawing muck and sea-weed, top-dressing meadows, making compost heaps, relaying wall, and attending a little to the war and politics, can't be expected to write much for the papers.

But last month, ye see, I had a special hindrance, and the way it came about was jest this. Mrs. Bunker was sitting by the fire one evening, reading the paper, when she stopped suddenly, took off those gold-bowed spectacles that Josiah gave her, and laid down the paper, and says she, "Timothy, I want to go to Washington. You see I have been knitting and sewing, drying and brewing, for the soldiers for over two years, and I should like to know where all the things that we have boxed up go to. Some say there is an awful waste of these things,—that the shirts are used for wadding to the cannon, that the wines and cordials go to the well soldiers instead of the sick ones, and the stores of the Sanitary Commission never see the inside of a hospital. I should like to see for myself, and while I am down there I should like to see John." "Agreed," says I, "We'll start for Washington to-morrow."

You see we went down south five years ago, and came home so well satisfied with Hookertown that we have hardly been out of the place since, for more than a day or two at a time. Sally Bunker has been the most contented woman in all my experience from that day to this. I was rather glad when I saw that she had got her mind on a visit. It very soon got wind that we were bound to Washington, and almost all the neighbors brought in their axes to grind, as if I should have nothing to do while I was down there but to turn the grindstone for 'em.

Among others, Jake Frink came, and said he would be much obliged if I would get him appointed keeper of the Hookertown light-house. He said he would take back all the uncivil things he had ever spoken against me, would forget the horse-pond lot, and would admit that I was the best farmer and most straightforward Justice in town. Says I, "No you don't, Jake Frink. That wont go down. But I am willing to lay your case before the President and give him my honest opinion."

It took Mrs. Bunker a week to get started, for she had to go down to Shadtown to see Sally and the grandchildren, as if she wasn't going to see 'em again in a year. We went round outside so as to see the Potomac river, Mount Vernon, and as much of the rebel country as was possible in so short a time. The valley of the Potomac surpassed all our expectations. It is a magnificent region, with every natural facility for agriculture and commerce, and the trades connected with them. We sailed all day up that river without seeing any thing like a village until we reached Alexandria. There were beautiful farming lands, still well wooded, and occasionally a fine planter's mansion, with its group of slave cabins. But for the most part the houses are dilapidated and look forsaken. How rapidly will a change come over this scene, when energetic men take possession, and villages spring up like magic along the banks of this noble river! There ought to have been a half million of people here instead of a handful of planters.

Mrs. Bunker had heard awful stories about the steep prices for board in Washington, six dollars a day at Willard's and hard to get in at that, and was a good deal worried lest the money should give out before we finished our visit. Now you see these high prices are only for the rich ones who don't care, and the green ones who don't know any better. We soon found that Washington is about the best place in the country for people to live independently. In Boston they ask you if you know anything; in New York, how much money you have got; in Philadelphia, who is your father? In Washington, they take you upon trust, until they find you out. As we did not calculate to stay long enough to be found out, it suited us exactly. Your respectability does not depend upon your keeping house, boarding at a hotel, or taking furnished rooms and having meals served to suit your convenience. To people who have backbone and can attend to their own marketing, living is not much dearer than in New York.

I kept my eyes opened while in the Capital, and was astonished to see the enormous waste they make of hay and provisions, and every thing else in this war. One would think that when hay is $30 a ton, they could afford to take care of it, but it is dumped down almost anywhere, and has to take its chances with the weather. Corn and oats fare pretty much in the same way. I judge that musty grain and hay must be plenty in the army. I saw a large herd of government cattle, perhaps fat when they were bought, but they had got to be rather lean looking specimens. Had the Potomac been the Nile, I should have thought of the lean kine of Pharoah. It was suggested by an observer that the purses of contractors were not lean, if the cattle were.

I attended to Jake Frink's business early; I went right round to the White House and found a colored man at the door, and says I, "Is Mr. Lincoln home?" Says he, "The President don't receive calls to-day." "Well," says I, "You jest tell him that 'Squire Bunker of Hookertown wants to see him on a little business." I got in by that trick. I expect he had seen my name in the *Agriculturist*, though I didn't know him from Adam. He received me with a smile in one corner of his mouth, as if I had been an old acquaintance. Says I, "Mr. Lincoln, I hain't got any ax to grind for myself, but one of my neighbors has—wants a light-house, and I promised him when I left home to see you about it." "Well," says the President, "that hardly comes under my direction; I shall have to refer you to the Light-house Department." "Well," says I, "I don't care what you do with it. I want to say that Jake Frink is rather a poor farmer, don't manage his own business well, and I don't think he would manage yours any better. His light don't shine on the farm, and I don't think he would make it shine in a Light-house." "'Squire Bunker, you are a brick, but you don't understand the way they do business. *If a man can't do any thing for himself, he thinks he is just fit to manage Uncle Sam's business.* I will give you, 'Squire Bunker, the Light-house in Hookertown, with great pleasure." I assured the President that I was still acting as Justice of the Peace, and should have to decline the honor.

Yours to command,

TIMOTHY BUNKER, ESQ.,

Hookertown, Feb. 10th, 1864.

NO. 71.—TIM BUNKER ON THE SANITARY COMMISSION AND THE WAR.

MR. EDITOR.—I was astonished to hear from your note of yesterday that there had been some considerable inquiry, if not more, about my not writing for the paper so much as common. I take the first leisure day I have had in four months to tell you all about it. You see, I always had my hands full to keep up with my farming and writing, and attending to the duties of Justice of the Peace, before John went to the war. You see, the boy had got to be mighty handy about every thing, from yoking a steer, to mending a broken window or cleaning a clock. And when he turned soldier, every little thing that the boy used to do fell back into my hands, and come to pile this on top of Court duties, and war and politics, I have hardly had time to find out whether my soul was my own or not. I rather guess 'tis, however, at least enough of it to give you a bit of my mind on the topics at the head of this letter.

You see, when I last wrote, I left off in the White House, a place that many a smart man, (and some that aren't so smart) has been crazy to get into, and never fetched. When I got home Jake Frink wanted to know if I had done his errand. I told him I thought I had done it up brown, and if he didn't believe it he might see just what I said in the papers. You see, he hasn't been into our house since. That is the way with some folks; you may do your best to serve 'em, and they will treat you with the blackest ingratitude and neglect. Somehow it hasn't been particularly lonesome at our house, though Jake hasn't called as usual. I hadn't time in my last letter to tell you about the Sanitary Commission business. You see, that was about half that took Mrs. Bunker to Washington; the other half was John, for I must own she has considerable of a woman's weakness about her. She is such a prudent sort of a woman in her own household that she can't bear to see a bit of anything wasted. Our dog was always *lean* when we kept one, for all the scraps went into the swill-pail for the pigs. Finally, she thought dogs didn't pay, and as I couldn't gainsay that opinion our dog turned up missing one night. As I noticed an uncommon bleating of sheep and skipping of lambs the next time I went to salt the flock, I kind of thought they had got the news and was holding a sort of Thanksgiving. The cats caught mice and fared better. Now, you see, Mrs. Bunker thought that her notions of economy and saving ought to be carried into all public matters. She said, "Gather up the fragments that nothing be lost," ought to be written as a frontispiece over the door of every public building and hospital in Washington, and everywhere else. Now there are a set of busybodies, who have nothing else to do but to find fault with the management of all public concerns, from the President's business down to the Justice's Court in Hookertown. They have sometimes criticized my judgments, though I never had an opinion reversed by a higher court since I sat upon the bench. You see, these idle folks—chaps like Jake Frink—would say, "it was no sort of use to send any thing to the soldiers, for it wasn't half the time they got any thing when it was sent. A good deal of it was stolen, lots of things were smashed by the Express Companies, and the jellies and jams got jammed into the wrong stomachs." You see, these stories worried my wife just as bad as if the milk was souring in her own pantry in dog-days. They didn't worry me much, for I always noticed that the folks who grumbled most about the Sanitary stores spoiling, were the very ones who hadn't given a red cent to buy them. A precious little Jake Frink and company care about the soldiers! He never gave a dime for Sanitary stores.

Well, you see, nothing would satisfy the woman, but she must go and see that nothing was wasted, and when she came to hear that John was wounded it brought matters to a focus, as Mr. Spooner would say, and we set right out for Washington. The hospitals about that city are about as thick as hay-cocks in a meadow on a summer afternoon, and it takes one near a week to see 'em all and find out all the particulars. Mrs. Bunker went into them about as thorough as if she was house-cleaning, and I guess the nurses thought the Inspector General had sent an agent to pry into things generally. She wanted to know if the things come straight, that had been sent to them by express from Hookertown, for she knew what the Sewing Society had sent, as she was one of the directresses, and packed up pretty much all herself. There were shirts and drawers, socks and blankets, cushions, ticks and sheets, pillow-cases, quilts and comfortables, and pretty much every thing that a sick man could wear or use on a bed. There were preserves in every variety, sugar, tea and coffee, candles, soap and towels, tin plates, basins and lanterns, etc.,—six barrels and nine boxes packed jam full. Now it so happened that the Hookertown supplies were on hand, and she had the satisfaction of seeing that everything had come straight. All the nurses agreed that the express folks brought things very carefully, and many of them would not take any pay for the trouble. Mrs. Bunker was astonished to find everything so neat and clean. When she went into the Columbian College Hospital and saw the doctor and his wife, and the motherly looking women that were nursing the soldiers, and the nice beds and the scrubbed floors, she declared it was equal to any thing in Connecticut housekeeping, which she thinks is about the limit of perfection. The Sunday after she got home, she looked up from the Bible where she was reading, and taking off the gold-bowed spectacles that Josiah gave her, she said, "Timothy, I declare, I used to think David was rather hard on mankind when he says, 'All men are liars.' But since I went down to Washington and saw how they lied about the Sanitary Commission, I think he wa'n't much out of the way. Things down there could not have been better managed if I had done it myself." I guess she is about right, and folks need not be afraid of doing too much for our soldiers. The poor fellows are fighting our battles, and we ought to do every thing we can for them when they are sick and wounded. Three years fighting has not made us poor; we have only grown rich and saucy. Hookertown is as chockful of fight as ever. We have some soldiers' graves among us, and some in old Virginia, and by the bones of our honored dead we are going to see this thing fought straight through.

Yours to command,

TIMOTHY BUNKER, ESQ.

Hookertown, Oct. 5th, 1864.

NO. 72.—TIM BUNKER'S RAID AMONG THE PICKLE PATCHES.

MR. EDITOR:—"What is in the wind now?" asked Seth Twiggs, as Mrs. Bunker and I started off down the Shadtown road.

"Smoke," said I, as Seth pulled out his stump of a pipe, and blew a puff into the air like a small locomotive just firing up. Old Black Hawk has n't been used much lately, and he went off considerable gay, as we struck the turnpike on Seth Twiggs' corner. Seth did not follow his big-bellied Dutch pipe a great while, but fell back upon his own tried and trusty clay stump. It is mighty hard for old dogs to learn new tricks, and Seth is one of 'em. My letter agin tobacco didn't have any more effect on him, than peas rattling on a tin pan.

"Well, I didn't mean that," said Seth. "Where are you gwine?"

"I am going down to Shadtown, to take the boat," said I.

"Then where?" asked Seth, perseveringly.

"And then to New York, and up into Westchester county, visiting. And if any of the neighbors get into a quarrel, jest tell 'em they'd better make up, for I shan't be back under a week, and there won't be any Court."

You see the way it came about was this:—Sally got a letter a few weeks ago from her cousin, who married Noadiah Tubbs, thirty years ago, and moved off to Westchester. Cousin Esther and Sally used to be about as thick as blackbirds in the pie, before they were married, but haven't met often of late. She hadn't more than read the letter, when she said:

"Timothy, it is a dozen years since I have seen Esther, and she used to be the best friend I had before I found you. And if you feel as if you could spare the time, I should like to go down and see her this winter."

"Agreed," says I. And we got ready and started off the next week.

Noadiah Tubbs (they call him Diah, for short, and sometimes, Uncle Di,) lives on the banks of the Bronx, about a dozen miles from the city. He is what they call in Hookertown a case, or hard customer. How in this world Esther came to marry him I never could see, and I am a little more than ever in the dark about it since our visit. Perhaps he's grown worse since he got married, or else I've grown better. I ought to be a good deal better after living so many years with Sally Bunker. At any rate, Diah and I seemed to be farther apart than ever. Why! the creature don't go to meeting more'n once a year, and then it is when he is going to be put up for representative or sheriff, when he thinks, may be, he'll get a few votes from church people, if he goes to meeting. I am sorry to say there is rather a bad state of morals all round Diah's neighborhood. The Westchester sinners, from what I see of 'em, are not a bit better than Hookertown sinners. The folks don't seem to have much idea of Sunday, except as a day of visiting, hunting, and fishing. Rum-holes are plenty, and I guess this state of morals accounts partly for the fact that Diah Tubbs has so run down to the heel.

But you need not suppose that Uncle Di is a fool, because he uses rather coarse language, and goes to the tavern oftener than he ought to. He is a pretty fair farmer, or would have been called so a dozen years ago. He knows a heap about raising cucumbers, which they call pickles in all this region. Whether they have heard that the world uses any thing else besides cucumbers for pickles, I could'nt say. I used to think, before I took to writing for the paper, that I had learned about all I could on farming matters, but I find, as I go about, that every region has some new kink in farming, some special crop that I've never paid much attention to. All around Diah's they grow cucumbers by the thousand. Almost every farmer near a railroad depot puts in an acre or two, and gets about as much clean cash from the patch as he does from the rest of the farm.

I see very soon that Uncle Di knew some things that I did n't, and as I wanted to learn, I got him started the first evening after I got to his house, on his favorite topic, raising pickles. There was a large dish of apples on the table when we begun, but not many of 'em left when we got through. Says I, "What do your folks call this the pickle crop for?"

"Wall," said Diah, "I don't zacktly know, but guess it's 'cause it's shorter than cowcumber. May be it's 'cause they grow 'em more for the pickle factories than to eat up fresh."

"Do they have *factories* for this business?"

"Sartain, big five-story house over the river, where they make 'em up by the million."

"And how many pickles do you suppose they raise in your town?"

"Wal, I could not tell, but it is an awful sight—enough to sour the crop of all creation, you'd think, if you should happen to be here in August, and see 'em going down to the depot. Most èvery farmer goes into it more or less, and would raise a great many more if he could get help just when he wanted it."

"How do you prepare the land for this crop?"

"Wal, there ain't much of a knack about that. I fix it pretty much as I would for corn, only I take more pains to make it mellow and light. If a green sward, it must be harrowed thoroughly, and the lighter you leave it the better."

"Is there any particular advantage in having the land fresh?"

"I never could see as it made much difference. Neighbor Bussing has 'em on the same land sometimes three years running. I 'spect more 'pends upon the dung than any thing else, and where you have pickles, you calculate to manure pretty high, and a good deal is left over for the second year."

"What kind of manure do you use?"

"Any I happen to have in the yard. It wants to be well rotted, and if ain't fine I fork it over until I make it so. Coarse stuff won't answer."

"How much, and how do you apply it?"

"If I have plenty of manure, and I believe in that article if I don't in any thing else, I spread on a good lot broadcast, and plow it in. I don't 'spose the crop gets the whole the first year. Then I put a good heapin' shovel-full in the hill."

"And how far apart are the hills?"

"I run the furrows pretty deep, just four and a half feet apart both ways, and make the hill at the crossing. One man drops the manure, and another follows with a hoe, mixing it a little with the soil, and covering it an inch or two."

"What time do you plant?"

"When I raise for nothing but pickles, I plant about the last week in June."

"Suppose it is a dry time. What then?"

"I give the manure a good soaking. It is pretty important to have the seed come right up. You see, the cowcumber is of such a nature that if it gets sot, it is of no use to try to start 'em. You must push 'em right along."

"And what variety do you plant?"

"We ain't got any pertikelar name for 'em. They ain't Clusters, nor London Greens, nor Russians. I guess they are a sort of mixture, for every man raises his own seed."

"Is there any particular knack in doing that?"

"Yes, there is. More 'n half the battle lies in raising the seed. I tried some seed I got in the city once, and didn't have any luck at all. It won't do to take the odds and ends for seed. If you want a lot of pot-bellies and nubbins, plant the seed of such, and you'll get 'em. I generally take the cucumbers that grow on the second and third joint, and let them ripen for seed, and don't allow any body else to see 'em. I put 'em where I can find 'em in the summer."

"How many do you have in a hill?"

"I plant from five to ten, and thin out at hoeing time to five or six."

"How many times do you hoe?"

"I cultivate and hoe but once, and it is pretty important that that should be done at just the right time. A day too late makes a great deal of extra work. I run a plow about three times between the rows just before the vines fall over and begin to run, then dress out with a hoe."

But I see that I can't tell you all that Uncle Diah said in this letter, and if your readers' teeth are not all set on edge, next month I'll give 'em some more pickles.

Yours to command,

TIMOTHY BUNKER, ESQ.,

Hookertown, Jan. 5th, 1865.

NO. 73.—TIM BUNKER'S RAID AMONG THE PICKLE PATCHES.—(*Concluded.*)

MR. EDITOR:—I began to give you some account last month about the way Noadiah Tubbs raised pickles up in Westchester County. I wanted your readers to hear him out, for when you get an old farmer to talking on a subject that he feels at home in, he always has something to say worth hearing. Daniel Webster learned something about growing turnips from the farmers of Old England, and a very plain boatman taught him in cod-fishing. Diah's morals don't exactly square with my notions, but I am willing to own that he knows more than I do about raising pickles. So you may just imagine that he sits there cocked up in his flag-bottomed chair in the corner, squirting tobacco juice into the sanded spit-box and "pickle eddication" into Tim Bunker.

"I wonder you don't cultivate your crop more; what is the reason?"

"Wal," said Diah, "There's two or three reasons. You see, you don't plow the ground till the weediest part of the season is over, about July 1st. Then the cultivating comes along the last of the month, and before it is time to cultivate agin, the vines are in the way. And besides, I allers sow turnips at the time of cultivating, to take the ground when the vines have done bearing. And in this way I often get a half crop of turnips and kill two birds with one stone, if not more; for the turnips take the place of weeds, don't tax the ground any more, and are a great deal better for the cattle."

"I hadn't thought of that, I declare! When do you begin to pick pickles?"

"It won't vary much from six weeks from the time of plantin."

"And how long does the season last?"

"It will hold on for six weeks or more, until frost comes sometimes."

"What do you do to keep the bugs off? I am always pestered to death with bugs on my vines."

"That is pretty easily managed where you have so many vines. Bugs might easily eat up a dozen hills in a garden where they would more'n have their mouths full in a two-acre lot. I generally sprinkle on a little plaster as soon as they get up in sight, and if this don't stop the bugs I go over them once or twice more. The plaster is good manure for 'em any way, and I s'pose a pinch of guanner in it would be better still. If I had hen manure plenty I should jest as lives have that. I calculate to keep the vines growing so fast that the bugs can't catch 'em."

"That's a good idea. I s'pose that accounts for the fact that we don't see so many vines destroyed in wet seasons as in dry. I never thought of that before. Now I should like to know a little about marketing the pickles, and as them apples are gittin rather low I'll let you rest."

"I ginerally make a market for 'em with some pickle maker in the city or over on the North River. He agrees to take 'em delivered at the depot at so much a thousand—assorted in barrels. We make three sizes. The big ones are for eating fresh, and I s'pose are sold in market by the pickle men for that purpose. The other two sizes are just the thing for pickles, and go to the factory. These are the fellers you see in jars in all the corner grocery stores. We pick all sizes together, and carry them to some convenient place under a shed, at the edge of the pickle patch, and there they are sorted and put in barrels and sent off to market."

"How often do you have to pick 'em?"

"Every other day is the rule. But sometimes a rainy day comes and stops the picking, which makes trouble. The pickles git a great deal bigger and it takes about a third more barrels to hold 'em, and you don't git any thing extra for your trouble. Some folks stop for Sunday, but that don't make any difference with me. I never could see but what pickles pick'd Sunday brought jest as good money as any other."

"Wal, now, I don't believe that suits Esther."

"No, it don't. She and the parson and all the children have a runnin' fight with me on that subject."

"I guess when you come to foot the bills in the final account, you'll find that all the money you've made by Sunday work has burnt a hole in your pocket and dropped out. But how many men does it take to attend to a pickle patch?"

"You ought to have at least four to the acre, and they'll have to be pretty smart to keep up with the work. It is hard on the back until you get used to it. You can work in boys pretty well, as they don't have so far to bend. You want to pick one-half of the patch one day, and the other half the next, and so on."

"What do you make your shed out of?"

"Most any thing will do for that. Four crotched sticks and two poles with rails laid across, and buckwheat straw or any refuse hay put on to make a cover and shed rain, will answer very well."

"How many pickles can you raise on an acre?"

"Well, there is about as much difference in pickles as there is in any thing else. Your success depends some on good seed, some on manure, and some on care, and a good deal on luck."

"Just what do you mean by luck?"

"It's what man hasn't any thing to do with. Some would call it the season, and some Providence. I call it luck."

"I guess there is a Providence in the pickle crop as in every thing else, and if the Almighty don't send rain, you'll come out at the little end of the horn."

"Well, it may be so. If every thing works right you may calculate on getting about three hundred thousand pickles to the acre. Sometimes I have known 'em to get four, but they must manure high and have uncommon good luck to do that. A good many fall short because they don't understand the business."

"About what do you get for your crop, taking them by the season?"

"I sold them last year for fourteen shillings a thousand, but some got as high as two dollars. I calculate I got a thousand dollars for my two acres, and the expenses were less than four hundred, and I had to hire every bit of labor. With good management and luck I should say a man might clear about three hundred dollars to the acre, to say nothing of the turnips, which come mighty handy."

"And what is the effect of the crop on the land? For I find that is a matter to be taken into the account. Some crops run the land terrible hard, and if you don't manure high, they'll make a desert of it."

"That's so. Tobacco, for instance. I've tried it time and agin, and it like to have spiled my farm. It took about all the manure I could rake and scrape for two acres of tobacco, and the rest of the land went dry. It aint so with pickles. They are pretty much all water, and a good deal of the strength of the manure goes over to the next crop. Then if they are well attended to, they leave the ground pretty clean. You see the weeds are all turned under the last of June, and agin when you cultivate the last of July. Then the turnips sown between the rows get the start of the weeds, and when these are pulled in November, you have a pretty clean field; I have allers noticed that grass and almost any other crop did well after pickles."

Esther's apple dish got low about this time and Diah's pond of pickle knowledge was in the same condition. I pumped him dry. Yours to command,

Hookertown, Feb. 10, 1865. TIMOTHY BUNKER, ESQ.

NO. 74.—TIM BUNKER ON "STRIKING ILE."

"Have you hee'rn the news, 'Squire Bunker?" asked Jake Frink, as he came into our house last evening, after a long absence.

You see, Jake has been mighty shy of our house ever since my trip to Washington, and the upsetting of his light-house, etc. It took some great excitement like the present oil fever to bring him round.

"No, I haven't. It is the latest news, neighbor Frink, to see you here. You're welcome."

"Wal," says Jake, "they du say that Deacon Smith has made five thousand dollars on ile within the last few weeks."

"And how did that happen?"

"It didn't happen at all. He made it by speculation in ile stocks. Ye see, he and a few men in Wall-street bought a lot of land for forty thousand dollars, and then bought an ile well, jest to sweeten it, and sold out sheers enuff to come to a quarter of a million, and talked about a working capital of a hundred thousand dollars, and all the work that capital did was jest tu work money intu their own pockets, and the Deacon's share of the spiles was five thousand dollars. I guess I shall want to hear the Deacon pray arter this!"

"Hear him pray!" exclaimed Sally, taking off her gold-bowed spectacles. "Little chance of that, Jake, for you haven't been inside of a meeting-house in a year."

Jake did not heed that shot, but proceeded.

"Now I should like to know, Squire Bunker, whether there is anything in this ile business, or whether it is all bosh. Did you see any ile when you was in the city?"

"Lots of it, neighbor Frink, and heard a great deal

more than I saw. There is no kind of doubt that the bowels of the earth is full of ile."

"And do you suppose, Timothy, it is prepared for the great conflagration of which the Bible speaks?" interrupted Mrs. Bunker.

"I couldn't say as to that. I guess it will light up a good many parlors and kitchens before it will help burn up the world. You'd be astonished to see the quantity that comes into the city from the West, and the quantity that goes out of it to the East. Why, what a change it has made in all our houses! Just think of the different sorts of lights we have had since we went to housekeeping! Tallow candles, with tow wicks that you used to spin from the tow from my hatchel, dipped in tallow about Christmas; then candles with cotton wicks, and run in moulds, six in a bunch; then whale oil lamps; then camphene and burning fluid, and lastly, kerosene, the best of all."

"Du tell if kerosene is the same thing that comes out of the ile wells! I thought they called it ketrolum, or some sich name."

"That is it, neighbor Frink, only kerosene is Petroleum, after it is purified at the factories."

"Wall, neow, du ye think there is any chance for me to make money easy in these ile companies?"

"I shall have to say yes and no according to circumstances; just as I would say about gold mining. There is, no doubt, plenty of gold in California, Idaho, and the Rocky Mountains in general. But it is my private opinion, that if all the money and labor expended in those regions had been applied to the soil in regular farming, or other common industrial pursuits, they would have produced more property and more happiness than can be found in those countries now. A few lucky adventurers have made fortunes, but the most who have gone thither have either failed, or got a bare support. Thousands upon thousands have lost capital and labor, and life itself, in the vain pursuit of sudden riches."

"I'm sorry to hear you talk so, Squire. Ye see I have tried the plan of slow riches for more 'n forty years, and it's no go. I've dug airly and late, and stuck tew my business as close as the next man, and I aint out of debt yit. And now if you say there is no chance for sudden riches, I am done for."

"Perhaps if you had stuck to the farm more and to the bottle less, the result might have been different."—"I don't see that," said Jake, gruffly.

"Well, your neighbors do, and it is no use to try to shift off the faults of the man upon the farm, or the business of farming. Nothing pays better in the long run. There is money in ile, just as there is in gold, only the ile business is not quite so risky. To those who know the ropes, I suppose there isn't any risk at all. The men who buy the land, and get up the companies, as a rule, make money. In the present fever heat of the business, there is no trouble about selling shares, and they mean to sell enough to pay for the land, and line their own pockets, whether they ever strike a drop of ile or not. If they are fortunate enough to strike ile, they make a good thing for their shareholders. If they do not, their stock is not worth a chaw of tobacco. They do not tell that it costs four or five thousand dollars to sink a well, and that thousands of these wells are bored without ever returning a red cent for the labor. They do not tell how many wells yield lots at first, and, after a while, 'kind o' gin out,' like the Paddy's calf. And what is a hundred acres of land worth, with a dozen dry wells on it?"

It is astonishing, Mr. Editor, to see how crazy people are getting on this subject. The Multicaulis fever, thirty years ago, wa'n't a priming to this. When I went through your city a few weeks ago, I did not hear much of any thing else talked about. The war was nowhere, dry goods didn't amount to much, and I couldn't get even a butcher to talk of beef cattle more than five minutes. Every old acquaintance I met offered me oil stocks, as if it was a medicine and I was ailing badly. I was told they were going to get up an exchange on purpose to sell ile stocks. The papers were all full of it, advertising companies with a capital anywhere from a quarter of a million up to ten millions. And it is not much better out here in the country. These things are advertised in the religious papers, holding out to everybody the prospect of sudden riches. The women get hold of the papers and read these advertisements just as if they were law and gospel, being in a religious paper, and indorsed by the editors, you see. I am afraid they read more about ile than they do about religion. It does seem as if everybody's face was shining with ile. They get all stirred up, and half the time forget to wash the dishes, or get the dinner into the wrong pot. They carry the matter to the minister, as they do all their other troubles, and he thinks there may be something in it. Then they tease their husbands to buy stock, and dream of rivers of ile and fine houses. "What is the use of scrubbing away at the wash-tub, or grubbing with a hoe, when you can have somebody pump money into your pocket just as easy as you pump water into a pail?"

Now you see, Mr. Editor, this business has gone about far enough. It is unsettling the foundations, as Mr. Spooner would say. It is well enough for people who have got money to throw away, to go into these speculations. They may make a heap of money, and they may lose every cent. Farmers, generally, are not of this class. There is nothing we want so much as more capital in *our* business. If I put a hundred dollars into tile drains, or into a mowing machine, or a stone digger, I am sure to get a good dividend. If I put it into ile stock, I may get three per cent a month, but more likely I shall not get three cents in as many years. Keep your capital where you can watch it. Drive at your business, if you would prosper. In farming, there is no ile like elbow grease.

Yours to command,

TIMOTHY BUNKER, ESQ.

Hookertown, March 10, 1865.

NO. 75.—TIM BUNKER'S VISIT TO TITUS OAKS, ESQ.

MR. EDITOR:—You see I hadn't more than got done with Diah Tubbs and his pickle patch, when I begun to grow uneasy for something else to talk about. Some folks can set round the fire and talk with the women all day, but I never could do up my visiting in that way. I knew I had got about all out of Uncle Di in one evening that I should get out of him if I pumped him till doomsday. So the next morning, after breakfast, I begun to inquire about the neighboring country and farmers. Says I,

"Uncle Di, your Westchester county is a great country. I have heard of it clear up in Connecticut. You ought to have some smart farmers round here that go in for fancy stock."

"Jest so. We have lots on 'em. Fellers that got rich in the city, and come out here and spend their money and call it high farming. I'll bet you a shad, every potato they raise costs 'em a dollar."

"How do you make that out?"

"Wal, ye see, they take perticuler pains to buy the roughest, stoniest place they can find, and next see how much money they can bury up in it. They blow rocks, tear down hills, drain swamps, fill up ponds that is, and dig ponds that ain't, and call 'em lakes; cut down trees that are stannin, and plant trees where there aint none; put the surface sile down to the bottom, and bring up the yaller dirt for the sake of making it black, and raise Hob generally with the land before they plant it. Here is Squire Oaks, jest above me, that has been rippin and tearin with his land for a dozen years and more, and I guess every acre he's got has cost him tew hundred dollars, if not more, and I can beat him on pickles, with all his manure and subsoiling."

"Well, now, 'spose we hitch up and go over and see Squire Oaks' place this morning. I want to learn something to carry back to Hookertown."

"What do you say, Esther?" inquired Uncle Di, looking up to headquarters.

"I think," says Mrs. Tubbs, "that Sally would like to see one of our country seats. Mr. Oaks has a fine conservatory, and the flowers are very attractive this winter." So it was arranged that we should visit the country seat of Titus Oaks, Esq., in full force.

I expected to find a man, city bred, with gloves on, and stove-pipe hat, and gold-headed cane, ordering men round, right and left. Instead of that, I found a man that might have been taken for a native of Hookertown, any where on Connecticut soil, and driving away at the dirt and stone, as if he wa'n't afraid of them.

"Good morning," said I, "Squire Oaks. I am glad to find a Justice of the Peace in these parts. I have thought that such an officer must have a good deal to do in this region."

"You were never more mistaken in your life," he replied. "They call me Squire, but I have no more claim to the title than my Alderney bull. The office must have been abolished some time ago around here. Every man does about what is right in his own eyes."

"Excuse me, sir, I do not like to hear a man speak evil of his birth-place."

"Praise the Lord, I was born in New-England, where a 'Squire' meant something, and scoundrels got their dues."

"Now, Squire," said I, "what have you got to show us? Any new notions around?"

"I tried an experiment last year on

CURING CLOVER HAY

and I would like to show you the result."

He took us out to the barn and showed us a bay, perhaps twelve by thirty feet, from which he was feeding his Alderney herd. It was well filled with as handsome clover as I ever saw. If I was not afraid of having my word doubted, I should say the handsomest. It was cut down in the middle with a hay knife, and you could see just how it was managed. There was about ten inches of clover, and then about two inches of old salt hay, in alternate layers. The clover had all the leaves on, nearly, and was as bright and green as on the day it was put in the barn. To show that the hay was as good as it looked, Squire Oaks pulled out a lock of it, and also a handful of Timothy from the opposite mow, and presented both to an old cow. She smelled of the Timothy first, and then opened her mouth for the clover, without stopping to take a second sniff. The same was done to an Alderney heifer, who might not be supposed to be so well versed in hay lore, with a like result. There was no mistake. It was tip-top clover.

"Now," says I, "Squire, how did you cure it? For this will do to tell in Hookertown."

"It is the easiest thing in the world," says he. "I cut the clover with a mower, when it was just in blossom, and let it lie in the sun till wilted. I then put it in cocks, and let it stand until the next day, when I put it into the barn. There was first a layer of salt hay, rather thin, then a thick layer of clover. It comes out just as you see it. I think one ton of that clover is worth two of hay, as it is usually cured. All the leaves and all the juices are there.

The salt hay, somehow, helps cure it. I do not attempt to explain the philosophy of it."

Farmers who have old stacks of this hay, and heaps of refuse straw about the barn, should save them, and try Squire Oaks' experiment. I guess there is more virtue in the dry hay than in the salt. It helps the ventilation, and makes the curing complete.

A NEW MULCH FOR STRAWBERRIES was shown us in the garden. This consisted of sods from a brake swamp, cut an inch or two thick, with a spade, so that they could be laid between the rows. He had been draining a piece of wet land, and had a plenty of these on hand. When fresh cut, they are free from seeds of weeds, and so sour that nothing will grow on them the first season. They are easily handled, keep the ground moist, and the berries clean. After a year's exposure, they may be spaded in, or removed to the manure heap.

TRELLIS FOR GRAPES.—Mr. Oaks has turned his ledges to good account in training grape vines all over them, by means of wires. These ledges, some of them, present a bare surface, of twenty or thirty feet, and as he could not very well remove them, he covers them with a mantle of green in summer, and has the purple clusters in autumn. This is a timely hint for the multitude of improvers in Westchester county and elsewhere, who are troubled with ledges. They were made on purpose for grapes.

HOW NATURE PLANTS A TREE.—He showed us an apple tree planted on Nature's plan—*i. e.*, as near to the surface as you can get it,—and a *spot* where a tree was planted on some gardener's plan burying the roots in a deep hole. The latter spot was vacant, while the tree was flourishing, and had made a very broad collar just above the surface of the soil. Titus Oaks, Esq., laid very great stress upon this mode of planting. "Nature," says he, "in growing an apple tree, first runs the seed through a cow's stomach, and deposits it in a thick vegetable paste, upon the surface of the earth, or a little above it. The following spring the seed sprouts and the roots find their way into the earth. Such trees make the hardiest stocks, and are the longest lived."

An Orchard upon a Gravel Bed.—This he regarded as one of the triumphs of his art. There was no mistake about the poverty of the soil, for it was made up of sand and gravel, as the adjoining bank showed. No one had ever got a crop from it before. There was just as little mistake about the apple trees. They were very thrifty, well grown trees, and fruitful. The gravel bed had been treated with muck from an adjoining pond. That was the secret.

We left, highly pleased with Titus Oaks, Esq., and his notions. He made us promise that we would not mention his name in connection with his improvements, a promise which we keep by taking his light out from under his bushel, and putting it upon your candlestick.

Yours to command,

Timothy Bunker, Esq.

Hookertown, April 1, 1865.

NO. 76.—TIM BUNKER ON THE PICKLE FEVER IN HOOKERTOWN.

Mr. Editor:—"I knew it would be so," said Mrs. Bunker, raising the gold-bowed spectacles from her eyes, as I came home from holding Court one night, "I knew it would be so. That paper is just like a whispering gallery, Timothy. Every thing you do and say in Hookertown is echoed from one end of the land to the other. Since you have been gone, three letters have come about pickles, and Seth Twiggs and Jake Frink have been in, and I guess Mr. Spooner has a touch of the fever, for he preached Sunday about the 'Lodge in a Garden of Cucumbers.'"

I had not more than got done supper when Seth Twiggs made his appearance in a cloud of very blue smoke, and he had n't got the first question fairly out before Jake Frink and Kier from the White Oaks knocked at the door, and Dea. Smith and Jeremiah Sparrowgrass followed. Thinks I to myself, I guess I shall have a meetin' tonight, whether the minister does or not. It was lecture night, and I suppose the Deacon stopped in on his way. I am afraid he did n't hear the bell, for he did n't start when it had done tolling.

"Now," said Seth Twiggs, bringing his pipe down on his knee with an emphasis that would have smashed it if had been worth anything, "Du ye really think three hundred dollars can be made on an acre of good Hookertown meadow, in pickles?"

"Is it clean cash?" asked Jake Frink with a dubious look. "Them fellers as deals in pickles is apt to be kind of sharp."

"Du ye think there is any chance for us up in White Oaks, 'Squire, to go into pickle business?" inquired Kier Frink, the hopeful son of Jake.

"Fellow-citizens," says I, "don't all talk at once, and I'll try and answer your questions. I've got three letters come in to-day's mail, on the pickle business, and I haven't had time to digest them yet. The policy of going into the cucumber trade depends altogether upon the facility of a market. You might grow cucumbers well enough in Iowa, but if you had to send them to New York to market, it would n't pay very well even at two dollars a hundred. A man must be within a short distance of a pickle factory if he purposes to deliver his crop from his own market wagon, or within easy reach of the factory by rail or steamer. Steamboat carriage is better and cheaper than railroad. Twenty-five cents freight on a barrel, probably, would not interfere with reasonable profits. The pay of the pickle men is as good as that of any other class of manufacturers. There are few in the business; their profits are supposed to be large. It is ready pay and clean cash, if you make that bargain with them. Pay as you go is the rule in pretty much all kinds of business now. That is one of the advantages of the war. A good many other folks besides the rebels have found out just where they stand."

"Where can we get seed?" asked Dea. Smith.

"That is one of the most important things in the business. I do not know of any one who makes a business of growing the seed to sell, but almost every farmer who has a pickle patch grows his own seed, and thinks it a little better than any thing else. If a man is going into the pickle business, it will pay him to visit Westchester County. He can hardly go amiss of farmers who have pickle patches in Yonkers, East Chester, West Chester, West Farms, and other towns. He can inquire for Noadiah Tubbs, who will tell him all about it. If he does not want to be at that trouble, he should send to the nearest good seed store. I have raised fine cucumbers from just such seed."

"Do you salt the cucumbers before you sell them?" inquired Sparrowgrass, with a refreshing greenness.

"No, Sir. That is the manufacturer's business. He wants fresh picked cucumbers to make pickles out of. Of course you do not want tight oak barrels, like whiskey casks, to pack your cucumbers in. The farmer generally buys up a lot of cheap flour barrels, when he is in town, at the baker's or grocer's, or at the hotel, and these, with a little coopering, will answer his purpose for a single season. They are sent to the purchaser or consignee, by rail or boat, full of cucumbers, and sent back empty by the same conveyance. The owner's name or initials should be put upon them."

"What sort of a bargain does the farmer make with the pickle man?" asked Seth Twiggs.

"That is just as he can light upon chances. If he is near the factory, he agrees to deliver at so much per thousand. If he sends by other conveyance, he agrees to deliver them at the nearest depot, or landing, or to pay the freight clear through, as the case may be. The terms will vary according to circumstances. Some prefer to send their crop to a commission merchant and run the risk of the markets."

"How about sorting?" asked Kier Frink.

"They commonly have a shed or hovel for this purpose where all the cucumbers are brought as fast as picked, and are assorted into three sizes, the largest for eating, and the two smaller for pickles. The 'nubbins' and 'yellow boys' will have to be thrown away or the pickle man will do it for you. If picked regularly, however, there will not be many unmerchantable."

One of my correspondents wants to know if night soil is good manure for this crop. He says: "I have got 261 one-horse loads of night soil; about three-fourths of it is composted with muck, and the other fourth is almost the pure article. Shall I plow in the former, and put half a shovelfull of the latter into the hill? My land is a clay loam—is that right?"

The trouble with the pure article is that it is quite too strong, and would be likely to rot the seed unless great pains were taken to mix it with the soil at the time of planting. I should prefer the compost in the hill, and either compost the rest or spread it, and plow it in. Such a quantity of night soil ought to put four acres in good condition. As to the preparation of land, look at Diah Tubbs' views in back numbers of the *Agriculturist.* A sandy loam is considered the best for all kinds of vines, but heavy crops are grown on clay lands. With night soil good pickles can be raised on any well-drained land.

He also wants to know who are reliable men engaged in this business. In Wilson's Business Directory he will find a list of pickle dealers, the most of whom have factories either in the city or out of town. Provost & Wells have a factory at West Mt. Vernon, and Broadmeadow & Stout at Dobbs' Ferry. The business is in very few hands, and judging from the large advance made upon the raw article, must yield a fair profit. Probably there is room for the enlargement of the business and for new men to make a living. Every man must judge for himself whom to deal with, and whether the pickle business will pay.

Yours to command,

TIMOTHY BUNKER, ESQ.

Hookertown, May 10, 1865.

NO. 77.—TIM BUNKER ON CURING PICKLES AND EATING THEM.

MR. EDITOR:—"It beats all what a fuss folks are making about pickles," said Seth Twiggs, walking into our house one hot July night, and taking his seat on the settee, where he was soon lost in his favorite cloud of smoke. "One would think," he continued, "that cucumbers was a new crop just imported from China, or some other furreign parts, insted of bein as old as the Bible. They're havin' a run about equal to Multicaulis and Rohan potato, I'm bound to say."

Speaking of Seth Twiggs' smoking, reminds me that I owe an apology to your readers, perhaps, to all the anti-tobacco part of them in particular, that I have said so much about his habit. For you see the thing is mighty catching. No sooner had I got the fashion set in the *Agriculturist* than all the letter writers in the political papers took it up, and every time they bring out their hero, General Grant, they must tell just how many times and how he smokes. You see, the General has not made his appearance in public since he got to be a great man without his cigar. The public are supposed to be interested in knowing just the length of his cigar, whether it is a long nine or not, its color, its cost, and the particular brand the General uses. Jake Frink says, "the tobacco men have bought up the General or his letter writer, and all this fuss about his smoking is an advertising dodge to get their cigars into market. It is a mean abolishun trick to raise the price of tobacco, and he 'spects it'll git to be so high that common folks can't have a chaw except on Fourth of July, or some sich special occasion."

I think there is considerable sense in what Jake says. Hookertown don't care a rush whether the General smokes or not, whether he smokes dollar cigars or steeped cabbage leaves, whether he smokes quietly or puffs away like a locomotive. The General's business has been fighting, I take it, for the last few years, and if he had used half the tobacco the letter writers have gin him credit for, he wouldn't have had any brains left to plan a campaign. They have run the thing into the ground.

Seth Twiggs' case is different. His business is smoking. If he has any other business, nobody has been able to find it out. He cultivates a little land, works in the garden some, and tinkers round a good deal; but this is only his amusement. The solid work on which he lays himself out is smoking. Now a man who assumes "the solemn responsibility" of writing for the papers, as Mr. Spooner would say, must regard the truth of history. The fact is, the Hookertown public wouldn't know Seth Twiggs without his pipe, and I had to introduce Seth's pipe or say nothing about him.

I like to have forgot Seth on the settee. "I'll bet there is fifty acres in pickles in Hookertown, this year," he added.

"Some folks are in great trouble as to how they'll cure 'em," I remarked.

"Du tell!" exclaimed Polly Frink, "I thought every body knew how to salt down cowcumbers."

"Not by a jug full," said I. "It is treated as a great secret at the pickle factories, and stores, and you might as well undertake to get ile out of a Wall Street Petroleum Company, as to get any light on the curing process out of them."

"I guess you didn't go to the right place, Esq. Bunker," said Seth. "For when I went down to the city to market my pickles I went all over the factory."

"And what did you see?" I asked. "Well, I saw a lot of vats, barrels, kegs, jars, and bottles, some of 'em full and some of 'em empty." "Did you ask any questions and did you get civil answers?" "Sartainly I did, lots on 'em. And I found out there wa'n't any secret about the brine, for it is the same rule my grandmother used to go by, and I guess it is about the same thing every housekeeper in Hookertown uses to-day,—brine strong enough to bear an egg, and the little pickles to lie in two weeks, and the big ones, three; that is about the whole of it, with a little variation to suit circumstances."

"Jest so," said Mrs. Jake Frink; "that is my rule, and I never knew it to fail. I've got pickles two years old now, and they are jest as good as ever. Ye see, I allers keeps my barrel open at the top, with a round board and a stone to keep the pickles in the brine. For a barrel of pickles you want jest about a peck of coarse salt. Turk's Island is the best, dissolved in water. That will jest about float an egg. If I want to keep them a long time in the brine, I look at 'em occasionally, and add a little more salt, if I think they need it."

"And what is to be done when you want to put them into vinegar?" I enquired.

"Oh, that is easy enough. You jest scald the cucumbers in a brass kettle, and let them stand a few hours, changing the water two or three times to take the salt out. You can tell by the taste when they are fresh enough."

"What do you have a brass kettle for?"

"They say it makes 'em green. My mother always used a brass kettle."

"And how is it about the poison?"

"Well, I never heard of it's hurting any body. If you have good cider vinegar, the green pickles will be wholesome enough. Every body in Hookertown cures 'em in this way, and we are not an ailin' set of people."

Aunt Polly is right about the vessel for freshening the pickles. A good deal more depends upon the vinegar than upon the vessel, and I suspect the brass kettle with its trace of verdigris is made to answer for all the atrocious compounds they put into the vinegar. The slops of the rum shops and drinking saloons, sulphuric, and other mineral acids, are put in liberally to give sharpness to the vinegar. This must be injurious to the stomach, and I suspect it is to prevent the public from learning the composition of the vinegar, that the pickle men affect so much mystery about their business.

Farmers have no apology for using any thing but home-made vinegar and pickles. They can always have the best, and plenty. A cucumber is little else than thickened water, a sort of sponge to hold vinegar. If good, it supplies the vegetable acid for which the system has so strong a craving in hot weather. The doctors tell us it regulates the bile, and for once I guess the doctors are about right. In the absence of fruits, which are not always to be had, keep pickles on your table the year round.

Yours to command,

TIMOTHY BUNKER, ESQ.,

Hookertown, July 10, 1865.

NO. 78.—TIM BUNKER ON THE COTTON FEVER AND EMIGRATION DOWN SOUTH.

MR. EDITOR.—Your notice in the May number took me considerably by surprise. The fact is, I have been so awful busy with my own affairs, and Hookertown matters, that I had pretty much forgotten the world outside. Court business, of course, I had to attend to. And then I never had so much advice to give in cases out of Court, since I have been Justice of the Peace. I have pretty much come to the conclusion that I am worth more to keep folks out of lawsuits than to settle cases after they come into Court.

You see, Hookertown has been in a great stew all winter, about going down South and raising cotton, and betwixt the meetings and the private talks around to the houses, there has not been much else done or thought on. You know our son John went to the war, and a lot more of the Hookertown boys, and they came home full of the matter, and they have kept the pot a boilin' ever since. To hear them talk about the Cotton States you would think there was never such a land lying out a'doors any where. Canaan wa'n't a touch to it. If it didn't flow with milk and honey, it did with cotton bales, which was enough sight better. Their heads were completely turned with the tall timber, the smooth, rich land, the magnolia blossoms, the cypresses, and the live oaks, and (would you believe it!) the pretty girls. Every one of 'em seems to have come home as uneasy as a fish out of water. It is mighty dull work squatting down in the land of steady habits after one has been tearing through the Cotton States with Billy Sherman and his troopers. John, for the first few days, said it seemed as if he should suffocate in Hookertown—there was nothing doing, or going to be done.

I talked with the boys in general, and my boy in particular, and argued agin the emigration scheme, and the more I argued the more sot they were in their way of thinking; and that wa'n't the worst of it, for they seemed to infect every body with the Southern fever, and one while, I thought they'd carry off Hookertown bodily—Mrs. Bunker and the grandchildren, and there wouldn't be any body left but Mr. Spooner, myself, and a few other old fogies. As it is, Hookertown has lost some of its best citizens, as well as some others that we could comfortabler spare.

I felt very bad when John stated the case pretty soon after he got home. "Now," says I, "my son, what is the use of your going down to Mississippi, to farm it, when you have got three hundred acres of as handsome land as lies in the Valley of the Connecticut, or as lies out doors anywhere, as to that matter. We old folks have been thinking, when you got back from the wars you would settle down on the old farm, and hand down the Bunker mansion and name to your children. It is kind o' weak in us, but we thought we should have somebody to lean on, when we got a little older. I can't always hold the plow, and mother's eyes will get past fine sewing and clear starching, one of these days."

There was a tear in John's eye as he got a glimpse of the picture we had been looking at during his long absence, and he said:—

"I expect to do jest as you say, father. I have always been brought up to mind, and I expect to mind you now. You and mother felt very bad about my going to the war, but on the whole, thought it was best; and when you come to look at this emigration down South on all its sides, you may think it is just about as necessary for me to go down there now as it was three years ago. I s'pose I shall feel worse about leaving Hookertown than you will, for you will have the dear old sod under your feet, and all the associations of your lives around you, the old home, the old church, and old friends, while I shall go mostly among strangers. You have taught me not to follow my feelings always, but to do my duty, and the precept and example have struck in pretty deep. Mr. Spooner has preached that way, and I have come to believe it. I didn't join the regiment because I had any appetite for fighting or seeing sights; I thought Hookertown was a part of my country, and the rebs were to be kept out of it. If I didn't go and meet them on Southern soil, they might come here, and be watering their horses in the Connecticut, which would not be so pleasant. We who went down there to fight have given you a life lease of your peaceful homes, and we feel as if we had a right to go and carve out homes for ourselves, in the land we have won by the sword. The boys talked it all over before they were mustered out, and we mean to go back, unless it is clear that Providence is against the movement.

"You who are on the stage have had your chance, and help'd make Hookertown what it is. You have cultivated and improved your farms, built your houses, and established your schools and churches, and got every thing going in good shape. The land is all occupied, and there isn't room here for more farmers. The farms are too small already. Your population will only grow in the cities and villages."

"But who is going to have my farm when I'm through with it?" I asked.

"Well, father, there is Timothy Bunker Slocum, a smart boy in his first pair of boots, and big enough to ride a horse and go to mill already. Sally thinks she's going to send him to college and make a minister of him, but unless I'm a good deal mistaken the Lord has made a farmer of him from the start, and if Sally undertakes to turn him off that track, she'll find she's having a sharp fight with the Almighty and give it up. These things run in the blood, and the Bunkers have always stuck to the soil, and haven't amounted to much in any other calling. Little Tim takes to a horse as naturally as a young Arab, and his voice has just the right coop for driving oxen. He is your own flesh and blood, and you ought not to feel very bad if a grandson takes care of the Bunker mansion when you have done with it.

"As I was saying, you have had your chance to make a home and build up society here. We want to take our chance down South where there is plenty of room. The South wants people, New England people, and brains especially, more than anything else. It is almost a wilderness, with only a few little clearings and scratches upon its surface. Its worn-out and abandoned fields are only worn out upon the surface. The riches of the soil are hardly touched yet. The forests are magnificent, and the climate probably quite as healthful as the Valley of the Connecticut, when it was first settled. It seems a pity that it should lie waste any longer. We want to start a new Hookertown down there, and are willing to take our chances of soil and climate. What is the use of conquering Canaan unless the people go over Jordan and possess the land?"

John said this, and a good deal more in the same vein,

and, as Mr. Spooner would say, there was in it considerable food for reflection. The more I argued, the warmer he grew. It was just like trying to put out a volcano with a squirt gun. "Ah," said Mrs. Bunker, with a sigh after John had gone out, "He isn't a boy any longer, Timothy. It is of no use talking. The fire burns in him, and who knows but the Lord has kindled it?"

I couldn't answer that. It was pretty clear that fire was there, and burning strong, and it seems to be spreading all through this region. It is a big subject, and of a good deal of importance to your readers, and with your permission I shall have to load and fire agin on it.

Yours to command,

TIMOTHY BUNKER, ESQ.

Hookertown, April 15th, 1866.

NO. 79.—TIM BUNKER ON THE COTTON FEVER AND EMIGRATION DOWN SOUTH.

MR. EDITOR.—I was a good deal taken aback by my talk with John, about which I wrote you in my last. You see, Mrs. Bunker and I had never thought of any thing else for him than our own home in Hookertown, and that he would want to live and die in the house in which he was born. We had not considered what a change three years was to make in him. He went away a boy; he came back a man, with notions of his own, and the reasons to back 'em. There was no disguising the fact that it was something more than a boyish freak that he had taken, to carve out for himself a new home in the sunny South. I turned the thing over in my mind, and I could not get round the argument. I had had my chance in Hookertown, and made my own home and fortune without any boosting. Why shouldn't he have his choice in a spot of his own choosing? He has seen the land and tried its climate, and was capable of judging for himself. If he could not stay at home without a feeling of constraint, why the sooner he was off the better. A contented mind is a continual feast, and without that a man must be a drudge anywhere.

So we give up arguing, and concluded that John had quite as good a right to dispose of himself as we had. If he felt he had a mission down South it might be as sacred as any other, and it didn't become us to stand in the Lord's way. Perhaps He had something better in store for John than Hookertown. They say old people, and some that are not quite so old, come to think that they live exactly in the center of creation, and that there is no spot quite equal to their town and their part of it. Even Mr. Spooner preached his New Year's sermon on being "Content with such things as you have," and undertook to show that the Western hemisphere was the best part of the world, that the North American Continent was greatly superior to the South, that the United States was the best part of the Continent, that Connecticut stood head and shoulders above all other States, and Hookertown was the cream of the land of steady habits. I don't want to stir up the jealousy of Boston, or any other respectable village, but I endorse Mr. Spooner's opinion. I thought all the while he was a preaching that he had a squint toward the folks who were so fast for going down South—and he owned as much afterwards. But preaching won't save a man who has got the cotton fever. You might as well undertake to preach total depravity out of him. It will work out.

"D'ye 'spose, Squire, there's any chance to make money in this cotton business?" asked Jake Frink this morning.

"Certainly," said I. "Growing cotton is just like any other business. Some men who have capital and skill will go into it and prosper, and others will fail, for the same reasons that they would fail in any thing. It does not require any more intelligence to manage a cotton plantation than it does to work a northern farm, and hardly so much. It has always been done by the rudest kind of labor. There is no doubt that the skill acquired in growing the dozen or more crops we raise here in Hookertown will come to a good market in the South."

"How much capital is required to raise cotton?"

"Just as much as to raise corn or potatoes, and the more one has the better he can make it pay, up to the point where he can command all the labor he can see to. There is no difficulty in growing cotton in a small way, if you are where you can use another's gin and press. But the better way is to have a large plantation, and use your own gin and press."

"I like the notion of using your own gin, Squire, for I don't think I should stand much of a chance of borrowing, unless folks down there are different from the Hookertown people."

"Very likely. But the gin you have in mind wont help the cotton harvest any more than it does the hay."

"Well, I don't see," said Jake despondingly, "as there's going to be any chance for me down there. Kier is going, and pretty much all the folks in the White Oaks, and I thought I might as well go along, but if it takes such a heap of money, I shall have to give it up."

I could not encourage neighbor Frink to join the expedition, for he and the class of men to which he belongs will not succeed either North or South. They are a good way past their prime, and their habits are bad.

But young men of good habits need not hesitate to go, even though they have small capital. Skillful labor will for a long time command a good price there, if labor is all that one has to put into the market. The unfriendliness of the climate to the white laborer is greatly overestimated. This story has been industriously circulated by interested parties, as an apology for slave labor. When I took Mrs. Bunker down to New Orleans seven years ago, I found the most of the labor about the wharves and cotton presses was performed by men of European birth. Irishmen and Germans were plenty as laborers and mechanics, and they suffered as little inconvenience from the heat as Africans. When I went up on to the cotton plantations, I found the planters employing Irishmen to ditch and drain where they would not put their negroes. I found Scotchmen and New Englanders settled there, and enduring the climate perfectly well. It is well known that multitudes of Germans and Hungarians have gone into Texas, still further South, and there raise cotton quite as safely and more economically than it could be done by slave labor. Our soldiers have stood the climate well, and it is my private opinion that labor in a cotton field isn't any harder or more dangerous than fighting. That's the opinion of the boys who have spent two and three years there in places where they couldn't always take care of themselves. I guess it will do to risk them when they can build houses of their own, and have the comforts of northern homes around them. The fact is, climate has the credit of a good deal of mortality that really belongs to whiskey. Of course in clearing up a new country there will be exposure to malaria and sickness. But when the forests are cleared and the swamps are drained, as they will be by northern skill, the risk of health and life will deter no one from going South.

Capital will be the great want of the emigrant to the South. There is plenty of cheap land to be bought, and plantations enough to be cheaply leased. Money must be had for this, and for stock and labor. According to John's figuring, a man wants forty-four dollars for every acre in cotton. If he was going in for 500 acres of cotton, the outlay would be

For stock, seed, and implements	$6 305
Supplies for 60 hands—say 1,200 bushels of corn, 120 barrels corn meal, 84 barrels pork, 15 bushels of salt, 10 months wages at 15 dollars a month, and incidentals	14,875
For rent of land at 10 dollars per acre	5,000
	$26,180

The stock and implements would be worth three-fourths their first cost or more at the close of the year, and this amount may be deducted for the second year's operations. Sometimes the cotton can be sold by Oct. 1st, and the money realized go to pay the expenses of the year.

The returns for such an investment will of course vary with the yield and the market price. The average crop, as planters estimated it under the old system, was—one bale upon alluvian, two-thirds of a bale upon "hard-bottom lands," and half a bale upon upland. With free labor this yield would probably be exceeded. The bale is rated at 400 pounds. At a bale per acre, and cotton at 30 cents, the crop on 500 acres would be worth $60,000. At a half bale per acre it would be worth $30,000. The lowest estimate gives near fifty per cent profit; the highest, near three hundred.

Here is great temptation for northern skill and capital. With any thing like a fair chance, money must be made at it. It isn't strange that the cotton fever rages and carries off our people. The boys have all started, and I suspect the girls will—be sent for.

Yours to command,

TIMOTHY BUNKER, ESQ.

Hookertown, Aug. 16th, 1866.

NO. 80.—TIM BUNKER ON THE FOOD QUESTION.

"I knew we should catch it to-day," said Seth Twiggs, as he came into our house on the evening of Thanksgiving Day, and seating himself comfortably upon the settle, blew a ring of smoke out of his mouth, as if it had been shot out of a rifle. "The Parson ginerally hits the nail on the head, and hit it square to-day, no mistake. We have sent off too many of our boys to the city. There isn't so much breadstuff raised in Hookertown as there was fifty years ago, and if it keeps on at this rate, somebody has got to starve by and by."

"That is to say, if every place is just like Hookertown," I responded.

Neighbor Twiggs' remark had reference to Mr. Spooner's Thanksgiving sermon, which was pretty much like all his sermons, whether on Sundays or not, "a word in season." You see, Mr. Spooner, like myself, belongs to the old school of folks, who have got so accustomed to making up our own minds on public questions, that we can't afford to take our opinions second-hand. You see, most people around here in Connecticut have got a dreadful hankering after city life and fashions. They want something better than farming for their sons and daughters, though, according to my notion, farming, taking the long run, pays better than any other calling upon the face of the earth. The boys that grow up around here are smart, and would probably do well at almost any thing, if they had a fair chance. But Hookertown can't hold 'em any more than a pot can hold boiling water. Some of them have gone down South to try their fortunes, some to the West, but more to the city, which threatens to swallow up the country, which is a good deal like a man swallowing his own stomach. You see, this state of things makes rather a dull look for the old parish, and worries the minister, and it works out in his sermons on Thanksgivings, and Fasts, and sometimes on Sundays. Some grumble about political preaching, and secular preaching, etc., but for my part, if a man has got any thing to say to make folks better, I never could see why it wa'n't jest as well to say it on Sunday as any other time. But the grumbling don't trouble Mr. Spooner much. He's as independent as a wood-chopper, and knows he can get his bread and take care of himself, if the Hookertown people turn him out of the pulpit to-morrow, which they have no notion of doing. He speaks right square out, and nobody has any more doubt as to which side of a question he is on, than they have about sunrise.

Well, you see this food question is what the philosophers call a poser. If bread and meat are all the while getting dearer, and labor is growing cheaper, and that is the settled tendency of society, you see the time is coming when labor wont buy bread, and somebody must perish. That is the way things are working now, and wise men should be looking for a remedy.

Mr. Spooner showed this very clearly. It has been the tendency in Europe for a great many years—England hasn't raised her own breadstuffs for more than 30 years. The great mass of her people are gathered in cities and large manufacturing towns, and there is not land enough left to raise a full supply of food for her population, even with their improved husbandry. She has to bring large quantities of wheat and other grains from the ports of the Mediterranean, and from across the Atlantic, to make up the deficiency. Now, if there should be short crops in these countries and in America, or if she should be at war with enemies strong enough to blockade her ports, nothing could prevent great distress and starvation.

The same social disease is beginning to work in this country. The price of food has more than doubled within a very few years, not only in cities but in the farming districts. Flour in Hookertown has been selling this fall at $15 a barrel, butter at 45 cents, and beefsteak at 30 cents per lb., and these things are just about a fair sample of everything else. Eight years ago these things could have been bought for less than half the money. This shows that mouths have multiplied faster than food. There are more consumers than producers. Farm labor in the same time has increased in value, but it has not kept pace with the increased price of food. Wheat has gone up from $1 to $2.50 a bushel—labor from five Yankee shillings to nine, which is an increase of more than one-half, and the labor is not near so good. The native born hired man of a generation ago, who worked for $12 a month and board, the year round, has pretty much disappeared, and we have in his stead the unskilled immigrant. This shows that labor is not comparatively as well rewarded. His day's work will not buy him as many comforts as it did 20 years ago. This shows that something is "rotten in Denmark," for the condition of the laboring class, and not that of the rich, is the measure of the prosperity of a country. It is a bad state of society where only a few are growing rich, and the many are just getting a living or suffering for the comforts of life.

Then, Mr. Spooner said, the Societies in the cities for the aid of children, were another indication of the same evil. Thousands are left every year in circumstances of extreme want, and there is no efficient remedy for their case but to find homes for them in the country, where they can help themselves. Thousands are sent off every year through these Societies, and a little is thus done to restore the disturbed balance of society.

The pith of the discourse was, that Hookertown was the center of the universe, that farming was the best business, that those who were engaged in it should be content with such things as they had, and be thankful for them. He had some sly thrusts at clam-shell bonnets, silks, satins, and ribbons, fast men, and fast women, and the general extravagance of the times. These, I suppose, were meant as sauce for the Thanksgiving turkey, and to help digestion.

"Well, Squire, what are you gwine to do about it? Food is getting higher every year, and labor don't keep up with it. The rich are growing richer, and the poor poorer. What are you gwine to do about it?" asked Seth Twiggs, as he knocked out the ashes of his third pipe and loaded again.

"Well," said I, "I am not going to whine about it. Of all remedies for a great public evil that of whining is the poorest. I have faith to believe that there is some way of deliverance from this and all other social evils. The high price of food is not going to last forever among this great people, with territory enough to raise breadstuffs for the world, were it only half tilled.

"All that Mr. Spooner says is as true as preaching. Things are a little unsettled just now, but they will come right after awhile. I have noticed that there is a tendency in Christian society to correct its own evils. Sometimes we have an outbreak of burglaries, bank robberies, and shop-lifting, and it seems as if society was going to ruin. But when the people get waked up, and a few of the thieves are convicted and sent to State's Prison, the times improve wonderfully. People are not going to live in miserable tenement houses, and suffer all the miseries of city poverty without learning something. Native born Americans certainly are not. I have noticed that many go to the city, do not succeed there, and come back again, wiser, if not better men. They find that their genius does not lie in the direction of trade, but they have a decided tact for making corn and potatoes grow. They support their families comfortably, and on the whole, are no worse for their city experience. Then I have noticed again, that a good many who succeed in the city, acquire a competence, and before they are spoiled, retire to the country to lead an industrious rural life. They become large producers of breadstuffs, and supply the city markets with fat cattle, sheep, and swine. They rejoice in their well-tilled farms, and in their flocks and herds. Then again, I have noticed that some of our very best small farmers and gardeners are city bred people, tradesmen, or mechanics, who from failure of health or disgust with the city, come into the country, near good markets, to support their families from the soil. They have thrifty habits, some capital, and succeed admirably by making the most of a little land. Thousands in these ways are changed from consumers into producers, every year. If multitudes flock to the city, multitudes come back to the country.

"And then there is a growing tendency among our city people to scatter themselves in the neighboring towns. A large part of the men who do business in New York, live out from five to fifty miles in the country. Some have small homesteads, but they are all to some extent cultivators, and draw a part of their support from the soil. And this tendency is on the increase, and will grow with the increased facilities for travel that every large city is making for itself. This will not only help to unburden the city, but will add to the production of the country, and help to make food cheaper."

"I shouldn't wonder if we had New Yorkers living in Hookertown, yet," said Seth.

"Stranger things have happened," said I.

"I shall beat 'em on cabbage tho', if the smartest of 'em come," said Seth, with an extra puff.

"It takes Dutchmen for cabbage. You should not brag!" I continued.

"Then there is another thing in connection with this

food question, which I have thought of a good deal. No man has begun to conceive of the great change which our improved farming tools are destined to make in the productiveness of human labor. A man is multiplied ten fold. We should have had a famine during the war, if it had not been for them, and food would have been a great deal dearer than it now is. The horse reaper and mower mean cheaper grain, and cheaper meats of every kind, that consume hay and grain. Every year is adding to these improved tools, and extending the fields of their usefulness. They come very slowly into use, but they are certainly coming; and they can not fail to do two things—to make farming pay better, and to cheapen the price of food. A vast deal of brain power is lavished upon these inventions, and it will have its reward in relieving the sweat of the brow.

"And then when steam gets into the field, as it must, upon the prairies at least, what may we not expect in the way of cheap Johnnycakes and bacon?"

"May I be there to see," exclaimed Seth, rising to go. "That is what other folks will do about it;—but what do you mean to do about it, Squire Bunker?"

"Do?" said I. "Why, I'll stick to the old farm, set my neighbors a good example, and die in the furrow. And if that ain't enough, I'll blow my trumpet in the *Agriculturist*, and set all the people from Maine to Texas, thinking on the food question."

"Good!" said Seth, as he went out. "That paper is the best tool yet out, to make bread cheap. It believes in brain manure."

Yours to command,

TIMOTHY BUNKER, ESQ.

Hookertown, Dec. 8, 1866.

NO. 81.—TIM BUNKER ON JIM CROW.

Mr. Editor:—It may seem an ungracious task to say a word agin this gentleman, when everybody is writing up people of color in gineral. Folks who, a year ago, could not express their disgust of the negro, in language strong enough, are now bawling for universal suffrage. Such sudden conversions I never saw in camp meeting. But I have been in favor of their voting this twenty years; so I've no prejudice agin color to influence my opinion on the crow question. You said you wanted all the Hookertown news, especially if it had any bearing on farming. Now you see, we have had a big ferment in the Farmer's Club up here on this question, which is certainly as old as I am, and I guess as old as the country. I thought it had been settled several times, but it is one of them questions that don't stay settled. I expect it is because we haven't got upon the right foundation yet. I have always noticed that any unsound opinion kept working in the public mind like bad food in the stomach. It wont stay down. Hookertown has spoke and I rather think Jim Crow is settled forever.

You see these creatures had been uncommon plenty last season, and we had all suffered more or less from their depredations in planting time, and this had been put down as one of the things that was to be discussed and settled in the Club this winter. "Jim Crow, shall he jump or no?" In old times in Connecticut they said no, and offered a premium on crows, and the boys used to hunt them, and bring the young ones by the basketful to get their pocket money. Then the men, who were science on birds, thought the crows killed a good many grubs, and paid their way and said we must not kill them.

Deacon Smith was chairman for the evening and stated the question. He said "it was admitted that the crow did some good and a great deal of mischief. The point was to find out whether he did more good or hurt.

Jotham Sparrowgrass said he did not think there was any question at all about it. He knew what he was about when he went to the Legislature at Hartford, well-nigh fifty years ago, and got the law passed to give a bounty on foxes and crows. He said both of 'em were the farmer's enemies, and he didn't know which was the worst. He said our fathers understood their cases, and killed them off as fast as they could lay hands on them. Talk about crows destroying bugs! He has shot 'em many a time, and he always found more corn and carrion in their crops than anything else.

Cicero Smith said he was astonished to hear such sentiments from his venerable friend. He thought the crow had not been made in vain. If it had not been for some good end he would never have been brought into existence, and been made so hardy and prolific. He was a very long-lived and very shy bird, so that with all the warfare which men had made upon them they were as numerous as ever. They were the farmers' friends, picking up a multitude of grubs and worms that preyed upon his crops, and acting the part of a scavenger in removing dead animals, that would otherwise pollute the atmosphere; they pulled up some corn, to be sure, but every laborer was worthy of his hire.

Mr. Spooner, our minister, said he found some difficulty with Mr. Smith's argument. A good many creatures had been made for a different state of the world than existed at present, and if we admitted that they were originally useful, it would not follow that they could not very well be spared now. He said they had found over in Shadtown, and in many other places, the remains of extinct birds, beasts and fishes. These fossils had had their day, and died out, or been killed off, because they had become nuisances. He was inclined to think that it was about time for man, who was lord of nature, to dispense with the services of the crow; he could join the great company of fossils without disturbing the balance of nature. He admitted he had been useful in the earlier ages, when animal life was more abundant, and the air was likely to be tainted with the effluvia of dead animals. But the farmer did not need such a scavenger now. Dead animals were exceedingly valuable for the compost heap, and he must be a very foolish cultivator who would allow them to waste unburied. Wolves and bears, and other wild animals, had disappeared from the State, without any suspicion that the Almighty had made a mistake in their creation. He thought that the crows could all be killed off without interfering with the divine purposes, according to which man has the responsibility of subduing nature, and ruling over it."

Jake Frink said he was agin crows, and had been from the start. He never had been on more than one side of this question. They pulled up his corn whether it was tar'd or not, and strings and scare crows had n't any more influence on 'em than on the wind. He had seen 'em light right on a stuffed man. He never'd found but one thing to fix 'em, and that was corn soaked in New England rum. That made the critters so drunk you could knock 'em over as easy as lame geese.

Seth Twiggs thought that was the best use neighbor Frink could put his rum to. If he kept it, he was mighty afraid that somebody besides the crows would become extinct. His opinion was that "carrion crow" expressed the character of the bird as well as his habits. He not only pulled up his corn, and bothered him to death with planting over, but he destroyed the eggs and young birds in his orchard. He was a thievish, blood-thirsty fellow, ready to kill any thing, that has not strength enough to defend itself against his attacks. He knew a good many of the small birds lived mostly on insects, for he had watched them when feeding their young. He thought the crow destroyed the grub killers, instead of the grubs, and he was glad to see folks getting waked up to his true character. He should go strong for smoking him out.

You see which way the current is setting up here. Every crow thinks his own young the whitest, they say; and I am perhaps a little prejudiced in favor of Hookertown, but it strikes me that there is about as much good common sense in our Club as there is in any scientific society. I have to admit that I have been on both sides of this question, but have found hard bottom at last. Our fathers were right in killing crows. The birds belong to the fossil age. There is no music in his caw. He prefers a dead carcass to a living one, and will devour a half pound of putrid flesh a day. We can make a better use of the flesh than to bestow it on this sneaking thief. He destroys our song birds and worm eaters in the nest. He is the pest of our corn fields and the scourge of our orchards, where the farmer's true friends build their nests. A strong petition is going up to the Legislature from Hookertown this spring for a big bounty on crows.

Yours to command,

TIMOTHY BUNKER, ESQ.

Hookertown, March 1, 1867.

NO. 82.—TIM BUNKER ON THE EIGHT HOUR LAW.

BIG FERMENT IN HOOKERTOWN.

MR. EDITOR:—We have been having considerable doings up here lately, and as you wanted me to keep you posted on Connecticut news in general, and Hookertown in particular, I send you some notes I took on the Eight Hour Convention. It was got up by Cicero Smith, and a few of the fellows that work with him, when they do anything, which is not often.

Big posters were stuck up on all the sign posts in town, calling upon mechanics and working people in general, to meet in the town hall, and assert their rights, just as if somebody had been trying to take away their rights. There was a full house. Shadtown was well represented by the fishermen, and the White Oaks turned out strong. Kier Frink and the coal men came down in their carts, and Hookertown street has not seen such a collection of broken down wagons, and gaunt, raw-boned horses, in many a day. It reminded one of the early days of the war, when they were holding big meetings to drum up recruits.

Judge Loring was appointed chairman, and Cicero Smith introduced a long string of resolutions, recommending eight hours as a legal day's work, and pledging the meeting for no man that was not in favor of an eight hour law. He said the time had come for the heavy burdens of labor to be lifted from the working classes; that they now did all the work, got poor pay, and had to live in humble abodes, on scant fare, and endure all the ills of poverty. They were ground down by capital to the lowest depths, and had no time for the cultivation of their minds, and for social enjoyments. He hoped to see the day when the men who did the work should have the money, and the fine houses, and the fast horses, and enjoy life like human beings. He was in favor of paying the laborer as much for his eight hours as he now received for ten, and if that was not enough, he would go as far as the fartherest in relieving his wants, and meeting his wishes. The only true foundation for a State was to glorify labor.

Seth Twiggs said he should like the latter part of the

gentleman's speech better, if he would illustrate it in his life. If any body got one hour's work out of Smith, it would be so much clear gain. "There is as many as two ways of glorifying labor. One is to make stump speeches to working people, and the other is to pitch in and work yourself." He thought a man who held a plow, or chopped wood all day, honored labor enough sight better than a man who was everlastingly talking about work and doing nothing. He didn't value the working of the jaws near so much as some other parts of the body.

Uncle Jotham Sparrowgrass said he didn't know as he understood this eight hour movement, but as fur as he did, he didn't think much of it. "It ain't any thing new. It was tried over on the Island more than forty years ago. There was a set of fellows then trying to get rid of work, and they come nearer to saying what they meant than folks did now. They wanted to divide up property equally all round, and said nothing about working for it. When I was a boy, folks who got ahead any, used to get up early in the morning and work as long as they could see, and milk the cows in the dark. If they got the chores done by nine o'clock and got ready for bed, they did pretty well. They hadn't much time to feel abused and talk about their rights. The main pint was to get a living and get ahead in the world. They may have carried work a little too far, but arter all, they were first-rate people, and better neighbors I never expect to find in this world." It seemed to him that the question was whether folks should work and thrive, or try to get a living without work. For one, he was in favor of work, and if he could find any thing to do that paid, he shouldn't be particular about the hours.

George Washington Tucker said he was glad there was somebody to consider poor folks. He had always worked hard and had nothing to show for it. He never owned a foot of land, and couldn't expect to without some change of times. He wanted more pay and less work, and he thought the eight hour plan was the best one that had ever been tried to relieve poor folks.

Jake Frink said he was a good deal bothered about the question. "Heaven knows I've hard work enough to git along. I've been trying to pay for my farm this thirty years, and hain't made it eout yit. And I've worked like a dog a good part of the time. But how working eight hours instead of twelve is gwine to help me, I can't exactly see. I rather guess there would be less corn in my bin, and pork in my cellar in the fall, than there is now. I have to hire some help in summer, and if a man quits in the middle of the arternoon, and leaves me to git up the hay and grain, I don't see how I'm gwine to be benefited. It looks considerable like a humbug. I bo't some patent manure onc't."

Dea. Little said he didn't like the looks of this question. "They tried the same thing in Sodom, and it didn't work well. The land was rich and produced big crops, and they had nothing to do but look on and see 'em grow. They come very near getting rid o' work, and took to serving the devil so that no decent man could live among them." Work was a good thing for sinners, and he never expected to live without it. He thought if his friend Tucker would pull harder at the hoe handle, and not so much at the bottle, he would be able to own land and a house, and to be quite comfortable. Idleness clothed a man in rags in Solomon's time, and he didn't expect to see a lazy man's wardrobe improve any in our day. "If you want any thing, work for it, and if you work long enough and hard enough, you are pretty sure to get it."

Rev. Mr. Spooner said he was troubled about the moral aspects of this movement. It was nothing new that men tried to escape the curse of toil. Nothing has called forth more ingenuity, but the curse still remains, and he doubted if man would ever be able to repeal the law, 'Six days shalt thou labor.' Eight hours was not a day's work under this law, whatever the civil statute might make it. The average length of the day was about twelve hours. Men were able to work more than eight hours, and did generally, without injury to health, and with much advantage to their fortunes. That was pretty good evidence that they ought to work more. Some people, he supposed, worked too long and too hard, but there was a far larger number who were ruined by idleness, and the vices that grew out of it. He thought the great want of the country now was more labor. If this measure was made a practical thing, it would take one-fifth from all the labor in the country, and that meant, when we come to sift it down, a deduction of one-fifth from every man's income. It was labor that gave value to capital. Men who had money could not loan it unless its use could be made productive by labor. The country was not ready for any such reduction of production and of income. The agitation of the question he thought was mischievous, and would only tend to embarrass the relations of capital and labor.

Last Sunday, Mr. Spooner preached a Sermon from St. Paul: "Neither did we eat any man's bread for nought, but wrought with labor and travail, night and day, that we might not be chargeable to any of you," in which he laid out the eight hour law in its grave clothes. Paul was a gentleman and believed in paying his way, which the eight hour folks don't. If we are going to have any thing besides victuals and clothes, we've got to work more than eight hours for it. Quitting work the middle of the arternoon in haying time wont go down. Even Jake Frink can see the bearing of that nonsense.

Yours to command,

TIMOTHY BUNKER, ESQ.

Hookertown, June 15, 1867.

NO. 83.—TIM BUNKER ON BASE BALL CLUBS.

"Don't you think they are running on't into the ground?" asked Seth Twiggs, as he stopped at my garden fence, when I was gathering squashes this morning. "I du declare there'll be a slim chance to get anybody to work, if things keeps on in this way. We shall be as bad off as they are among the Indians, where the women do all the drudgery, and the men play all the time they ain't fightin'. I hired Kier Frink and another White Oaker to come down and help me husk, and they had to leave right away arter dinner to go to a base ball match. They said they wouldn't stop for double wages, for they could make more money on the ball ground betting. They knew which side was gwine to win. Pretty state of things!" Seth thought the case was so clear that he didn't wait for an answer, but walked off in his usual cloud of smoke. This evening, Mrs. Bunker took up the Hookertown Gazette, and read, "Shadtown victorious! the White Oaks nowhere!! The score stood 27 to 9. Great interest has been taken in this match, from the well-known fact that both parties had been training for it for a month past, and large sums had been staked upon the result. It is said that the White Oakers practiced by moonlight while they were burning their coal pits, and the picked nine of the Shadtown Club have made a business of playing ball six days in a week for the last month. Of course, they bore off the honors."

"Honors!" exclaimed Sally, lifting her gold-bowed spectacles to the top of her forehead, and looking over to me. "When we were young, Timothy, it used to be an honor for a young man to lay a straight furrow, or to mow a wide swath. But now they've beat their plowshares into ball clubs, and the loafers that can play ball best carry off the honors. It seems to me, Timothy, that we are getting considerable ahead of the days of prophecy. The ploughshares and pruning hooks is the Bible idea of a perfect state of society. When grown up men exchange plowed fields and orchards for the ball ground, and make a bat stick their coat of arms, I think they are progressing the wrong way."

This set me to thinking about this base ball business. For it has ceased to be a mere amusement, and, with some people, has got to be as much of a business as catching fish or making brooms. I believe in the division of labor and in new kinds of business, but it is a question whether this is going to add anything to the common wealth or happiness. I believe in athletic sports and games of skill, and have no doubt that there is a place for them in every well-regulated society. Base ball, as we used to play it when I was a boy at school, was a very healthful recreation. It was a change from sedentary habits that the boys needed. I should think it might be a good thing for college boys and clerks in the city. But what do people want of it whose lives are already full of labor? It can only add to their weariness, and detract from the interest and pleasure that every man should take in his daily toil. After a man has spent three or four hours in a game, he is pretty well used up for the day, and is in rather poor trim for work next morning. Base ball, as it is played now, is getting to be a great nuisance.

It seriously interferes with the business of life. Seth Twiggs' case is just what has happened to me a dozen times this summer, and is happening all over the country. When I get a gang of men into the hay field, and have the hay all ready to go into the barn, I do not want to have half of them quit at three o'clock in the afternoon for a ball match. It breaks up all my plans for the day, and necessarily leaves a part of my hay to stand out over night. Over in Shadtown, they build ships, and when a man gets a contract to drive his ship through in a given time, it's a great vexation to have a part of his force absent two or three days in a week, to attend a ball match. Many kinds of mechanical labor are done by contract, and it subjects a contractor to very serious loss if he cannot depend upon his laborers.

It is a great waste of time and money, and few men can afford it. Most laboring men need the avails of their six days' work for the support of their families and for the accumulation of capital enough to carry on business for themselves. One day in the week is a serious loss to them. But if a man joins a base ball club, the loss of time is only a small item. He must have a suit expressly to play ball in, costing, say twenty-five dollars. Then, there must be a club-room, nicely fitted up, where the members meet for business, and on state occasions, when they receive guests from abroad. Then they must have their entertainments—which means sprees. Then they must, of course, accept all invitations to attend matches, no matter at how great a distance. Come to foot up the initiation fees, taxes, traveling expenses, sprees, and lost time, a young man finds himself three or four hundred dollars out of pocket at the close of the year. This may be all very agreeable pastime, but how few can afford it, even in the city! And if they could, there are still more serious objections to it.

It leads very naturally to bad company. I know the young men that make up the ball clubs of Hookertown, Shadtown, and the White Oaks, and I have seen their guests. They are not such men as I should want my John to associate with. Some of them are what they call gentlemen's sons, with plenty of money and no business, which is very bad. Others have business, and neglect it to play ball, which is still worse. Some are average farmers and mechanics, rather green at the play, not yet spoiled, but in a fair way to be. Others are confirmed loafers, rather seedy, and far on the downhill road. They are vulgar and profane; but pitch, bat, and catch splendidly, for the game is their only business. It can't do a young man much good to be brought in contact with such characters. The manners and morals of the ball ground are much more likely to mar than to mend him. The tendency of the game, as now managed, is towards idleness, gambling, and dissipation. It makes good ball players, but bad farmers and mechanics, bad husbands and fathers. I am not ready to have the plow beams whittled into ball clubs just yet.

Then it is rather a low aim in life. There is something noble in making a first-rate farmer. That means cheaper bread and meat for the nation. To be a good mechanic is praiseworthy. It means better homes for the people, and better tools to do their work. But to be a first-rate ball player, or to be one of a champion nine—what does it amount to? If Shadtown beats the White Oakers all hollow, who is the better for it? General Trowbridge came through Hookertown last week in his splendid turn-out, and when opposite the widow Taft's, a little noisy cur came out, and barked at his carriage, as if he thought he could stop it. He succeeded, and the General jumped out, and walloped the cur soundly, and sent him yelling through the gate. This brought the widow to the door in a somewhat excited state: "Wall, Gineral, that's a big victory for you! You've whippt a one-eyed cur." It strikes me that the base ball victories are about on a par with the General's. Shadtown is triumphant, but the White Oakers still live.

Yours to command,

TIMOTHY BUNKER, ESQ.

Hookertown, Oct. 25, 1867.

NO. 84.—TIM BUNKER ON REAL ESTATE IN THE WHITE OAKS AND HOOKERTOWN.

" 'Taint worth so much by a hundred dollars as 'twas eight years ago, when you married the widder," said Uncle Jotham Sparrowgrass to Kier Frink, as he stopped his horse to blow on Hookertown street yesterday.

"That's so," said Kier, sticking his old boot into the nigh wheel of his coal cart, for a rest. "But what's a poor feller tu du, when property is all the while fallin', and money's gettin' more skase? Ye see, when I fust went into the White Oaks to live, coalin' was a good bizness, and a feller had a chance to make suthin' extra on swappin' horses and pitchin' quates. But neow every body is so poor they can't pay the boot in a trade, or the stakes, when they git beat in quates. Tell ye what 'tis, Uncle Jotham, there ain't coppers enuff in the White Oaks on ordinary okashuns to buy a decent glass of likker. I'm gwine to sell eout airly, and come on to the street to live, and so keep from comin' onto the town."

"Mighty slim chance for ye here," said Seth Twiggs, hauling out a tinfoil package from his pocket, and thrusting in his pipe and forefinger at the top. "Ye see, the widder's eighty acres wouldn't buy five here, throwin' in the widder, young ones, and all. Property's riz here worse than emptins, the last ten years."

"Wal, I guess the old man wont hold on furever," said Kier, looking up the hill, where Jake Frink still leads a slipshod life.

"It's poor bizness waitin' for dead men's shoes," said Uncle Jotham. "Better run that coal cart oftener, and swop hosses less. Pitchin' quates and takin' the stakes in likker don't pay in the long run. Land ain't worth much in the White Oaks or anywhere else, unless you work it.

They work the land down here and pretty much everything else. Any thing, or anybody, gets lick'd that lies idle."

"Yes, yes," said Kier, "I remember them lickin's. That's what started me off to the widder's, where things went easy."

"And folks round here take the *Agriculturist*," chimed in Seth Twiggs, whose pipe by this time was in full blast. "More'n forty copies come to the Hookertown post-office, and 'taint more'n twelve years ago there wa'n't but three, and I was the fourth man that took it, and I shouldn't 'ave done it if it hadn't been for the woman. Ye see, she offer'd to pay for it if I couldn't. She laff'd consumedly when I set up readin' on't the fust night it cum till smack twelve o'clock."

"A pretty state of things we'll have here in Hookertown shortly!" exclaimed George Washington Tucker, who had now joined the party. "What with your Agriculturists, and old Bunker's experiments, and everybody aping him, and snappin' up every bit of land that comes into market, there wont be any chance for a poor feller to live in town. Rents have more than doubled in five years."

"Doubled!" exclaimed Benjamin Franklin Jones. "I've got to pay a hundred dollars for my place this year, and ten years ago I got it for twenty-five. Some say it's the war, and some say it's short crops. But that's all nonsense. Tim Bunker and the paper is at the bottom of the whole of it. You see, when that salt mash was reclaimed, and the bottom knocked out of that horse-pond at the foot of Jake Frink's hill, everybody took to drainin' as if their everlasting fortune was gwine to be made right off. There aint a swamp anywhere within five mile of Hookertown neow, but what is as dry as a bone, and kivered with the tallest kind of herd's grass or corn. Sich a hankerin' arter land I never expected to see. Folks aint no plentier than they used to be, but land is a deal skaser, and growin' more so. There's no kind of a decent chance for poor folks to live."

This talk of my neighbors shows the drift of public opinion on the real estate question. In some communities farming lands have risen and quadrupled in value within the last twenty years. In others, they are worth no more than they were a hundred years ago, and hardly so much. Jones has got hold of the philosophy of it, though he is not much of a philosopher, where his own affairs are concerned. In the White Oaks, and places of that kind, land is cheap because cheap people own it, who think a good deal more of shooting-matches, horse-races, and poor whiskey, than they do of farming. As Kier Frink says, "there aint a man of 'em but would sell his soul for a chaw of tabaker." Kier is a little disgusted just now, and perhaps the statement is a little harsh. But it stands to reason that the land isn't worth much unless you work it, and get something out of it. If it bears nothing but wood, cut off for coal once in thirty years, everybody presumes that is all it is good for. Nobody that has capital wants horse jockeys, gamblers, and loafers, for neighbors, and so land is cheap in the White Oaks. Land is worth any sum you can make it pay the interest on, and take care of itself, and it isn't worth a cent more. Some is dear at ten dollars an acre, and other is cheap at $400 for farming purposes. And it does not depend altogether on its original character. Poor land can be made productive by right treatment, and pay its way as well as that which is good. That horse-pond lot was poor property for Jake Frink at twenty dollars an acre. He did not get his interest from it at that price. It certainly is worth three hundred to me, aside from the abatement of a nuisance, which it always was, until it was drained. A variety of causes have made land dearer about Hookertown. There are more people and of course more purchasers of homes. The place has felt the effect of the war, and of a depreciated currency, which makes almost every thing dearer. But this cause has affected the price of land less than most other property. Improved husbandry has more to do with it than anything else, and in this matter agricultural societies, papers, and books, have had their influence. A good farmer put down in any community, raises the price of land all around him. If he gets eighty bushels of corn to the acre, and makes it worth three hundred dollars, his neighbors will not long be content with twenty-five. Big crops raise the reputation of the land. They tell every year upon the purse of the owner, and when he wants to add to his acres, and comes into the market to buy adjoining land, he cannot buy at the old prices. He has been all the while working against himself as a purchaser, and raising the price of his neighbors' farms. Just beyond Shadtown there is a big plain, where any quantity of land could have been bought twenty years ago, for fifteen to twenty dollars per acre. It was difficult for farmers to get rid of it, even at these prices. It is now worth an hundred dollars an acre. A fish oil factory in the neighborhood made cheap manures, and started a better style of farming. Here in Hookertown, we have not only cheap fertilizers, but a constantly increasing class of reading and thinking farmers, who are all the while putting more *brains* into the soil, which starts crops faster than bony fish. The Farmers' Club is active, and Deacon Smith and Mr. Spooner keep talking, and Seth Twiggs smokes out a good many errors in the course of the year. The draining and the manure, and the new tools and seeds, tell their own story, and, as Jones says, "everybody has a hankering arter land." Farms, like putty, has riz. The *Agriculturist* subscription list has riz also, from one to forty, and real estate agents, if they were fair, would vote it a medal. Hoping they will do the clean thing, I am,

Yours to command,

TIMOTHY BUNKER, ESQ.,

Hookertown, June 15th, 1868.

INDEX.

www.ingramcontent.com/pod-product-compliance
Lightning Source LLC
LaVergne TN
LVHW020220110826
845151LV00003B/767

* 9 7 8 1 4 2 5 5 3 3 2 9 8 *